THE CAMBRIDGE COMPANION TO
AMERICAN CIVIL RIGHTS LITERATURE

The Cambridge Companion to American Civil Rights Literature brings together leading scholars to examine the significant traditions, genres, and themes of civil rights literature. While civil rights scholarship has typically focused on documentary rather than creative writing, and political rather than cultural history, this *Companion* addresses the gap and provides university students with a vast introduction to an impressive range of authors, including Richard Wright, Lorraine Hansberry, Gwendolyn Brooks, James Baldwin, Amiri Baraka, and Toni Morrison. Accessible to undergraduates and academics alike, this *Companion* surveys the critical landscape of a rapidly growing field and lays the foundation for future studies.

Julie Buckner Armstrong is professor of English at the University of South Florida St. Petersburg. She is the author of *Mary Turner and the Memory of Lynching* and editor of *The Civil Rights Reader: American Literature from Jim Crow to Reconciliation*. Armstrong has also contributed to such journals as *African American Review, Mississippi Quarterly, MELUS, Southern Quarterly, Flannery O'Connor Review*, and *Georgia Historical Quarterly*.

A complete list of books in the series is at the back of this book.

D0222202

THE CAMBRIDGE
COMPANION TO

AMERICAN CIVIL
RIGHTS LITERATURE

THE CAMBRIDGE COMPANION TO

AMERICAN CIVIL RIGHTS LITERATURE

EDITED BY

JULIE BUCKNER ARMSTRONG
University of South Florida St. Petersburg

CAMBRIDGE
UNIVERSITY PRESS

32 Avenue of the Americas, New York, NY 10013-2473, USA

Cambridge University Press is part of the University of Cambridge.

It furthers the University's mission by disseminating knowledge in the pursuit of
education, learning, and research at the highest international levels of excellence.

www.cambridge.org
Information on this title: www.cambridge.org/9781107635647

© Cambridge University Press 2015

First published 2015
Reprinted 2016

Printed in the United States of America by Sheridan Books, Inc.

A catalog record for this publication is available from the British Library.

Library of Congress Cataloging in Publication Data
The Cambridge Companion to American Civil Rights Literature / [edited by]
Julie Buckner Armstrong, University of South Florida St. Petersburg.
pages   cm. – (Cambridge Companions to Literature)
Includes bibliographical references and index.
ISBN 978-1-107-05983-2 (hardback) – ISBN 978-1-107-63564-7 (paperback)
1. American literature – 20th century – History and criticism.   2. Civil rights
movements in literature.   3. Civil rights in literature.   4. Civil rights movements –
United States – History – 20th century.   I. Armstrong, Julie Buckner, editor.
PS228.C55C36   2015
810.9'35873–dc23   2014038368

ISBN 978-1-107-05983-2 Hardback
ISBN 978-1-107-63564-7 Paperback

CONTENTS

NOTES ON CONTRIBUTORS

NILGÜN ANADOLU-OKUR is associate professor of African American Studies at Temple University. She is the author of *Contemporary African American Theater: Afrocentricity in the Works of Larry Neal, Amiri Baraka, and Charles Fuller* (2011) and multiple articles on African American theater and literature, the Underground Railroad, abolitionism, and universal women's rights.

JULIE BUCKNER ARMSTRONG is professor of English at the University of South Florida St. Petersburg, where she teaches African American, American, and women's literatures. She is the author of *Mary Turner and the Memory of Lynching* (2011), editor of *The Civil Rights Reader: American Literature from Jim Crow to Reconciliation* (2009), and co-editor, with Susan Hult Edwards, Houston Roberson, and Rhonda Williams, of *Teaching the American Civil Rights Movement: Freedom's Bittersweet Song* (2002).

GERSHUN AVILEZ is assistant professor in the Department of English and Comparative Literature at the University of North Carolina, Chapel Hill. He is completing a book on artistic radicalism and the legacies of the Black Arts Movement. His published work appears in the journals *African American Review* and *Callaloo* and the edited collection *Representing Segregation* (2010).

JEFFREY LAMAR COLEMAN teaches American literature at St. Mary's College of Maryland. He is editor of *Words of Protest, Words of Freedom: Poetry of the American Civil Rights Movement and Era* (2012) and author of *Spirits Distilled: Poems* (2006). Coleman is a founding associate editor and poetry editor for *The Journal of Hip Hop Studies*; he is currently completing a manuscript of poems titled *Peace, Love & Soul* and a chapter on African American protest music for *The Black Intellectual Tradition in the Twentieth Century*.

BARBARA MCCASKILL is associate professor of English and co-director of the Civil Rights Digital Library at the University of Georgia. She has co-edited two collections of essays about nineteenth- and twentieth-century African American literature and culture, and she has edited the 1860 narrative of black abolitionists

William and Ellen Craft. Her book about the couple is titled *Love, Liberation, and Escaping Slavery: William and Ellen Craft in Cultural Memory* (2014).

CHRISTOPHER METRESS is associate provost for academics at Samford University. His work on the intersections of literature and the civil rights movement has appeared in such journals as *Southern Quarterly, African American Review, Mississippi Quarterly*, and *Southern Literary Journal*. He is the editor of *The Lynching of Emmett Till: A Documentary Narrative* (2002) and co-editor (with Harriet Pollack) of *Emmett Till in Literary Memory and Imagination* (2008). He is currently at work on a series of essays about white southern writers and the civil rights movement.

SHARON MONTEITH is professor of American Studies at the University of Nottingham and was a Rockefeller Humanities Fellow at the University of Memphis. Her publications include *Advancing Sisterhood? Interracial Friendships in Southern Fiction* (2000); *American Culture in the 1960s* (2008); *Gender and the Civil Rights Movement* with Peter Ling (1999/2004); *South to a New Place: Region, Literature and Culture*, with Suzanne Jones (2002); *The New Encyclopedia of Southern Culture: Media*, with Allison Graham (2011); *The Cambridge Companion to the Literature of the American South* (2013); and *SNCC's Stories: Narrative Culture and the Southern Freedom Struggle of the 1960s* (2014), as well as articles and essays on interdisciplinary southern studies.

BRIAN NORMAN is associate professor of English at Loyola University Maryland, where he also founded the program in African and African American Studies. He specializes in twentieth-century American and African American literature and their relationships to social movements. He is the author of *Dead Women Talking: Figures of Injustice in American Literature* (2013), *Neo-Segregation Narratives: Jim Crow in Post–Civil Rights American Literature* (2010), and *The American Protest Essay and National Belonging* (2007). He is also co-editor of *Representing Segregation* (2010) and is currently working on a book about collaboration in American literature and culture.

ROBERT J. PATTERSON is associate professor of English and director of the African American Studies Program at Georgetown University. His first book, *Exodus Politics: Civil Rights and Leadership in African American Literature and Culture* (2013), reflects his research and teaching interests in African American studies, literature, civil rights historiography, and black religious studies. Patterson has published articles in *South Atlantic Quarterly, Black Camera, Religion and Literature*, and the *Journal of Feminist Studies in Religion*; he also co-edited a special issue of *South Atlantic Quarterly*, Black Literature, Black Leadership. He is currently working on a second book, *Between Resistance and Reinscription: Black Popular Culture and the Intimacy of Politics*.

ZOE TRODD is professor of American literature in the Department of American and Canadian Studies at the University of Nottingham. She works on American and African American protest literature and visual culture, and her books include *American Protest Literature* (2006), *To Plead Our Own Cause* (2008), *Modern Slavery* (2009), *The Tribunal: Responses to John Brown and the Harpers Ferry Raid* (2012), and *Picturing Frederick Douglass* (2015).

CHRONOLOGY

The following chronology of publication dates and major events situates this volume's literary discussions within a broadly defined civil rights history. The one-hundred-fifty-year time span (1863–2013) reflects changing ideas of freedom, equality, and citizenship from slavery's end until just before the book went to press. Only a few literary works appear here; for a lengthier list, see the Guide to Further Reading.

1863 On January 1, Abraham Lincoln issues the Emancipation Proclamation, freeing slaves from the states that had seceded from the Union; many do not receive the news until the Civil War's end in 1865.

1865 Post–Civil War Reconstruction begins; Thirteenth Amendment to the U.S. Constitution outlaws slavery; the first Ku Klux Klan is formed in Pulaski, Tennessee; former Confederate states establish Black Codes (laws that proscribe African American public behavior) to begin the "Jim Crow" era.

1866 The first Civil Rights Act counters Black Codes.

1868 The Fourteenth Amendment grants citizenship and "equal protection" under the law to all citizens, including former slaves.

1870 The Fifteenth Amendment protects African American men's right to vote.

1871 The Civil Rights Act or "Ku Klux Klan Act" temporarily suspends Klan activities.

1875 The Civil Rights Act of 1875 prohibits discrimination in public transportation, accommodations, and jury selection.

1877   The Compromise of 1877 signals Reconstruction's end; federal troops leave the South.

1892   Tuskegee Institute (now University) records a record number of lynchings at 230; later, historians will refer to this year as the "nadir" of race relations: Frances E. W. Harper publishes *Iola Leroy*, a novel that describes black life before and after the Civil War.

1896   In the *Plessy v. Ferguson* decision, the U.S. Supreme Court institutionalizes racial segregation by allowing for "separate but equal" public facilities; the National Association of Colored Women (NACW) is formed.

1901   Charles Chesnutt publishes *The Marrow of Tradition*, based upon massive white-on-black violence in Wilmington, North Carolina, during 1898.

1903   W. E. B. Du Bois publishes *The Souls of Black Folk*, which proclaims, "the problem of the Twentieth century is the problem of the color-line."

1909   The National Association for the Advancement of Colored People (NAACP) is formed.

1910s   The "Great Migration" of African Americans from the Jim Crow South to urban centers of the North and Midwest begins.

1910   Du Bois founds the *Crisis* magazine, an important venue for civil rights writing.

1915   After the success of D. W. Griffith's film *The Birth of a Nation*, the Ku Klux Klan re-forms in Stone Mountain, Georgia; Carter G. Woodson founds the Association for the Study of African American Life and History (ASALH) to promote black accomplishments.

1916   The NAACP produces Angelina Weld Grimké's anti-lynching play *Rachel*.

1919   During "Red Summer," white-on-black violence spreads across U.S. cities; the Commission on Interracial Cooperation (CIC) is founded; the first Pan-African Congress is convened.

1920   The Nineteenth Amendment gives women the right to vote.

1920s	The Harlem or "New Negro" Renaissance signals an explosion of African American cultural and political activity.
1922	The Dyer Anti-Lynching Bill passes the U.S. House of Representatives but fails in the Senate under threat of filibuster; subsequent anti-lynching bills proposed over the next two decades also fail.
1925	The Krigwa Little Theater Company forms (it closes in 1927).
1931	Nine African American youths are falsely accused and convicted of raping two white women in Scottsboro, Alabama; the case becomes an international symbol of Jim Crow justice.
1937	Abel Meeropol publishes "Strange Fruit"; Billie Holiday's later recording of this anti-lynching song will become highly popular.
1940	Richard Wright publishes *Native Son*.
1941	A. Philip Randolph organizes the March on Washington Movement.
1942	The Congress of Racial Equality (CORE) is founded.
1946	President Harry S. Truman establishes the President's Committee on Civil Rights; Ann Petry publishes *The Street*.
1947	CORE initiates the Journey of Reconciliation to challenge segregation on interstate buses; the Committee on Civil Rights issues a report, "To Secure These Rights."
1948	President Truman desegregates the U.S. military.
1950	Gwendolyn Brooks becomes the first African American to win the Pulitzer Prize (for her book of poems, *Annie Allen*).
1951	The Civil Rights Congress issues a petition to the United Nations, "We Charge Genocide: The Crime of Government against the Negro People."
1952	Ralph Ellison publishes *Invisible Man*.
1954	In *Brown v. the Board of Education of Topeka, Kansas*, the U.S. Supreme Court rules that segregation in public schools is unconstitutional; the first White Citizens' Council is formed shortly afterward in Indianola, Mississippi.

1955   In *Brown II*, the U.S. Supreme Court rules that schools should desegregate "with all deliberate speed"; in December, Rosa Parks is arrested in Montgomery, Alabama, for refusing to give up her seat on a bus to a white person; a resulting boycott of the city bus system lasts more than a year and catapults a local minister, Martin Luther King Jr., into the national spotlight; fourteen-year-old Emmett Till is killed in Money, Mississippi, after allegedly whistling at a white woman; an all-white jury finds two local men not guilty in his death and, later, the men confess to killing him; James Baldwin published *Notes of a Native Son*.

1956   Southern congressmen issue a "Southern Manifesto" opposing integration.

1957   The Civil Rights Act of 1957 protects African American voters; nine African American students integrate Central High School in Little Rock, Arkansas, under the protection of federal troops; the Southern Christian Leadership Council (SCLC) is formed.

1959   Lorraine Hansberry's *Raisin in the Sun* becomes the first play by an African American produced on Broadway.

1960   The Civil Rights Act of 1960 protects voting registration; in Greensboro, North Carolina, four African American youths initiate the sit-in movement at a Woolworth's lunch counter; the Student Non-violent Coordinating Committee (SNCC) is formed; Harper Lee publishes *To Kill a Mockingbird*.

1961   Inspired by CORE's 1947 Journey of Reconciliation, Freedom Riders test segregation laws in interstate bus travel across the South; surviving attacks in Anniston and Birmingham, Alabama, they persist until they are arrested in Jackson, Mississippi; SNCC initiates a direct action campaign in Albany, Georgia; Hoyt Fuller revives the periodical *Negro Digest*.

1962   Riots erupt at the University of Mississippi to prevent James Meredith from enrolling.

1963   Civil rights protests take place across the South throughout the year; in Birmingham, Alabama, nonviolent protestors – many of them part of the "Children's Crusade" – are attacked with police dogs and fire hoses; while there, Martin Luther King Jr. is arrested and writes "Letter from a Birmingham Jail" to defend direct action tactics; in June, NAACP organizer Medgar Evers is murdered in Jackson, Mississippi; Eudora Welty writes "Where Is the Voice Coming From?" in response and publishes it a few weeks later; in August, 250,000 attend the March on Washington, where King delivers the "I Have a Dream" speech; in September, a bomb explodes in Birmingham's Sixteenth Street Baptist Church, a hub of civil rights activity, killing four girls; in November, President John F. Kennedy is assassinated in Dallas, Texas.

1964   During Freedom Summer, young adults from across the country converge on Mississippi for voter registration drives; three civil rights workers are murdered in Neshoba County; the Mississippi Freedom Democratic Party is not seated at the Democratic National Convention, calling attention to local voting rights and other abuses; the Twenty-Fourth Amendment abolishes the poll tax, originally instituted after Reconstruction to prevent poor African Americans from voting; the Civil Rights Act of 1964 prohibits discrimination based on race, religion, sex, and national origin; Martin Luther King Jr. is awarded the Nobel Peace Prize for his civil rights work; *Dutchman*, by Amiri Baraka (writing as LeRoi Jones), opens off-Broadway; Malcolm X delivers "The Ballot or the Bullet" address in Detroit, Michigan; Malcolm X and Alex Haley publish *The Autobiography of Malcolm X*.

1965   Malcolm X is assassinated in February; in March, Alabama state troopers beat back an attempted Voting Rights March from Selma to Montgomery, Alabama; a second one, weeks later, is successful; in August, President Lyndon B. Johnson signs the Voting Rights Act into law; other important legislation includes "affirmative active" for federal employees and government contractors; during the summer, riots erupt in the Watts section of Los Angeles; also this year, Dudley Randall launches the Broadside Press and Amiri Baraka opens the Black Arts Repertory Theatre/School (BARTS).

1966   James Meredith organizes the "March against Fear" in Mississippi; after he is shot, SNCC, CORE, and the SCLC continue the march; SNCC leader Stokely Carmichael popularizes the phrase "Black Power" during a Greenwood rally; the Black Panther Party for Self Defense is founded in Oakland, California; Martin Luther King Jr. initiates an anti-poverty campaign in Chicago; the National Organization for Women (NOW) is formed.

1967   In *Loving v. Virginia*, the U.S. Supreme Court rules that laws banning interracial marriage are unconstitutional; former NAACP head council Thurgood Marshall is sworn in as the first African American Supreme Court justice; Carl Stokes becomes the first African American mayor of a major city (Cleveland, Ohio); riots erupt in Newark, New Jersey, and Detroit, Michigan; John O. Killens publishes *'Sippi*; Douglas Turner Ward, Robert Hooks, and Gerald S. Krone found the Negro Ensemble Company (NEC) theater group in New York: Don L. Lee (later Haki Madhubuti), Johari Amini, and Carolyn Rogers found Third World Press; Hoyt Fuller and others form the Organization of Black American Culture (OBAC), a collective of writers, artists, historians, educators, intellectuals, and activists.

1968   Dr. Martin Luther King Jr. is assassinated in April while participating in a sanitation workers' strike in Memphis; U.S. senator Robert Kennedy is assassinated; the Civil Rights Act of 1968, known as the Fair Housing Act, is passed; Ralph Abernathy leads 50,000 demonstrators to Washington, D.C., for the Poor People's Campaign; Ann Moody publishes *Coming of Age in Mississippi*; Eldridge Cleaver publishes *Soul on Ice*; Amiri Baraka and Larry Neal publish *Black Fire*, a Black Arts Movement anthology; Tom Dent and Kalamu ya Salaam found the poetry and theater collective BLCKARTSOUTH.

1969   Black Panther Party leader Fred Hampton is killed by Chicago police; the first Black Studies Department is founded at San Francisco State University; massive demonstrations against the Vietnam conflict are held in Washington, D.C.; the Stonewall Riots in New York galvanize the gay rights movement.

1970   Protests against the Vietnam War at Kent State University in Ohio and Jackson State College (now University) in Mississippi result in the shooting deaths of unarmed students; feminist rallies across the nation call for passage of an Equal Rights

Amendment and highlight the need for reproductive freedom; Toni Cade (Bambara) publishes *The Black Woman: An Anthology*.

1971   News reports reveal that the FBI conducted a secret operation, called COINTELPRO, to discredit and disrupt civil rights and other domestic political groups from 1956 to 1971; the Congressional Black Caucus is formed; Morris Dees and Joseph J. Levin Jr. found the Southern Poverty Law Center (SPLC).

1972   Shirley Chisolm becomes the first African American woman to run for president; the first National Black Political Convention is held in Gary, Indiana; Title IX of the 1972 Education Amendments provide equal opportunities in funding for males and females in public schools.

1973   In *Roe v. Wade*, the U.S. Supreme Court rules that a woman's right to an abortion in the first or second trimester is protected under the Fourteenth Amendment.

1976   ASALH establishes National Black History Month; Ntzoke Shange's experimental play *for colored girls who have considered suicide/when the rainbow is enuf* opens off-Broadway; Alice Walker publishes *Meridian*; Robert S. Hayden becomes the first African American to be named Consultant in Poetry to the Library of Congress (later the position is renamed "U.S. Poet Laureate").

1977   Robert Chambliss becomes the first of several men to be tried and convicted for his role in the 1963 Birmingham church bombing that killed four girls, the first of many similar civil rights "cold case" prosecutions.

1982   A public battle against a Warren County, North Carolina, toxic waste dump draws national attention to the issue of environmental racism; ratification of the Equal Rights Amendment fails.

1983   President Ronald Reagan signs legislation creating a federal holiday to honor Martin Luther King Jr.

1984   Jesse Jackson founds the National Rainbow Coalition (later renamed Rainbow/PUSH) – a political organization connected to his 1984 U.S. presidential campaign that embraced voters from a broad spectrum of races and creeds.

1986   The Anti–Drug Abuse Act of 1986 establishes a 100:1 sentencing disparity between crack and powder cocaine, resulting in a discrepancy in punishments between races.

1987   National Women's History Month is established.

1991   The Civil Rights Act of 1991 is enacted to help prevent employment discrimination; Clarence Thomas replaces Thurgood Marshall on the U.S. Supreme Court after controversial hearings focus on allegations that he sexually harassed a former employee, Anita Hill; Los Angeles, California, police beat Rodney King, an African American, during his arrest; the next year, when the officers are found not guilty of using excessive force on King, the city erupts in violence.

1993   Toni Morrison becomes the first African American awarded the Nobel Prize for Literature.

1994   Florida state legislature passes the Rosewood Claims Bill, compensating survivors of a 1923 massacre for the loss of their town; President Bill Clinton institutes a policy of "Don't Ask Don't Tell" (DADT), which allows gays and lesbians to serve in U.S. military forces but forces them to keep their sexual orientation secret.

1995   The Nation of Islam sponsors a Million Man March in Washington, D.C.

1996   California's Proposition 209 bars affirmative action in public hiring, contracting, and college admissions, an important test case for the practice; President Clinton signs the Welfare Reform Bill (known formally as the Personal Responsibility and Work Opportunity Reconciliation Act of 1996); Clinton also signs the Defense of Marriage Act (DOMA), which bans federal recognition of same-sex marriage.

1997   President Clinton begins the Initiative on Race, a yearlong dialogue in local communities across the country.

1998   James Byrd, an African American, is chained to the back of a pickup truck by two white men and dragged to his death in

Jasper, Texas; Matthew Shepard, a gay white man, is beaten by two men and left hanging on a fence to die in Laramie, Wyoming; both incidents draw widespread attention to the problem of hate crimes.

2000   During the close, and later disputed, presidential election between George W. Bush and Al Gore, thousands of African Americans are prevented from voting in Florida because their names have been accidentally purged from voting lists.

2001   On September 11, al-Qaeda-coordinated airplane hijackings and attacks bring down the World Trade Center in New York, damage the Pentagon in Washington, D.C., and crash United Airlines Flight 93 in Shanksville, Pennsylvania, killing approximately three thousand, and renewing national debates on the meaning of "freedom" and "civil liberties"; Anthony Grooms publishes *Bombingham*.

2005   The U.S. Senate apologizes for its failure to enact anti-lynching legislation during the twentieth century; Hurricane Katrina floods the city of New Orleans and devastates the Gulf Coast, calling attention to the relationship between economics and the federal government's response to national emergencies.

2007   Virginia's state legislature issues an apology for slavery, making it the first of several states to do so; a rally in Jena, Louisiana, draws tens of thousands to protest the prosecution of six African American youths known as the Jena Six for assaulting white youths who hung nooses in a local tree; before the year's end, between fifty and sixty noose incidents throughout the country recall this powerful symbol of Jim Crow violence; in two decisions, the U.S. Supreme Court prohibits assigning students to public schools solely for the purpose of achieving racial integration and declines to recognize racial balancing as a compelling state interest.

2008   U.S. Senator Barack Obama, from a racially mixed background, is elected president; the U.S. Congress apologizes for slavery and Jim Crow laws.

2009   President Obama is awarded the Nobel Peace Prize; the Matthew Shepard and James Byrd Jr. Hate Crimes Prevention Act expands the U.S. federal hate crimes law to include crimes motivated by a victim's actual or perceived gender, sexual orientation, gender identity, or disability.

2010   President Obama signs federal legislation allowing openly homosexual Americans to serve in the U.S. armed forces; the Fair Sentencing Act reduces the disparity between crack and powder cocaine to an 18:1 ratio; statistics released the next year show increases in the U.S. federal prison population of nearly 800 percent since 1980; Arizona passes a strict anti–illegal immigration law; although the U.S. Supreme Court strikes down portions of the law as unconstitutional, the measure prompts other states to pass equally strict laws of their own.

2012   An unarmed Florida teenager, Trayvon Martin, is shot and killed by volunteer neighborhood watch patrolman George Zimmerman, calling attention to issues of racial profiling and "stand your ground" defense laws; Zimmerman is found not guilty the following year.

2013   In *Shelby County v. Holder*, the U.S. Supreme Court strikes down sections of the 1965 Voting Rights Act as unconstitutional; in *Windsor v. the United States*, the Court grants federal recognition of same sex marriage.

ACKNOWLEDGMENTS

Authors and editors have their names on book covers, but they know that the process of bringing any project to fruition is collaborative. Many individuals assisted with the production of this volume. Ray Ryan, Senior Editor at Cambridge University Press, initially contacted me to do this *Companion*, so I must credit him with the idea and thank him for his wise counsel along the way. Editorial Assistant Caitlin Gallagher was a model of patience, answering many questions during the production process.

Several contributors offered helpful feedback at different stages. Christopher Metress and Barbara McCaskill have been with me from the start – commenting on the initial proposal and signing up first to write chapters. Chris, Zoe Trodd, Sharon Monteith, and Jeffrey Coleman provided helpful feedback on the introduction, and Sharon gave me pointers on the fiction chapter. Each contributor has made working on this volume a joy; the book is truly the sum of its individually strong parts.

I have benefited at several points from the work of students at the University of South Florida St. Petersburg. Foremost among them is Jay Boda, who prepared the Chronology and Guide to Further Reading. Much credit also goes to Kyle Pierson, who helped with all stages of manuscript preparation while working as my graduate assistant. Matthew Jackson helped with several miscellaneous tasks, from proofreading endnotes to helping me prepare the author questionnaire. Emily Handy and Alex Maldonado, artists with a much better visual sense than mine, helped select the cover image.

Last, the two people always due the most credit for any book to which my name is attached are Thomas Hallock and Zackary Armstrong-Hallock. Tom, also an academic, reads multiple drafts of everything I write. I cannot imagine life without an in-house editor. Likewise, I do not want to imagine life without Zack, my constant reminder to work less and play more. Both Tom and Zack keep me focused on what is right, beautiful, and true.

JULIE BUCKNER ARMSTRONG

Introduction

In July 1963, a few weeks before the March on Washington for Jobs and Freedom, several well-known artists began meeting to discuss how they might use their talents in service of the civil rights movement. The artists – Romare Bearden, Hale Woodruff, Norman Lewis, Charles Alston, and others – called themselves "Spiral," after the Archimedean spiral that moves outward and upward. Spiral held one exhibit in 1965, "First Group Showing: Works in Black and White," a subtitle that reflects both a color palette and a political statement. In a nation sharply divided over race, oppositions clash, confront, and sometimes meet in shades of gray. Spiral's significance lies less in this show than in the group's example of collective creative energy directed toward progressive social action.[1] Many similar alliances of artists, writers, and performers formed during the 1960s believing that the arts could, and should, inspire change. From the artist, through the work, to the audience, and into the community (outward and upward), *movement* would flow.

Take, for example, the painting *Freedom Now*, Reginald Gammon's selection from Spiral's 1965 show, which serves as a cover image for this volume. Gammon portrays a demonstration, with its bottom section focusing on faces in the crowd, and its top on marching feet clad in boots and sneakers. Signs at the top, left, and right form a triangular visual field with fragmented words: two clearly say "Now," and one presumably says "We Demand Integration and Freedom." By cutting off the words, Gammon invites audience members to finish the statements, articulating for themselves why these protestors have taken to the streets. Viewers therefore become part of the demonstration, other wide-open mouths participating in the call and response that the painting's title signifies:

What do we want? *Freedom!*
When do we want it? *Now!*

Freedom Now serves a dual function with respect to this volume. As part of the Spiral exhibit, the painting exemplifies understudied connections between the civil rights movement and the arts. As a cover image, Gammon's piece emphasizes words (protest signs) and action (marching feet) – or, more pointedly, words *as* action (open mouths demanding "Freedom Now!") – highlighting one of the book's key themes. Audre Lorde's 1977 essay, "The Transformation of Silence into Language and Action" expresses the idea best. Facing a possible cancer diagnosis and, thus, her mortality, Lorde realized, "I was going to die, if not sooner then later, whether or not I had ever spoken myself. My silences had not protected me. Your silence will not protect you."[2] The opposite of silence – speaking her truth, speaking up, speaking out – became Lorde's way of countering invisibility, fear, alienation, and powerlessness. For Lorde, language provided, in the face of death, a profound articulation of life.

The *Cambridge Companion to American Civil Rights Literature* introduces readers to a rich resource for understanding one of the most significant instances of "the transformation of silence into language and action." The scholarly essays collected here look at fiction, poetry, drama, and related cultural productions from and about the United States' long civil rights movement. Many of these texts respond (whether intentionally or not) to a question that Richard Wright famously asked in his 1945 memoir *Black Boy*: "Could words be weapons?"[3] The answer was a resounding "Yes," as scores of writers seized upon the power of words as weapons, bridges, balms, and tools for bearing witness, making sense, and remembering. Continuing the admonitions of Wright and Lorde, the many works examined here confront discrimination, marginalization, violence, and death with the most powerful weapon of all: language.

The *Cambridge Companion to American Civil Rights Literature* appears at an auspicious time for looking at the relationship between language and action. The book's publication date of 2015 marks several anniversaries in a long civil rights history. One hundred fifty years ago, in 1865, the Thirteenth Amendment to the U.S. Constitution outlawed slavery. It was the first of three "Reconstruction Amendments" that clarified the place of blacks in a nation founded, at least in principle, on ideals of freedom and equality (the Fourteenth, ratified in 1868, guaranteed due process and equal protection under the law; the Fifteenth, ratified in 1870, granted voting rights to black men). The year 2015 also marks fifty years since the Selma-to-Montgomery March and passage of the Voting Rights Act. On March 7, 1965, activists attempted a fifty-mile protest walk from Selma, Alabama, to the capitol in Montgomery. State and local police beat them back in an attack so brutal that the day came to be known as "Bloody Sunday." A subsequent protest, beginning weeks later, drew thousands – this time walking under the protection of U.S. Army troops, federal marshals, and federally commanded

Alabama National Guardsmen. The situation in Alabama drew national attention to the need for legislation to prevent voting discrimination. During the following months, while Gammon's *Freedom Now* and other Spiral works were on view at New York's Christopher Street Gallery, a bill wound its way through the U.S. Senate and House of Representatives, under constant threat from white southern congressmen. In August 1965, President Lyndon B. Johnson finally signed the Voting Rights Act into law.

Such anniversaries stand as reminders that the fight for civil rights in this country remains a series of gains and losses extending beyond one short period of "movement" during the mid-twentieth century. The Reconstruction Amendments met multiple forms of resistance. Many states quickly passed laws to undermine them. Known colloquially as "Jim Crow," after a popular racist caricature during the time, these laws strictly circumscribed black public and political behavior. The penalties for violating Jim Crow ranged from imprisonment – often a new form of slavery through labor camps and debt peonage – to violence and death. The year 1892, commonly known as the "nadir" of U.S. race relations, recorded the highest number of lynchings on record.[4] A few years later, in 1896, the U.S. Supreme Court gave legal sanction to Jim Crow, institutionalizing "separate but equal" racial segregation with its *Plessy v. Ferguson* ruling. That decision would not be reversed until 1954, when the Court ruled in *Brown v. Board of Education* that segregation in public schools was inherently unequal and therefore unconstitutional. During the decade that followed, the civil rights movement – a multifaceted effort that included grassroots activism and federal legislation – dismantled de jure, or legalized, Jim Crow.

A question that many civil rights scholars ask today is whether Jim Crow exists de facto – in fact. The year in which preparations for this volume officially got under way, 2013, turned out to be pivotal for that debate in particular and for civil rights gains, losses, and definitions more generally. In January, Barack Obama was sworn in for his second presidential term – a key marker of what many call a "post-racial" era. In June, the Supreme Court's *Shelby County v. Holder* decision struck down a provision of the 1965 Voting Rights Act that required federal monitoring in certain districts, calling it no longer necessary in a post–civil rights age. Critics of the decision (foremost among them, 1965 Selma-to-Montgomery march leader John Lewis, now a U.S. Representative from Georgia) argued that it would disenfranchise certain citizens based on race, ethnicity, and class. The constellation of political, legal, and social forms of discrimination that exist in a supposedly "colorblind" society has come to be known as the "New Jim Crow" (or, alternatively "Juan Crow" and "Jane Crow"). Perhaps the most contentious is a prison system that has grown exponentially during the past few decades, with sentencing and incarceration rates for black and brown males disproportionately higher than those of whites. Also controversial is the question of whose equality counts under the civil rights banner. In 2013, two Supreme Court rulings paved the way for same-sex marriage, with supporters hailing the decisions as part of a "new civil rights movement." Those who disagree with the application of such terminology believe that doing so takes away from the distinctive effort to eliminate legalized Jim Crow that took place during the 1950s and 1960s. How to define the current moment – post–civil rights, New Jim Crow, new civil rights – remains debatable. More certain is that American definitions of freedom and equality undergo continual revision, especially as those definitions refract through the prisms of race, class, gender, sexuality, and other intersecting subjectivities. The times we inhabit have outpaced our language.[5]

This volume considers the relationship of literature to such a tangled history. For many years, civil rights scholars have observed what one might call a "trade gap" in the academic exchange of ideas.[6] Writing in 2000, Charles Eagles described how civil rights historiography privileged analysis of political and social issues over the cultural and intellectual. Four years later, Richard H. King agreed, noting that "the 'full' history of the Civil Rights Movement is not being confronted" when literary, art, and music criticism is left out.[7] More recently, an explosion of works – from anthologies, to monographs, to articles and special issues of journals – has begun to rectify the literature side of this disparity.[8] Although recognizing that a comprehensive overview of what has now become an extensive field of inquiry is nearly impossible, the *Cambridge Companion to American Civil Rights Literature* brings together leading thinkers to survey significant traditions, genres, themes, and critical approaches, suggesting along the way the variety of questions that remain to be asked. In particular, scholars realize that the relationship between literature and civil rights extends well beyond creative productions merely reflecting political developments or critical analyses contributing to academic conversations. As Christopher Metress explains, literary representations offer "valuable and untapped ... material artifacts." Rather than functioning as adjuncts to history, these important resources have their own "cognitive value ... in the production of social memory."[9]

Metress provides a conceptual framework for understanding literary productions in two different ways: as historical evidence (an artifact) and as a process (producing social memory). Other scholarship replicates this division. A foundational article by Barbara Melosh argues for viewing civil rights novels beyond their (then current) status as pedagogical tools, as add-ons to history courses. Instead, Melosh describes them as "primary resources" that present "historical evidence of ideology." Margaret Whitt teaches civil rights through literature, explaining that "literature can help us 'feel' history."[10] For both Melosh and Whitt, literary works hold a status equal to, or greater than, other kinds of documents because they provide truths that rise above facts. If some scholars see civil rights literature as evidence or artifact, others view it as a process: how readers understand or engage with the world around them. In *Down from the Mountaintop*, Melissa Walker describes how black female novelists writing during the 1970s and 1980s bring readers into a conversation that Martin Luther King Jr. initiated with the title of his 1967 book, *Where Do We Go from Here?*[11] Similarly, for historian Richard H. King, civil rights literature invites readers to ask wide-ranging moral and epistemological questions. In "Politics and Fictional Representation," King writes, "literature can inform us in the deepest sense about certain ethical and political dimensions of the way we 'are' in the world.... At its best fiction can illuminate certain dimensions of the experience of politics that otherwise might have remained hidden."[12] Walker and King, then, take further the idea that literature acts as evidence, offering reading as a process of exploring new realms of experience, imagination, and identity.

As the term "new realms" suggests, scholars often rely on spatial metaphors to describe acts of reading civil rights literature. Writing in *History and Memory in African American Culture*, Geneviève Fabre and Robert O'Meally employ French historian Pierre Nora's concept of *lieux de memoire* or "sites of memory." *Lieux de memoire* can be any space, object, or practice (cemeteries, churches, rituals, sayings, monuments, symbols, texts, and so on) that stand at the crossroads of personal and collective memory. Because *lieux de memoire* often form counter-narratives to official or mainstream histories, interacting with them involves thinking critically about one's relationship to a particular past.[13] Readers of civil rights literary texts become active participants rather than passive consumers of memory and meaning. In *The Nation's Region*, Leigh Anne Duck also uses a metaphor of place – a "site for forms of analysis and understanding" – to describe southern literature. Readers entering its spaces navigate the difficult ideological waters where segregationists insist "that apartheid constituted a vital cultural trait" and others "create a venue for more democratic and radical visions."[14] One should not, however, confuse a spatial metaphor with one located in a specific place. In a book that examines literary responses to Medgar Evers's murder, Minrose Gwin utilizes a term from trauma studies, "frames of remembrance," to consider broader relationships. Gwin asks "how such a moment as the Evers assassination becomes a continually shifting frame of remembrance that reveals just how incompletely and imprecisely the border is spliced historically between past and present – and spatially between the U.S. South and the rest of the world – when it comes to cultural memory of human-inflicted trauma in a long and ongoing civil rights movement."[15]

The discussion so far might seem to some readers a jumbling confusion of nouns and verbs. How can a literary work be a thing (a material artifact) and a process (one that also gets described as a place)? Perhaps it is more helpful to think of literature as an imaginative space where the interaction between reader and text results in transformation. The act of reading has the potential to change how readers see themselves, their communities, and their histories. Literature asks readers to step outside of themselves to imagine new ways of seeing and being in the world. Literature produces dynamic engagement through emotional, intellectual, and aesthetic difficulty. "Your silence will not protect you," Audre Lorde reminds us. Language operates as a form of action: the word conjures freedom – now.

Civil rights literature, then, offers a means of working through questions of historical complexity as well as local and global significance. In doing so, literary representations offer an alternative to what scholars call civil rights "consensus memory." This way of constructing a story about the past continues to dominate popular culture and to vex the paradigm shifters of new civil rights studies, determined to provide more nuanced historical accounts. Briefly, the consensus story starts in 1954, when the *Brown v. Board of Education* decision prompted national leaders such as Martin Luther King Jr. to direct a nonviolent movement to end segregation. Events such as the Montgomery Bus Boycott (1955), the Freedom Rides (1961), the Birmingham Campaign (1963), Mississippi's Freedom Summer (1964), and the Selma-to-Montgomery March (1965) resulted in positive changes to law and custom. The late 1960s rise of Black Power and the 1968 death of King represented a decline in this movement's values and a fragmentation of its aims, leaving it essentially broken and ineffectual by the mid-1970s. Civil rights scholars from multiple disciplines have asked what this narrative says and what it leaves out – for example, stories of grassroots efforts, economic justice, self-defense, radicalism, and connections to other movements nationally and internationally. For example, in *The Civil Rights Movement in American Memory*, Renee C. Romano and Leigh Raiford ask, "What kind of civil rights movement is produced through this consensus memory and what vision of the present does it help to legitimate, valorize, or condemn?"[16]

For one, the dominant narrative offers a "satisfying morality tale" about the "natural progression of American values," historian Jacquelyn Dowd Hall explains, but one that is too "easy." Hall argues for making "civil rights harder ... harder to simplify, appropriate, and contain." Hall is concerned in particular with having the movement's meaning co-opted by forces determined to reverse its achievements.[17] Her message becomes clear in the conflicting understandings of civil rights seen in the 2013 *Shelby County v. Holder* decision and U.S. Representative John Lewis's reaction to it. The Supreme Court ruling assumed a movement whose goals were met, making federal monitoring of voting rights no longer necessary in places where Jim Crow laws formerly disenfranchised large portions of the population. Lewis, however, perceived a need to remain vigilant in an ongoing struggle between civil rights gains and losses.

A phrase from the title of Hall's article, "the long civil rights movement," has become a catch phrase for something more than extending chronology. *When* one brackets dates of the civil rights movement is often a function of *what* one considers that movement to be. When Hall connects the 1954–1968 "consensus narrative" to progressive politics of the 1930s and a "movement of movements" that took place during the late 1960s and early 1970s, she implicitly, if not overtly, extends the black freedom struggle to include such objectives as economic justice, gender equality, and gay rights.[18] Writing in the journal *Souls*, Peniel E. Joseph makes a related point, that "popular and historical narratives have conceptualized [1954–1965] literally and figuratively as 'the King years,'" a story that "obscures and effaces as much as it reveals and illuminates." While Joseph has a focus different from Hall's, specifically Black Power, he too expands ideas of the civil rights movement. His article and a later, more in-depth study demonstrate how Black Power developed alongside nonviolent direct action campaigns of the late 1950s and early 1960s. Instead of describing a "declension narrative" that sees figures such as Malcolm X and the Black Panthers as less acceptable stand-ins for the consensus narrative's more palatable figures (i.e., King or Rosa Parks), Joseph describes Black Power as a radical attempt to connect African American political discourse to international anti-colonial movements.[19]

Pinpointing the *when* and *what* of the civil rights movement is a subject of continual scholarly debate. Two articles might sum up that debate's extremes. On the one hand, Leon Litwack's "'Fight the Power': The Legacy of the Civil Rights Movement" offers a very broad view. Litwack states, "The civil rights movement began with the presence of enslaved blacks in the New World, with the first slave mutiny on the ships bringing them here."[20] Litwack takes his discussion into the present day with the appearance of the New Jim Crow in examples such as the prison-industrial complex, the decline of urban infrastructures, and crucial points of crisis such as the federal government's indifference to human suffering in the aftermath of Hurricane Katrina in 2005. On the other hand, Richard H. King in "The

Civil Rights Debate" clearly narrows the civil rights "movement" from 1954 to 1968. During this time period, individuals "sought during a sustained fashion ... to destroy the Jim Crow system of segregation and disfranchisement." This work differs markedly from the longer civil rights *"struggle"* (emphasis in original).[21]

The discussion prompts a question. If the *Cambridge Companion to American Civil Rights Literature* offers literary works as a solution to the problem of consensus memory, then what, if any, definition of civil rights ("movement" or "struggle") underlies the project? The most pragmatic approach might be to follow Brian Norman's lead in *Neo-Segregation Narratives: Jim Crow in Post Civil Rights American Literature* and understand "civil rights" as both a "useful" and "slippery" term.[22] This Cambridge Companion looks primarily at literature about events that took place from the post–World War II through the Black Power eras – traditional "movement" years – while recognizing that these events arose from very broad historical and artistic contexts that began in slavery and continue today, and that also include a diverse array of actors and stakeholders. Not all the chapters contained here agree on "when" and "what" the civil rights movement means. For the most part, however, they recognize that something transformational and sustained (to borrow Richard King's word) happened from the mid-1950s to the early 1970s. Some writings distinguish between a civil rights or black freedom *struggle* and a civil rights movement; some do not. Most agree that making such distinctions is more difficult when one discusses literature rather than history. A case in point involves works that look back at earlier events for, of course, writers often return to the past to address contemporary concerns. Where the chapters included here do converge is less upon what constitutes a historical time period and more on the value of literary and cinematic representation for civil rights study. As Robert J. Patterson and Erica R. Edwards explain in their introduction to a 2013 special issue of the *South Atlantic Quarterly*, the "strategies of close reading and methodologies of cultural studies" that literary scholars employ offer provocative challenges for reconceptualizing a significant and complex story.[23]

This volume's chapters are organized loosely by literary tradition and genre. Contributors discuss works from the mid-nineteenth century to the present, demonstrating the variety of materials available for civil rights literary study and different critical approaches to examining these texts. The first selections establish historic and artistic frameworks for understanding civil rights writing. Chapter 1, Zoe Trodd's "The Civil Rights Movement and Literature of Social Protest," shows how writers from peak decades of civil rights activism draw upon strategies of literary protest that writers such as Frederick Douglass and Harriet Jacobs developed during the abolitionist movement. Gwendolyn Brooks, Ann Petry, Robert Hayden, and Ralph Ellison provide examples of "spatio-symbolic" representation, where spaces that initially symbolize segregation, confinement, and other forms of social marginalization transform imaginatively into places of opposition, opportunity, and freedom. By making connections to literary abolitionism, Trodd explains, such writers perform two important functions. They turn "the no-place of America's margins into a site of resistance," and they expand the civil rights "movement's temporal boundaries" beyond conventional perspectives.

The second chapter in this volume, by Brian Norman, raises similar questions about time and space. Norman employs a range of texts to trace three primary strategies that black writers have used to represent a Jim Crow that has proven surprisingly durable and protean across the twentieth century. Authors such as Nella Larsen, in *Passing* (1929), and Richard Wright, in "Big Boy Leaves Home" (1935), reveal the physical and psychological violence that results from crossing the color line. Other works – notably Zora Neale Hurston's 1937 *Their Eyes Were Watching God* and Alice Walker's 1983 *The Color Purple* – show characters rejecting the color line altogether. In a different form of rejection, some writers "get out," to quote George Schuyler's 1931 satirical novel *Black No More*, turning to international or fantastical settings. In all three cases, Norman explains, "The Dilemma of Narrating Jim Crow," is both an artistic problem (how to represent compulsory segregation without reinscribing it) and a spatial one (how to negotiate a system that insists upon races knowing their "place").

The two chapters that follow examine the relationship between the civil rights and Black Arts movements. As GerShun Avilez explains, writers, artists, and intellectuals of the late 1960s and early 1970s focused in particular on creating a black public sphere where arts organizations, publication venues, and university curricula would enact social change. One might, in fact, trace the development of a companion to civil rights literature back to the formation of the first Black Studies program at San Francisco State University in 1969. Through an in-depth reading of Barry Beckham's 1972 novel *Runner Mack*, Avilez shows how writers from the period responded to repeated disappointments at creating real civil rights change. Mack's surrealist novel departs from typical Black Arts Movement realism, but its characters' decision to attempt revolutionary destruction – "takin' over the muthafuckin' country" – seems reasonable, given the way American dreams too often become nightmares.

Within the past few years, scholars have begun to re-examine the African American stage within a longer performance tradition. Nilgün

Anadolu-Okur's chapter for this volume situates Black Arts Movement theater within that context. Lorraine Hansberry's 1959 classic play *Raisin in the Sun* is almost synonymous with the phrase "civil rights literature," and for the Black Arts Movement writers who followed, theater was a form of revolutionary struggle. Anadolu-Okur's essay looks at this period as a turning point for black theater and, more broadly, in African American culture. Works such as Leroi Jones/Amiri Baraka's *Dutchman* (1964), Ntozake Shange's *for colored girls who have considered suicide/when the rainbow is enuf* (1976), and Charles Fuller's *Zooman and the Sign* (1980) show African Americans negotiating an unprecedented "ownership of agency."

Anadolu-Okur's chapter provides a transition point where the volume shifts from literary movements to literary genre as a lens for examining civil rights issues. The next chapters look specifically at fiction, poetry, and film from the movement's "classic phase" to consider different strategies for representing transformational social change. My own contribution surveys the landscape of civil rights fiction – defining and providing examples of different types, and outlining typical plots and themes. The chapter considers why a controversial novel such as Kathleen Stockett's *The Help* (2009) is so popular for teaching movement history. I propose as alternatives texts such as John O. Killens's *'Sippi* (1967), Alice Walker's *Meridian* (1976), and Anthony Grooms's *Bombingham* (2001) that are complex and nuanced like the movement itself.

The next chapter, by Christopher Metress looks at a specific fictional form: the white southern movement novel. Here, Metress examines how white southern novelists wrestled with the social and structural reconfigurations that were taking place during the turbulent years of 1954 to 1968. Canonical writers such as Flannery O'Connor, William Faulkner, and Robert Penn Warren produced a variety of personal and literary responses to the changing times. These writers, however, did not directly engage with the civil rights movement in their fiction. Many lesser-known figures, including Elizabeth Spencer, William Bradford Huie, Shirley Ann Grau, and Jesse Hill Ford, produced movement-related works that were widely read. Metress's chapter looks at novels by two writers all but forgotten today – Lettie Hamlett Rogers and Elliot Chaze – to provide a literary perspective on an understudied subject: the range of views white southerners held about the mid-century's confrontation with race.

Following Metress, Sharon Monteith examines cinematic engagements with the civil rights movement. For many audiences, film provides a vehicle for popular understandings of the movement itself, and more generally, of mid-century race relations. As Monteith has argued elsewhere, the movement became a "media event … and now it is being replayed as a cinematic event."[24] In this chapter, she critiques the most comforting and comfortable of fictional films for the ways in which they help to foster a very partial form of consensus memory, and she shows how *The Help* (2011), and *The Butler* (2013) may be understood within a longer film history. Monteith makes the case for a variety of genres, including overlooked films, and even examines films that never quite made it to the screen, as she takes a position about the extent to which cinema has or has not grappled with civil rights history.

In the volume's final chapter on genre, Jeffrey Coleman makes a compelling argument for paying more critical attention to civil rights movement poetry. Poetry was the dominant genre during a pivotal historical moment. Major national and international figures composed poetic responses to almost every significant civil rights event. Poetry offers some of the most aesthetically, intellectually, and emotionally rich civil rights material. To demonstrate his point, Coleman provides an overview of key figures and themes, and offers an in-depth analysis of Michael S. Harper's "Here Where Coltrane Is," a meditation on the intersections of music and mourning for four young victims of a 1963 church bombing in Birmingham, Alabama.

This volume closes with two chapters that expand civil rights literary study outward into new directions. Robert J. Patterson continues the book's focus on genre, using first-person writings to explore the intersections between race, gender, sexuality, and rights. Works such as Toni Cade Bambara's *The Black Woman: An Anthology*, Kaluma Ya Salaam's "Women's Rights Are Human Rights," and Huey Newton's "A Letter from Huey to the Revolutionary Brothers and Sisters about the Women's Liberation and Gay Liberation Movements" attempt to destabilize patriarchal and heteronormative hierarchies that reproduced oppressions and, by extension, undermined the movement's desire for black communal advancement. Although Patterson focuses primarily on writings from the 1970s, he draws connections between ideas expressed in these works and those from a long tradition of memoir and autobiography from the nineteenth century to the present to show how ideas of civil rights are deeply intertwined with the complex individual identities of those who fight for them. By establishing these connections, Patterson makes a point similar to Trodd's: that civil rights writers adapt and carry forward to new generations literary strategies from their activist forebears.

The final chapter brings full circle ideas expressed in this volume's beginnings. Like Trodd, Barbara McCaskill looks at space as trope of the movement's possibilities; like Norman, she examines how literature negotiates a supposedly "post-racial" landscape. McCaskill examines three contemporary works: Lila Quintero Weaver's graphic novel and memoir *Darkroom* (2012), about growing up Latina in segregation-era Alabama; Tayari

Jones's novel *Silver Sparrow* (2011), set in the New South's cultural epicenter, Atlanta, Georgia; and *Beyond Katrina* (2010), poet laureate Natasha Trethewey's memoir about Gulfport, Mississippi. In each, place functions as a way to ground explorations of extending the movement's chronology beyond the "classic years" of the 1950s and 1960s and of expanding civil rights activism to include such issues as immigration, economics, environmentalism, and criminal justice. Weaver, Jones, and Tretheway focus in particular on questions of identity. If "black" became a way to label, marginalize, and deny rights to a certain segment of the U.S. population during the Jim Crow era, then how does that label function in a supposedly post–civil rights world? The question is not so easily answered when one considers the interplay of race, gender, class, and the tenuous label "post."

The publication of a *Cambridge Companion to American Civil Rights Literature* does not intend to close out conversation on the topic. Quite the opposite: this gathering of selected essays makes clear how much ground remains to be covered. Ample opportunities for further inquiry exist because the study of literature itself has undergone transition – one result being the emergence of interdisciplinary fields such as civil rights literature. Freshly minted PhDs excepted, most literary scholars working today were trained to teach and write about national literatures in specific chronological periods (Modern American literature, British Romanticism, and so on), with specializations in authors, genres, critical approaches, or specific areas (Shakespeare, the novel, feminist theory, African American literature). Although plenty of excellent work has examined civil rights and, more specifically, the movement, in literature, few scholars have described themselves as "specialists" in this "field" because the field, per se, did not exist. Not quite African American literature, not quite southern literature, hovering on the line between modernism and post-modernism, civil rights literature does not fit neatly into traditional categories of literary study. As those categories continue to expand, prospects open up for more work and for more individuals to pursue those lines of inquiry.[25]

Chapters below touch on multiple topics that merit additional investigation. The cover image alone, Gammon's *Freedom Now*, hints at the rich relationship between civil rights, text, and the visual arts. Chapters by Norman, McCaskill and myself discuss graphic narratives, a topic that easily could have been its own chapter. McCaskill, Anadolu-Okur, and Coleman make specific references to music in their chapters. The open mouths in the bottom half of Gammon's painting also look as if they might be singing a freedom song – directing readers to the deep connections between civil rights literature and music, which extends through poetry to hip-hop and spoken word. Coleman describes his chapter on poetry as a "state of the field" essay. His anthology, *Words of Protest, Words of Freedom*, made the important first step of assembling an archive; the next steps involve asking what these materials reveal. Coleman's work leads to an important point. Anthologies of fiction and poetry exist, but no comparable volume exists for civil rights movement drama – although the study of African American performance has made exciting new strides during the past few years.[26] Metress examines the work of white southern novelists, but no one has yet tackled overtly segregationist rhetoric and its resulting literary productions.[27] Fruitful areas of exploration also include connections to other ethnic literatures, especially with regard to what Sarah Eden Schiff calls "power literature."[28] Important connections remain to be made to freedom struggles or social justice movements in other countries – this is especially true for scholars of the Global South, as Monteith makes clear in essays that link civil rights in Mississippi and the 1964 Freedom Summer project to France, the Caribbean and to the U.S.-Canadian border and that compare civil rights struggles in Selma, Alabama; Paris, France; and Aberystwyth, Wales.[29] Literary scholars might do more with documentary writings such as journalism and autobiography, for the lines between "art" and "artifact" in many of these works are often very blurred, as Monteith and Allison Graham demonstrate in their 2011 volume on southern media in the series *The New Encyclopedia of Southern Culture*. And, as chapters by Patterson and McCaskill reveal in this volume, first-person writings often provide the best perspective into the complexities of the phrase "civil rights."

Different kinds of complexity – intellectual, artistic, and emotional – lie at the heart of this book. Civil rights literature ultimately does not compel readers because they seek to join a growing academic discourse, to build résumés, teach courses, or find research topics for those courses. This literature draws readers because, in multifaceted ways, it transforms the silence Lorde speaks of into language and action. The result is a triumph of art and life: the depth, beauty, and power of the word.

NOTES

1 Lauren Haynes and Emily G. Hanna, curators, *Spiral: Perspectives on an African-American Art Collective* (Birmingham, AL: Birmingham Museum of Art, December 5, 2010–April 17, 2011).
2 Audre Lorde, "The Transformation of Silence into Language and Action," in *Sister Outsider: Essays and Speeches* (New York: Crossing Press, 1984), p. 40.
3 Richard Wright, *Black Boy* (New York: World Publishing, 1945), p. 218.
4 The term "nadir" comes from Rayford W. Logan, *The Negro in American Life and Thought: The Nadir, 1877–1901* (New York: Dial Press, 1954). On racial violence during this time period, see *Phillip Dray, At the Hands of Persons Unknown: The Lynching of Black America* (New York: Random House, 2002).

5 Writing in the foreword to Michelle Alexander's book *The New Jim Crow: Mass Incarceration in the Age of Colorblindness* (New York: New Press, 2012), Cornel West says that "the very discourse of colorblindness ... has left America blind to the New Jim Crow" (x). See also Charles Johnson, "The End of the Black American Narrative, *The American Scholar* 77.3 (Summer, 2008): 32–42; Ashraf Rushdy, *The End of American Lynching* (New Brunswick, NJ: Rutgers University Press, 2012), pp. 169–75; and Koritha Mitchell, "Love in Action: Noting Similarities between Lynching Then and Anti-LGBT Violence Now," *Callaloo* 36 (2013): esp., 706–9. Each discusses the need for new narratives or new discourse that more adequately describes the contemporary moment.

6 The term "trade gap" comes from early American studies. See Eric Slaughter, et al., "The 'Trade Gap' in Atlantic Studies: A Forum on Literary and Historical Scholarship," *William and Mary Quarterly* Third Series 65.1 (Winter 2008): 135–86.

7 Charles Eagles, "Toward New Histories of the Civil Rights Era," *Journal of Southern History* 66 (2000): 834; Richard H. King, "The Civil Rights Debate," in *A Companion to the Literature and Culture of the American South*, ed. Richard Gray and Owen Robinson (Malden, MA: Blackwell, 2004), p. 221.

8 In addition to the many chapters by individual contributors from this volume see *Words of Protest, Words of Freedom: Poetry of the American Civil Rights Movement and Era*, ed. Jeffrey Lamar Coleman (Durham, NC: Duke University Press, 2012); *The Civil Rights Reader: American Literature from Jim Crow to Reconciliation*, ed. Julie Buckner Armstrong (Athens: University of Georgia Press, 2009); *Short Stories of the Civil Rights Movement*, ed. Margaret Earley Whitt (Athens: University of Georgia Press, 2006); Minrose Gwin, *Remembering Medgar Evers: Writing the Long Civil Rights Movement* (Athens: University of Georgia Press, 2013); Brian Norman, *Neo-Segregation Narratives: Jim Crow in Post–Civil Rights American Literature* (Athens: University of Georgia Press, 2010); Brian Norman and Piper Kendrix Williams, eds., *Representing Segregation: Toward an Aesthetics of Living Jim Crow, and Other Forms of Racial Division* (Albany: State University of New York Press, 2010); Christopher Metress and Harriet Pollack, eds., *Emmett Till in Literary Memory and Imagination* (Baton Rouge: Louisiana State University Press, 2008); Christopher Metress, ed., *The Lynching of Emmett Till: A Documentary Narrative* (Charlottesville: University of Virginia Press, 2002); Robert J. Patterson and Erica R. Edwards, eds., Black Literature, Black Leadership Special Issue, *South Atlantic Quarterly* 112.2 (2013); Brian Norman and Piper Kendrix Williams, eds., Representing Segregation Special Issue, *African American Review* 42.1 (2008).

9 Christopher Metress, "Making Civil Rights Harder: Literature, Memory, and the Black Freedom Struggle," *Southern Literary Journal* 40.2 (Spring 2008): 140. Metress's article builds upon an essay of Jacquelyn Dowd Hall's, "The Long Civil Rights Movement and the Political Uses of the Past," discussed later in this chapter.

10 Barbara Melosh, "Historical Memory in Fiction: The Civil Rights Movement in Three Novels," *Radical History Review* 40 (Winter 1988): 145; Whitt, *Short Stories*, p. x.

11 Melissa Walker, *Down from the Mountaintop: Black Women's Novels in the Wake of the Civil Rights Movement, 1966–1989* (New Haven, CT: Yale University Press, 1991).

12 Richard H. King, "Politics and Fictional Representation: The Case of the Civil Rights Movement," in *The Making of Martin Luther King and the Civil Rights Movement*, ed. Brian Ward and Tony Badger (New York: Washington Square Press, 1996), p. 163.

13 *History and Memory in African-American Culture*, ed. Geneviève Fabre and Robert O'Meally (Oxford: Oxford University Press, 1994), pp. 3–10.

14 Leigh Anne Duck, *The Nation's Region: Southern Modernism, Segregation, and U.S. Nationalism* (Athens: University of Georgia Press, 2006), p. 246.

15 Gwin, *Remembering Medgar Evers*, pp. 18–21. Gwin takes the term "frames of remembrance" from Iwona Irwin-Zarecka, *Frames of Remembrance: The Dynamics of Cultural Memory* (New Brunswick, NJ: Transaction, 1994).

16 Renee C. Romano and Leigh Raiford, eds., *The Civil Rights Movement in American Memory* (Athens: University of Georgia Press, 2006), pp. xiv–xv. Scholarship on the new civil rights movement studies is extensive. Good starting points are Eagles, "Toward New Histories of the Civil Rights Era"; King, "The Civil Rights Debate"; and John Dittmer, "The Civil Rights Movement," in *The African American Experience: An Historical and Bibliographical Guide*, ed. Arvarh E. Strickland and Robert E. Weems (Westport, CT: Greenwood Press, 2001), pp. 352–67.

17 Jacquelyn Dowd Hall, "The Long Civil Rights Movement and the Political Uses of the Past," *Journal of American History* 91 (2005): 1235.

18 See Van Gosse, "A Movement of Movements: The Definition and Periodization of the New Left," in *A Companion to Post-1945 America*, ed. Jean-Christophe Agnew and Roy Rosenzweig (New York: Blackwell, 2006), pp. 277–302. For a critique of the long movement thesis, see Sundiata K. Cha-Jua and Clarence E. Lang, "The 'Long Movement' as Vampire: Temporal and Spatial Fallacies in Recent Black Freedom Studies," *Journal of African American History* 92 (2007): 265–88. Cha-Jua and Lang criticize the "long movement" idea for the way it erases conceptual differences between movements. Because it keeps finding new life beyond its specific place and time, a long civil rights movement is effectively "undead."

19 Peniel E. Joseph, "Waiting till the Midnight Hour: Reconceptualizing the Heroic Period of the Civil Rights Movement, 1954–1965," *Souls: A Critical Journal of Black Politics, Culture, and Society* 2.2 (Spring 2000): 7; and *Waiting 'Til the Midnight Hour. A Narrative History of Black Power in America* (New York: Henry Holt, 2006).

20 Leon Litwack, "'Fight the Power': The Legacy of the Civil Rights Movement," *Journal of Southern History* 75.1 (February 2009): 5.

21 King, "The Civil Rights Debate," p. 222.

22 Norman, *Neo-Segregation Narratives*, p. 4.

23 Robert J. Patterson and Erica R. Edwards, "Black Literature, Black Leadership: New Boundaries, New Borders," *South Atlantic Quarterly* 112 (2013): 219.

24 Sharon Monteith, "The Movie-Made Movement: Civil Rites of Passage," *Memory and Popular Film*, ed. Paul Grange (Manchester, UK: Manchester University Press, 2003), p. 120.

25 A case in point arises from the controversy generated over Kenneth Warren's *What Was African American Literature?* (Cambridge, MA: Harvard University Press, 2011). A subsequent roundtable (Glenda R. Carpio et al., What Was African American Literature? *PMLA* 128 [2013]: 386–408) focused the question on literary responses to Jim Crow – when Warren's point is that writing by black Americans often exists outside the relationship to slavery, Jim Crow, civil rights, and other dynamics of oppression and resistance. Conversely, Brian Norman makes a clear case in *Neo-Segregation Narratives* that responses to Jim Crow often exist outside African American literature.

26 For new ways of thinking about performance and social action, see Soyica Diggs Colbert, *The African American Theatrical Body: Reception, Performance, and the Stage* (New York: Cambridge University Press, 2011); Koritha Mitchell, *Living with Lynching: African American Lynching Plays, Performance, and Citizenship, 1890–1930* (Champaign-Urbana: University of Illinois Press, 2011); Lisa Woolfork, *Embodying Slavery in African American Culture* (Champaign-Urbana: University of Illinois Press, 2008).

27 See Keith D. Miller, "Martin Luther King Jr. and the Landscape of Civil Rights Rhetoric," *Rhetoric and Public Affairs* 16.1 (Spring 2013): 179.

28 Sarah Eden Schiff, "Power Literature and the Myth of Racial Memory," *Modern Fiction Studies* 57.1 (Spring 2011): 96–122.

29 On "the Global South" see Suzanne W. Jones and Sharon Monteith, eds., *South to a New Place: Region, Literature, Culture* (Baton Rouge: Louisiana State University Press, 2002); Jon Smith and Deborah Cohn, eds., *Look Away! The U.S. South in New World Studies* (Durham, NC: Duke University Press, 2004); Annette Trefzer and Katherine McKee, eds., Global Contexts, Local Literatures: The New Southern Studies, Special Issue, *American Literature* 78.4 (2006). On civil rights in the global South, see Sharon Monteith, "How Bigger Mutated: Richard Wright, Boris Vian and 'The bloody channels through which one pushes logic to the breaking point,'" in *Transatlantic Exchanges: The South in Europe and Europe in the South*, ed. Richard Gray and Waldemar Zachariesz (Vienna: Austrian Academy, 2007), pp. 149–66; Sharon Monteith, "The Bridge from Mississippi's Freedom Summer to Canada: Pearl Cleage's *Bourbon at the Border*," in *Cultural Circulation: Canadian Writers and Authors from the American South – A Dialogue*, ed. Waldemar Zacharasiewicz (Vienna: Austrian Academy of Arts and Sciences, 2013), pp. 155–75; Sharon Monteith, "Turning South Again: Conjuring Mississippi's Freedom Summer in Sans Souci, Trinidad," in *The U.S. South in Motion*, ed. Constante Groba (Valencia: Universitat de Valencia, 2013), pp. 145–56; and Sharon Monteith, "A Tale of Three Bridges," in *The Transatlantic Sixties: Europe and the United States in the Counterculture Decade*, ed. Greg Kosc, Clara Juncker, Sharon Monteith and Britta Waldschmidt-Nelson (Berlin: Verlag, 2013).

I

ZOE TRODD

The Civil Rights Movement and Literature of Social Protest

In 1957, W. E. B. Du Bois described a long civil rights movement – what he called the fight for black citizenship – that began in 1876 and continued to his present day. A decade later, Martin Luther King, Jr., explained that African Americans had been "fighting more than a hundred years" for "full emancipation" and that the struggle would endure. Civil rights movement literature performed the same expansion of the movement's temporal boundaries. It built on earlier literary protest traditions, namely, literary abolitionism, to perform its cultural work, and it also used the memory of past activism to create a protest ancestry for civil rights. In the poetry of Gwendolyn Brooks and Robert Hayden, the fiction of Ann Petry, and the essays and fiction of Ralph Ellison, with its protest memory and revision of earlier protest aesthetics, we can identify the shape of a centuries-long movement for equality.[1]

Identifying this open loop of repetition-with-difference helps to challenge narratives of the civil rights movement that begin in the mid-1950s and end a decade later. The imposition of a beginning in 1955 and an end in 1965 gives the movement a "ghostliness," as Jacqueline Dowd Hall observed in 2001. Confined to "a brief moment in time," visible only while King marched through the South, the movement recedes "into a grainy, washed-out past" and becomes "remote" and "digestible," Hall added. More myth than history, it feels several stages removed. Noting this problem again in 2005, Hall demanded a new narrative of what she termed the "long civil rights movement." She called for an expansion of chronological barriers – for a narrative of the movement that explores "the continuities between the 1940s and the 1960s" and goes beyond the "tragic denouement" trope of a 1965 ending. In the protest memory of civil rights literature lies an even longer narrative, one that goes further back, beyond the 1940s, to anti-slavery texts of the nineteenth century.[2]

This shared use of literary abolitionism was a key civil rights aesthetic. Writers knew that form could protest. It could challenge racist imagery, reassign the meanings of white supremacist symbols, and undermine narratives of the past that shaped power dynamics in the present. And from a vast range of possibilities, they chose tropes that abolitionists had tried and tested. They adapted those tropes for their own protest moment, using abolitionist aesthetics to claim a literary heritage of dissent and to argue that America had not fulfilled the promises of Emancipation.

The Protest Literature Tradition and the Long Civil Rights Movement

Protest writers have long asked America to *be* America. Raging and reasoning, prophesying and provoking, reporting ills and proposing remedies, their literature has given distinctive shape to long-accumulated grievances, created space for argument, and shattered the boundaries of acceptable belief. It has also fused aesthetics and ideologies into a poetics of engagement. Some writers explained how this fusion worked in practice. For example, Langston Hughes noted of one of his poems that it was "marked by conflicting changes, sudden nuances, sharp and impudent interjections, broken rhythms, and passages," so as to evoke a "community in transition," while Gwendolyn Brooks once commented that she wrote off-rhyme for "an off-rhyme situation." Making aesthetic choices express cultural change and social conflict, Hughes and Brooks crafted a politics of form. Like numerous protest writers, they negotiated a space between socially conscious representation and formalism.[3]

Aware of this particular balancing act between literary form and political content, several other writers confronted it head-on. Du Bois famously declared in 1926: "I do not care a damn for any art that is not used for propaganda." In other lesser-known articles from the same period he was careful to qualify this assertion and explain what he meant by a propagandist "use" of art. In 1924, he insisted that protest writers were "not prostituting art to propaganda, rather we are lifting propaganda to the high realm of art." Two years later he further resisted the idea that writers must choose between "Beauty" and "Propaganda," noting that it was doubtful if "there can be a search for disembodied beauty which is not really a passionate effort to do something tangible." As far as Du Bois was concerned, any divide between art and propaganda was artificial: rather than simply using art for propaganda, art should *be* propaganda and propaganda had *become* art. Fellow NAACP (National Association for the Advancement of Colored People) member and protest writer William Pickens agreed. "*Art and Propaganda always do exist side by side,*" he observed in 1924. And, like Du Bois, Pickens had a qualification for his statement. "Here's what the near-artists stumble over," he continued: "*it is the function of art to conceal the propaganda as to make it more palatable to the average recipient, while yet not destroying its effect*" (italics in the original). Neither Du Bois nor Pickens understood the term "protest literature" as an oxymoron. Writers should lift propaganda to the realm of art, in Du Bois's words, or at least conceal propaganda *with* art, in Pickens's.[4]

This negotiated space – the gap between "protest" and "literature" in the very term "protest literature" – is at the heart of civil rights texts. A struggle of ideas took place during the long civil rights movement, and writers expressed those ideas through symbols and motifs, embodied them in imagery, rhythm, rhyme scheme, syntax. Yet until recently, scholars used the label "protest" to signal well-meaning but artistically limited writing. Jerry Bryant offers a typically dismissive evaluation, observing that when black novelists stopped campaigning against lynching (which he thinks happened during the Harlem Renaissance) this produced "real novels, great improvements over the well-meaning but floundering fiction of the earlier period." In fact, scholars have often termed protest literature "propaganda" or "polemics." Judith L. Stephens referred to "protest (or propaganda)," as though "propaganda" always lurks in parenthesis after any mention of "protest." Margaret Ann Reid's book subtitle offers "polemics" as another synonym for "protest." Other scholars use the terms "social document," "problem literature," or "social viewpoint art," and one, Maryemma Graham, mentions a "tradition of 'protest' literature," with scare quotes around "protest" that introduce a skeptical modifier. Some have expressed frustration at the very designation "protest writer," with Melba Joyce Boyd explaining that when Frances Harper is "pigeonholed" as a "protest poet," this discredits her "literary merit." While protest writers themselves – Du Bois, Pickens, Hughes, Brooks, and numerous others – refused to decouple art and protest, scholars have often ignored the complex harmony of that marriage.[5]

Recently, however, two scholars have reassessed the relationship between politics and form. They examined, respectively, the genre of American protest literature and the American protest essay. In 2006, John Stauffer offered a genre definition for "American protest literature." He pointed out that there has been "no common understanding of protest literature; the term has been used to mean virtually all literature … or no literature." Either, Stauffer explains, "all novels [are] a form of protest" (and so the term "protest literature" becomes tautology), or else "literature [is] a hermetic text, divorced from politics and ideology" (the term an oxymoron). Stauffer defines protest literature as the texts that have critiqued society and suggested "either implicitly or explicitly, a solution to society's ills." He also identifies three rhetorical strategies that protest literature employs: empathy, shock value, and symbolic action. The following year, Brian Norman examined the

American protest essay. Like Stauffer, Norman points to the dominant strain of critical thought that separates art and protest. Literary scholars dismiss protest literature as too immediate or polemical, he observes. Insisting, however, that "writers do not jeopardize their art when they assume the mantle of political advocacy" and that "*protest* defines a formal tradition in its own right," Norman reveals an "American protest imaginary." He argues that the American protest essay fuses elements of the European personal essay and American political oratory to produce an aesthetic of inclusion. The form has engaged national myths, denounced the failure of those myths to become reality, and worked for their final realization – seeking "collectivity in the face of division." Norman also argues that protest essays share a five-strand protest aesthetic.[6]

Stauffer's "symbolic action" and Norman's "protest imaginary" are visible in civil rights literature's plethora of spatio-symbolic representations between the early 1940s and the early 1970s. Writers imagined segregation to encompass schools, neighborhoods, buses, and lunch counters, but also the dreams and ambitions of individuals, economic opportunities, and cultural representations. As Hughes affirmed in a 1964 poem, the space at the heart of the desegregation struggle was also symbolic: "There is a dream in the land / With its back against the wall ... Our dream of freedom," he writes, creating a spatio-symbolic confinement of the "dream" by a "wall." Writers, including Hughes, blended material space with the figurative space of the public sphere: employment opportunities, the ballot box, history books, Hollywood, and the media. In their spatio-symbolic protest literature, desegregation meant an end to all forms of marginalization and entry into what King repeatedly termed a "choice place" or the "promised land."[7]

One major element of this civil rights aesthetic was the spatialization of social margins. A geo-political literary landscape of manholes, coal-bunkers, basements, sewers, kitchenettes, shacks, and boxes offered a vision of the cultural periphery. Writers imagined confined and segregated places as the margins of social space. But in developing this politics of form, writers were also representing the problem of historical marginalization: what King protested in 1967 as history books that ignore "the contribution of the Negro in American history." Spatio-symbolic representations literalized the dark underworld of American public memory – the dumping ground for that ignored history – and the margins of representational space.[8]

Protest writers tried to overturn these confinements and exclusions. Seeking liberation from the hidden spaces of historical representation, they remembered history's exclusions and challenged the narrative of American progress. In particular they re-narrated the history of slavery. Collapsing the white wall of amnesia and nostalgia, writers depicted segregation as slavery by a different name. Far from a hidden, walled-up past, slavery shapes the segregated, walled present. Yet even more pervasive than the memory of slavery in civil rights literature was the memory of *resistance* to slavery. Writers protested neo-slavery but also located the movement alongside abolitionism and their literature alongside anti-slavery literature. As Hughes insisted in 1966, Frederick Douglass was "not dead." Writers turned Douglass and others into early desegregationists, thereby challenging historical margins (by remembering slavery and abolitionism) and social margins (by applying abolitionist protest rhetoric to the desegregation struggle).[9]

The relationship of desegregation literature to Douglass and other abolitionists ran deeper still. The black history that writers remembered was itself a history of spatio-symbolic representation. As bell hooks notes, "many narratives of struggle and resistance, from the time of slavery to the present, share an obsession with the politics of space.... [F]reedom [is] always and intimately linked to the issue of transforming space." hooks suggests that African Americans should build on these past strategies of resistance. Civil rights literature did just that. As writers imagined the spaces of segregated America, they drew upon a strand of the abolitionist aesthetic: the fusion of concrete boundaries with the abstract boundaries of citizenship. In abolitionism's usable past was a model of spatio-symbolic protest, and writers used this past as a tool for the open future. Countering the idea that the horizon represents the future, that only open space represents hopeful time, they turned the no-place of America's margins into a site of resistance. They adapted the spatio-symbolism of abolitionist literature to challenge America's historically segregated spaces with the deep space of its protest past.[10]

The Abolitionist and Civil Rights Politics of Form

Literary abolitionism has a series of confined spaces. From Henry Brown's box, the Underground Railroad, and Nat Turner's "cave," to the "loophole" in Harriet Jacobs's *Incidents* (1861), Frado's tiny L-shaped room in Harriet Wilson's *Our Nig* (1861), and the "holes and crevices" in Douglass's *The Heroic Slave* (1853), this abolitionist trope expressed the problem of being "slaves in the midst of freedom," as Martin Delany put it in 1855. It literalized the physical confinement and social marginalization of millions of black people. For example, William Pennington's *The Fugitive Blacksmith* (1849) describes the "mental and spiritual darkness" of slavery in Maryland, its "total moral midnight," which Pennington only comprehends while in the safe space of "six months' concealment" during his flight to freedom.

Pennington reverses this symbolism of dark space with a memory of hiding for "hours in a wood, or behind a fence," to escape his master's "eye" – of chosen invisibility and confinement. Then he transforms the *master's* space into one more horrific because it collapses as history sweeps through. He describes the "dilapidated dwelling" of a man who "has been guilty of great cruelties" and who is dead or moved away:

> the once fine smooth gravel walks, overgrown with grass ... the once finely painted picket fences, rusted and fallen down – a fine garden in splendid ruins – the lofty ceiling of the mansion thickly curtained with cobwebs – the spacious apartments abandoned ... the crying cricket and cockroaches.

Borders are breached, for the "walks" are overgrown and the ceiling is hidden. Boundaries are insecure, for the "fences" have fallen down. The master's space is shattered, abandoned, and invaded. Pennington follows this description with an account of the "decline of slaveholding families." The "old master declines" and slavery has so affected the families of slave-holders that the "decline" in his family line is equally "rapid and marked." In "almost every point of view," Pennington explains, "the children of slaveholders are universally inferior to themselves." Juxtaposing a "dilapidated dwelling" and this familial declension, Pennington suggests that *slavery*, rather than the slave, is about to enter the dead space of history – becoming extinct.[11]

Other anti-slavery literature went still further with its spatio-symbolism, turning closets, garrets, boxes, and crevices into the forgotten spaces of history's house. For example, Wendell Phillips prefaces Douglass's *Narrative* (1845) with an assertion that space is endlessly unsafe for the slave ("there is no single spot – however narrow or desolate – where a fugitive slave can plant himself and say 'I am safe'"), and Douglass goes on to describe slavery's spatial dynamics. Covey controls all space through surveillance, Douglass observes: "He was under every tree, behind every stump, in every bush, and at every window." In *My Bondage and My Freedom* (1855), he describes slavery's spatial confinements in detail: the "holes and corners" around the plantation, the "out-of-the-way places" and the "'tabooed' spot ... separated from the rest of the world." He locates this "spot" amid the apparent "boundlessness of slave territory," with its deliberately "vague and indistinct" geography. Slaves occupy a tiny corner that a never-ending no-man's land segregates from the rest of the world. Douglass adds that slavery circumscribes movement within this space. While freemen might "contemplate a life in the far west, or in some distant country," the "slave is a fixture; he has no choice, no goal, no destination; but is pegged down to a single spot, and must take root here, or nowhere." Slaves have no spatial destination.[12]

Repeatedly, Douglass imagines slavery itself as a physically confined or marginalized space. A slave is "a man going into the tomb ... buried out of sight" and slavery is "a stone prison." In conversations with white boys, he imagines his fixed social and physical position as a literal location "on a curb stone or a cellar door." While sitting at the margins ("curb stone") or at the entrance to a dark hole ("cellar door"), he observes that the boys are free to "go where [they] like" but he is "a slave for life." Douglass even notes that the plantation is "a little nation of its own, having its own language, its own rules, regulations and customs." It is an entirely discreet space, "far away from all the great thoroughfares" so that no "foreign or dangerous influences" can disrupt the "natural operation of the slave system." Controlling space, the slave owners maintain their power. Then, in his third autobiography, *The Life and Times* (1881/1892), Douglass took up the theme again. Slavery is a "house of bondage," "a horrible pit," "a life of living death," a "dark corner" of a "dark domain."[13]

But Douglass lays out the transformation of slavery's controlled space. For example, he hides in the tight space of a closet and finds a vantage point from which to reverse the master's controlling gaze. Through the closet's "cracks," Douglass can see but not be seen. In a speech that he printed at the end of *My Bondage,* he describes slavery as a "dark cell" but insists that "we are opening the dark cell, and leading the people into the horrible recesses of what they are pleased to call their domestic institution." His descriptions of the Underground Railroad – and of his own change in status through moving from one space to another, from Baltimore to New York – are further calls for spatial resistance. And his eventual decision to be "the thin edge of the wedge to open for my people a way in many directions and places never before occupied by them" reveals his belief that he might seize control of slavery's space.[14]

One hundred years later, civil rights literature revived this abolitionist aesthetic of spatio-symbolism. Setting up the stakes, numerous writers summoned images of literal confined space and employed metaphors of confinement, turning the South's physical space into figurative space. For example, in *Coming of Age in Mississippi* (1968), Anne Moody comments on the White House's failure to create civic space for African Americans by juxtaposing a description of her "dreams" with a memory of "Mr. Carter's big white house" and the "rotten wood two-room shacks" where her family lived. Other writers shifted their gaze to the North. Gwendolyn Brooks focused many of her poems on confined spaces in northern black belt areas and expressed spatial confinement through form as well as imagery. For example, in "The Birth in a Narrow Room" (1949), Brooks describes the birth of a girl into a space that will make her say: "How pinchy is my room!

How can I breathe!" This "pinchy room" mirrors the narrow selection of sounds in the sixteen-line poem. The sounds of "w" and "ch" dominate the first stanza's sound. The sounds of "p" and "b" dominate the second stanza, with some overlap of the first stanza's dominant sounds. The only lines free from these four sounds ("I am not anything and I have got / Not anything, or anything to do") are cramped instead by the thrice repetition of "anything."[15]

When not making form express confinement, Brooks turns literal space into figurative space. For example, she asks in the poem "Kitchenette Building" (1945): "could a dream ... sing an aria down these rooms / Even if we were willing to let it in?" She returns to spatio-symbolism in "A Lovely Love" (1960), which examines those who are "definitionless in this strict atmosphere" and builds up to this vision of symbolic space through literal spaces: "alley ... a hall ... stairways ... a splintery box ... cavern." The definitionless space exists on a local scale in "Beverly Hills, Chicago" (1949), where the poetic voice wonders "if one has a home" and asks for admittance to "our mutual estate," and on a national, civic scale in "The Blackstone Rangers" (1968), which notes of a Chicago street gang that "their country is a Nation on no map." Brooks also explored the confinements of *memory*. "The Sundays of Satin-Legs Smith" (1945) depicts the past as an oppressive force that further confines space in the present: "The pasts of his ancestors lean against / Him. Crowd him." In "The Lovers of the Poor" (1960), the homes are a "sick four–story hulk ... with fissures everywhere," filled with "soil that looks the soil of centuries," and people who are the "puzzled wreckage / of the middle passage."[16]

Yet Brooks countered these confinements of history in other poems, where the past is a tool for spatial transformation. In "The Anniad" (1949), the one mention of a "room" comes within the long poem's only parenthesis, again creating a confined space through form: "(Not that room! / Not that dusted demi-gloom!)" The poem then ends with a woman "kissing in her kitchenette / The minuets of memory." Here, the rhyme scheme affirms the power of memory to open a new space by only half-rhyming "memory" with "thoroughly" and by separating the rhyme across seven lines, while all other lines in the forty-three-stanza poem contain tightly packed rhymes (usually separated within the seven-line stanzas by two or three lines, often coming together in a two-line rhyme). The trochaic tetrameter catalectic poem contains thirty rhyme schemes but only in the final stanza, as Brooks ties together a seemingly confined space and memory, does the poem have to stretch fully across itself in order to rhyme. This stretched space at the poem's end is even more noticeable because of the internal rhyme of "minuets" with "kitchenette." Already rhymed with "sweat" and "violet" from lines three and four of the stanza, "kitchenette" is given the extra echo of "minuets," embedded within the poem's last line, while "memory" stretches back to line one. The fact that the poem's first release from a tightly packed rhyme scheme comes amid a description of a "minuet," a methodical, structured dance, signals through an ironic juxtaposition of form and content one final rebellion against the formal constraints of Brooks's chosen conventions.[17]

Brooks overturns confined space again in "The Bean Eaters" (1960). An old couple lives in a "rented back room" and finds in memory an open space. All lines in the three-stanza poem are rhymed except for the line "rented back room" and the two-word line "And remembering ..." The ellipsis, coming after "remembering," implies a space of memory, and is an echo of the space created by the open word "room," never closed out by a rhyme. Tied together as this tightly structured poem's only outlets, the words "remembering" and "room" form a memory-room within the poem's space. Sometimes, suggests Brooks with these two poems, the past could be an open space rather than a confining force.[18]

Ann Petry's *The Street* (1946) performs another spatio-symbolic reversal through memory. The novel sets up the problem of confined space, transforms literal space into figurative space, and then offers the glimmer of a solution. The novel's first chapter repeatedly returns to the confined spaces in Lutie Johnson's building – the hallways are so narrow "she could reach out and touch them on either side without having to stretch," and the stairs are "dark high narrow." This imagery recurs throughout: the apartments are "dark, filthy, traps" with "little hallways," "ratty little rooms," and walls that seem to "come in toward her." They have "row after row of narrow windows – floor after floor packed tight with people." She dreams of Harlem's residents as rats moving through the streets, each one with a "building chained to its back," crying "'Unloose me!'" Petry goes on to make the confined spaces signify a loss of choice (Lutie sees her choice of living space as "a yard wide and ten miles long" – narrow like the building's hallways) and so a loss of futurity; of open horizons, of possibility. Lutie "can't see anything ahead of me except these walls that push in against me."[19]

Yet, like Brooks, Petry offers an alternative. One chapter consists mostly of a flashback. Lutie enters the confined space of a subway car, where people have to make "room for themselves where no room had existed before," and remembers seeing her white employer's house for the first time (when she realized that she herself had spent her life sleeping "in cubicles that were little more than entrances to and exits from other rooms"). She recalls that looking at the house "made her feel that she was looking through a hole in a wall at some enchanted garden." Lutie could see and hear the people, but cannot "get past the wall" which prevents her "from mingling on an equal footing." Then the chapter ends and she emerges from both the subway and her memories, as though the "room" that the passengers created has been – for her – the space of memory. Soon after this flashback, Petry starts to hint at an end to walls: there are "broken places in the fences" in her neighborhood, so that things creep through into the backyards; Lutie sees children playing tag in the streets, moving with ease across the sidewalks together; and "grown-ups" lounge "in chairs in front of the houses" so that the street becomes "an outdoor living room." Lutie's vision of this communal "living room" feeds her awareness that there were many streets with people "packed together like sardines in a can." And in fact, she continues to realize, "it wasn't just this city," but any city "where they set up a line and say black folks stay on this side ... jammed and packed and forced into the smallest possible space." The space of memory and her glimpsed possibility of communal space have shifted Lutie toward a collective empathy.[20]

In the wake of this shift, she starts to create her own space. Singing in a club she thinks of "leaving the street with its dark hallways, its mean, shabby rooms." Her hatred of the buildings becomes politicized. She sees that in "every direction ... there was always the implacable figure of a white man blocking the way." When one man attempts to exploit her, she notes that it was "a pity he hadn't lived back in the days of slavery, so he could have raided the slave quarters for a likely wench," and immediately after making this historical connection, she imagines that the confined buildings were "the North's lynch mobs ... the method the big cities used to keep Negroes 'in their place.'" She goes on to realize: "From the time she was born, she had been hemmed into an ever-narrowing space, until now she was very nearly walled in and the wall had been built up brick by brick by eager white hands." She imagines "countless children" in the same situation – "behind the same wall already." And, from this newly politicized and historicized perspective, comes the image again of a communal space, this time from a white woman. Miss Rinner sees (in a direct echo of the earlier image of outdoor "living rooms") furniture standing in front of buildings, people lounging "as informally as though they were in their own living rooms." The notion of entering the nation's living room, leaving its basements and garrets, now pervades black *and* white America.[21]

Eventually, faced with a white man who has the final brick "needed to complete the wall that had been building up around her for years," so that she "would be completely walled in," Lutie strikes back. In her mind as she kills is an image of "rows of dilapidated old houses; the small dark rooms; the long steep flights of stairs; the narrow dingy hallways." She feels she is "striking at the white world which thrust black people into a walled enclosure." Lutie buys a ticket and leaves for Chicago. And as the train starts to move, she traces on the window a "series of circles that flowed into one another." She remembers that she drew these circles when she first learned to write and a teacher told her: "I don't know why they have us bother to teach your people to write." She continues to move her finger, "around and around," so that when she wonders "by what twists and turns of fate she had landed on this train," she has already drawn those twists and turns – the circles "showed up plainly on the dusty surface." In spite of the white teacher, Lutie is now writing the story of how she ended up here.[22]

Even more important, Petry brings the novel full-circle by returning to the memory of Lutie's grandmother and to Granny's *own* memories. In the novel's first chapter, Lutie had remembered Granny's tales "that had been handed down" and if you "tried to trace them back, you'd end up God knows where." A few minutes later she had found herself singing "an old song that Granny used to sing": "'Ain't no restin' place for a sinner like me." Then, at the novel's end, she suddenly remembers "all the stories she had ever heard," decides that "there wasn't any excuse for her," and begins a life on the run – completing the old song. The circles that flow into one another on the train window are not only connected spaces, those elusive visions of black people forming a communal "living room," but also a circle of time, back to the novel's own beginning and into the deep space of memory. Lutie escapes for Chicago *and* into the indefinite space of Granny's tales, traceable back to God knows where.[23]

Abolitionist Memory-Spaces

Although Brooks and Petry did not offer *abolitionist* memories that might shatter confinement, other writers did summon slave resistance and abolitionism as they crafted new spaces. Here, civil rights literature did not just draw on an abolitionist aesthetic of earlier protest movements but it also used explicit abolitionist memories to locate itself in a protest tradition – opening a space of protest memory even as it depicted and protested the confined spaces of segregated America. For example, in 1940 Robert Hayden had written anti-lynching poems and positioned Gabriel Prosser as a model of rebellion. Now, during the peak decades of the desegregation struggle, he awakened more abolitionist figures, eventually explaining in 1967 that these history poems affirmed "the Negro struggle as part of the long human struggle toward freedom." The movement was a centuries-long "struggle toward freedom," said Hayden, and it encompassed the lives of the abolitionist figures in Hayden's desegregation-era poems (written between the late 1940s and the 1970s): Douglass, Turner, John Brown, and Harriet Tubman. He even explained that he used the present tense in historical poems because "there is no past, only the present. The past is also the present." His abolitionist heroes are active participants in the contemporary struggle because the abolitionist past is a living history.[24]

Hayden's poem "John Brown," written in 1978 to accompany a reissue of Jacob Lawrence's 1941 series of twenty-two paintings that chronicle the anti-slavery activist's life and death, reveals his deep familiarity with abolitionist literature. The poem sets up a harmony of abolitionist voices. He inserts Shields Green's reference to Brown as "De Old Man," as quoted by Douglass in *The Life and Times*. He adapts Brown's last prison letter in the lines: "the crimes of this guilty / guilty land." In describing Brown as a "fire harvest," he echoes Henry David Thoreau's warning on October 30, 1859 (that "when you plant, or bury, a hero in his field, a crop of heroes is sure to spring up"). And his vision of Brown's "Hanged body turning clockwise / in the air ... visions prophesied," echoes Herman Melville's poem "The Portent" (1866), where Brown's body is "Hanging from the beam, / Slowly swaying" – his "shadow on the green" a portent (or prophesy, as Hayden writes).[25]

Hayden mined this abolitionist literature and then adapted its spatio-symbolic aesthetic in history poems that perform a descent into memory. For example, "The Diver" (1962) executes a generalized memory descent, moving through a "dead ship" with its "lost images / fadingly remembered." Images of a discarded, unused past reappear in "Sub Specie Aeternitatis" (1962), with its series of "hidden passageways and rooms." The specific memory of slavery haunts several other poems. In "The Ballad of Sue Ellen Westerfield" (1962), the family history reveals that Sue Ellen "had not been a slave ... because her father wept and set her mother free." In "Middle Passage," first published in 1944 and revised in 1962, Hayden remembers the original confined space of the slave ships ("there was hardly room 'tween-decks for half / the sweltering cattle stowed spoon-fashion there"). He locates the legacy of that confinement in the literal foundations of American life (*"Deep in the festering hold thy father lies / of his bones New England pews are made"* [italics in original]). But while slavery haunts Hayden's poetic vision, abolitionism is equally present as a shaping force. After all, the slave ships in "Middle Passage" are part of a shifting history: "Shuttles in the rocking loom of history, / the dark ships move." And there on the ship, a different history emerges in the form of the Amistad slave rebellion. Hayden claims Cinquez as a figure who will impact lives beyond his own ("life that transfigures many lives"). Similarly, in "Sojourner Truth" (1975), the poem's central figure walks "out of slavery" as an "ancestress" (though "childless") – offering an abolitionist inheritance.[26]

Continuing through the history of abolitionism, Hayden imagines the lives of numerous other abolitionist heroes as ongoing. In "The Ballad of

Nat Turner" (1962), Turner feels time stop and so waits, biding "my time," and in "Frederick Douglass," first published in 1947 and revised in 1962, the conjunction "when" builds a living history. The first long periodic sentence resists any end-point: "When it is finally ours, this freedom, this liberty, this beautiful / and terrible thing ... this man, this Douglass ... shall be remembered." Hayden then emphasizes the ongoing presence of Douglass, who we will remember "not with statues' rhetoric ... but with the lives grown out of this life, the lives / fleshing his dream of the beautiful, needful thing." His poem "Runagate Runagate" (1949), about Harriet Tubman, does include images of spatial confinement: the fugitive is running and hoping to "reach that somewhere," while the slave catchers know that slaves will "dart underground when you try to catch them, / plunge into quicksand, whirlpools, mazes." But as Hayden locates Tubman alongside "Garrison Alcott Emerson / Garrett Douglass Thoreau John Brown," he inserts extra spaces between the names, as though inviting additions to that list, and includes a present-tense instruction to his contemporary reader: "Mean to be free ... Mean mean mean to be free." In the spaces between the names is room to "flesh out" the abolitionist dream – that of Douglass and the others listed – and so reach "that somewhere" beyond the underground.[27]

Ralph Ellison was a second key architect of abolitionist memory-space during the civil rights movement. Ellison's politics remain under debate. For decades, scholars dismissed him as removed from political protest. But Ellison himself wrote of the "Negro Freedom Movement" in 1964 that he was "enlisted for the duration," adding that his writing was "action in the Negro struggle for freedom" and that *Invisible Man* (1952) was "a social action in itself." Around the same time, he explained that he had "always tried to express or to create characters who were pretty forthright in stating what they felt the society should be." He added that fiction is "a serious and responsible form of social action itself." Elsewhere he insisted that there is "no dichotomy between art and protest," and that being a novelist offers "the possibility of contributing ... to the shaping of the culture as I should like it to be." One of Ellison's contributions was to tie the civil rights aesthetic of spatio-symbolism to the memory of abolitionism. Challenging the no-place of black history in America's record and of black people in American society, closing the gap between the Emancipation Proclamation and achievement of real freedom, he crafted a spatio-symbolic abolitionist history. He offered that history to the movement because, as he explained in 1963, the abolitionist struggle continued: "No Negroes have had any illusion that we've had equality ... [we've been] fighting for a long time ... for an increase in our participation as citizens," he told an interviewer.[28]

Ellison built his spatio-symbolic abolitionist memory out of a belief that American historical memory was full of gaps. He protested that "Americans can be notoriously selective in the exercise of historical memory" and discussed the "realities of American historical experience which were ruled out officially." This "officially" excluded history was the *black* experience, he went on to explain. Black history was not in the textbooks, and as a result, Ellison concluded, African Americans have had a "high sensitivity to the ironies of historical writing" and a "profound skepticism concerning the validity of most reports on what the past was like." But though official history has excluded the black past, it still exists nonetheless. Especially in the work of novelists and in the oral tradition, there was an "internal history" alongside "official history." America's "unwritten history looms" and is "always with us," he warned. Some Americans had forgotten, but black people had not: "Negro American consciousness is ... a product of our memory, sustained and constantly reinforced by events, by our watchful waiting." Here he offered black memories of Douglass as a one example of unofficial history.[29]

This was not his only invocation of slavery. For Ellison, it was the key element of American history. In 1955 he explained that slavery built the country and in 1958 he insisted that black Americans "take their character from the experience of American slavery and the struggle for, and the achievement of, emancipation." He saw both a personal and a political connection to this history. In one speech he referenced his grandfather's slave status, adding that northern men died "to set me free," then emphasized the broader political implications of this history for the movement: the outcome of the Civil War was not yet decided and the 1960s might yet mark a new era. After all, he concluded, American society "has undergone a profound change" since 1954.[30]

Even more pervasive than his histories of slavery were his celebrations of abolitionist resistance during the 1950s and 1960s. In 1953 he discussed the differing responses of Thoreau and Ralph Waldo Emerson to the Fugitive Slave Law, and in 1958 he referenced abolitionist responses to the Civil War. In two pieces from 1964 he discussed Lydia Maria Child's abolitionist writings and remembered wondering why his parents named him after Emerson, rather than Douglass. A few years later, he compared contemporary print culture to William Lloyd Garrison's *The Liberator* and black newspapers from the 1850s. Affirming a living abolitionist history, he added that Americans needed to find out "who Frederick Douglass is today, who Nat Turner is today ... who Sojourner Truth is.... Patterns repeat themselves as long as human circumstances endure." Like numerous other civil rights writers, Ellison saw slavery enduring and believed that abolitionism must endure too.[31]

Looking at the abolitionist past and America's present, Ellison tried to break down the barrier between. In particular, he returned to the abolitionist tradition of literalizing history's gaps and America's loophole of inequality as holes or confined spaces. In various essays, he imagines that African Americans are in "the underground of the American conscience" and the "deepest recesses," beneath "the threshold of social hierarchy" and "outside the bounds of humanity." In one essay he describes the "confines of our segregated community," and in another the "no-man's land created by segregation." In his notes for *Invisible Man* he explains that "Negro life is a world psychologically apart." And in "Harlem Is Nowhere" (1948), his most extended spatio-symbolic meditation in essay form, he describes black life as a process of falling into "a great chasm." Black Americans have "no stable, recognized place in society," he explained: "one 'is' literally, but one is nowhere ... a 'displaced person' of American democracy." Confirming that literal space symbolizes social and historical space, he adds that a basement in Harlem is an "underground extension of democracy" and that the realities of Harlem, its crumbling buildings and cluttered streets, are a "symbol of the Negro's perpetual alienation" in the United States.[32]

He used these spatio-symbolic chasms, underground chambers, and displacements to protest the limits of Emancipation. One spatio-symbolic essay describes an encounter with Lincoln's corpse, in a time that seems to be the nineteenth century. Ellison dreams he is dressed like "a young slave" and has "fallen from a high place" to find "Negroes" gathered "around a great hole" in which lie horrors. It is the grave of Lincoln's intentions; a site where the intentions of Emancipation were holed up. As Ellison himself summarizes the dream, it is about the "fruits" of "neglected labors withering some ninety years" and America's "capacity for true heroism [cast] into the grave." He uses the same imagery in *Invisible Man*. The narrator's underground space is in a "section of the basement shut off and forgotten during the nineteenth century" – another site where the abolitionists' dream was holed up. Again, the hole contains an erased black past and a stillborn future. It symbolizes the no-place of an unachieved utopia. Ellison echoes this idea toward the end of the novel, when the Invisible Man tells Norton: "Take any train. They all go to the Golden D–." A symbolic utopia, the destination of all trains, the Golden Day is unfinished, a "D–." American history is not only full of gaps and erasures, but suspended in its progression. The years since Emancipation are an ellipsis, or a blank space like that after the colon at the novel's end:

And it is this which really frightens me:
Who know but that, on the lower frequencies, I speak for you?

The decision to break the line implies that what "really frightens" the narrator *is* this blank space after the colon. After all, he has been into history's hole, the site "shut off and forgotten during the nineteenth century," and now is struggling to emerge.[33]

The hole imagery therefore symbolizes white America's Swiss-cheese historical memory and the liminal space between a statement of ideal and its achievement. One feeds the other: in forgetting the history of slavery and abolitionism, America has failed to deliver on the promises of Emancipation. Across the novel, Ellison creates a series of other no-places, whether the imagery of the factory basement, the New York subway, or the Brotherhood's belief that some individuals belong "outside of history," in the "void." Yet believing, as he explained in a speech, that "we do not bury the past ... [we] modify it," Ellison also took up the task of reclaiming history's underground space. He provides glimpses of the abolitionist history buried in this "void": the old couple's manumission papers and their tintype of Lincoln; the portrait of Douglass in the office; the narrator's observation that he was "in the cards ... eighty-five years ago," when the slaves were "told that they were free." Then Invisible Man discovers that the only way to escape from history's hole – unrecorded and unfinished history – is to turn it into a creative space. In his manhole, he burns his identity papers. "Once he recognizes the hole of darkness into which these papers put him, he has to burn them," Ellison explained in an essay. He added elsewhere that the narrator's task is to find "an awareness of how [he] relates to his past and the values of the past": Invisible Man is symbolically destroying America's official history, its flawed narrative of equality and freedom, and writing from his hole a *whole* story. He unearths a buried black history and crafts its pieces into a new narrative. Armed with this new history, he can emerge.[34]

The Invisible Man emerges into an ongoing freedom struggle – one begun, according to the movement's literature at least, by the abolitionists 150 years earlier. As it adapted a key protest aesthetic from literary abolitionism and summoned the abolitionists themselves as early desegregationists, civil rights movement literature summoned a palpable protest past and rejected the notion of activist discontinuity. Though the 1860s produced what Eric Foner calls a "new American Constitution," its text became "dead letters" (as Foner adds). By reusing abolitionism, protesters wrote in that Constitution's margins: *not yet free*. Then they wrote new free papers, their own protest literature, with the ink of the original emancipation struggle.[35]

NOTES

1 W. E. B. Du Bois, "What Is the Meaning of 'All Deliberate Speed'?" November 4, 1957, in *Newspaper Columns by W. E. B. Du Bois*, Volume II, ed. Herbert Aptheker (White Plains, NY: Kraus-Thomson, 1986), p. 999; Martin Luther King, Jr., "Honoring Dr. Du Bois," February 23, 1968, in *W. E. B. Du Bois*

Speaks: Speeches and Addresses, 1890–1919, Volume I, ed. Philip S. Foner (New York: Pathfinder, 1970), p. 19.

2 Jacqueline Dowd Hall, "Mobilizing Memory: Broadening Our View of the Civil-Rights Movement," *Chronicle of Higher Education*, July 27, 2001: B7–8; Hall, "The Long Civil Rights Movement and the Political Uses of the Past," *Journal of American History* 91 (2005): 1253–54.

3 Langston Hughes, *The Collected Poems of Langston Hughes*, ed. Arnold Rampersad and David Roessel (New York: Vintage, 1995), p. 387; Gwendolyn Brooks, *Report from Part One: An Autobiography* (Detroit: Broadside Press, 1972), p. 158.

4 Du Bois, "Criteria of Negro Art," *The Crisis*, October 1926: 296; Du Bois, "On Being Dined," *The Crisis*, June 1924: 56; Du Bois, review, The Crisis, January 1926: 141; William Pickens, "Art and Propaganda," *The Messenger*, April 1924: 111.

5 Jerry Bryant, *Victims and Heroes: Racial Violence in the African American Novel* (Amherst: University of Massachusetts Press, 1997), p. 128; Judith L. Stephens, "The Harlem Renaissance and the New Negro Movement," in *The Cambridge Companion to American Woman Playwrights*, ed. Brenda Murphy (New York: Cambridge University Press, 1999), p. 107; Margaret Ann Reid, *Black Protest Poetry: Polemics from the Harlem Renaissance and the Sixties* (New York: Peter Lang, 2001); Maryemma Graham, "Introduction," *Complete Poems of Frances E. W. Harper* (New York: Oxford University Press, 1988), p. xxxiii; Melba Joyce Boyd, *Discarded Legacy: Politics and Poetics in the Life of Frances E. W. Harper, 1825–1911* (Detroit: Wayne State University Press, 1994), p. 23.

6 John Stauffer, "Foreword," in *American Protest Literature*, ed. Zoe Trodd (Cambridge, MA: Harvard University Press, 2006), pp. xii–xiii; Brian Norman, *The American Protest Essay and National Belonging: Addressing Division* (New York: State University of New York Press, 2007), pp. 40, 12, 19, 6.

7 Hughes, *Poems*, p. 542.

8 King, *Where Do We Go from Here: Chaos or Community?* (New York: Harper and Row, 1967), p. 41.

9 Hughes, *Poems*, p. 549.

10 bell hooks, "House, 20 June 1994: Housing without Boundaries: Race, Class, and Gender," *Assemblage* 24 (1994): 23.

11 Martin R. Delany, *The Condition, Elevation, Emigration, and Destiny of the Colored People of the United States: Politically Considered* (1852, rpt., New York: Arno, 1968), p. 155; James W.C. Pennington, *The Fugitive Blacksmith* (London: Charles Gilpin, 1849), pp. 44, 42, 3, 70, 72–73.

12 Douglass, *Narrative of the Life of Frederick Douglass* (Boston: Anti-Slavery Office, 1845), pp. xv, 60; Douglass, *My Bondage and My Freedom* (New York: Miller, Orton and Mulligan, 1855), pp. 101, 62, 64, 281, 176.

13 Douglass, *Bondage*, pp. 177, 301, 156, 64, 62; Douglass, *The Life and Times of Frederick Douglass* (Boston: De Wolfe and Fiske, 1892), pp. 85, 105, 217, 42.

14 Douglass, *Bondage*, pp. 87, 409; Douglass, *Life and Times*, pp. 623.

15 Anne Moody, *Coming of Age in Mississippi* (New York: Laurel Editions, 1971), pp. 11; Brooks, in *The Essential Gwendolyn Brooks*, ed. Elizabeth Alexander (New York: Library of America, 2005), p. 28.

16 Brooks, pp. 1, 75, 56, 57, 94, 14, 72, 73.

17 Ibid., pp. 41, 47.

18 Ibid., p. 60.

19 Ann Petry, *The Street* (New York: Houghton Mifflin, 1998), pp. 4, 12, 6, 73, 79, 230, 193, 19, 83.

20 Ibid., pp. 27, 38, 41, 73, 142, 206.

21 Ibid., pp. 222, 315, 322, 323–24, 332.

22 Ibid., pp. 423, 430, 435, 436.

23 Ibid., pp. 1516, 17, 432, 434.

24 Hayden, *Robert Hayden: Collected Prose*, ed. Frederick Glaysher (Ann Arbor: University of Michigan Press, 1984), pp. 74–75, 124.

25 Hayden, *Collected Poems: Robert Hayden*, ed. Frederick Glaysher (New York: Liveright, 1985), pp. 149–153; Henry David Thoreau, "A Plea for Captain John Brown," October 30, 1859, in *The Tribunal: Responses to John Brown and the Harpers Ferry Raid*, ed. John Stauffer and Zoe Trodd (Cambridge, MA: Harvard University Press, 2012), 106; Herman Melville, "The Portent (1859)," in *The Tribunal*, pp. 476.

26 Hayden, *Collected Poems*, pp. 3, 22, 13, 48, 49, 51, 53–54, 136.

27 Ibid., pp. 57, 58, 62, 59, 61, 60.

28 Ralph Ellison, *The Collected Essays of Ralph Ellison*, ed. John F. Callahan (New York: Modern Library, 2003), pp. 187, 188, 183; Allen Geller, "An Interview with Ralph Ellison," October 25, 1963, *Tamarack Review*, Summer 1964: 227; Ellison, *Essays*, pp. 212, 224; Geller, "Interview," p. 225.

29 Ellison, *Essays*, 598; Ellison, in *Conversations with Ralph Ellison*, ed. Maryemma Graham and Amritjit Singh (Jackson: University Press of Mississippi, 1995), pp. 152, 154; Ellison, *Essays*, pp. 598, 171.

30 Ellison, *Essays*, pp. 214, 292, 421, 423, 428, 429.

31 Ellison, *Conversations*, p. 153; Ellison, *Essays*, pp. 92, 104, 280, 195, 460, 461, 463.

32 Ellison, *Essays*, pp. 90, 782, 458, 52, 170, 343, 323, 325, 320, 321.

33 Ibid., pp. 37, 34, 44, 46; Ellison, *Invisible Man* (New York: Vintage Books, 1952), pp. 6, 578, 581.

34 Ellison, *Invisible Man*, pp. 434, 429, 15; Ellison, *Essays*, pp. 417, 219; Ellison, *Conversations*, p. 233.

35 Eric Foner, "The Second American Revolution," *In These Times*, September 16–22, 1987: 12–13.

2

BRIAN NORMAN

The Dilemma of Narrating Jim Crow

In the 1896 U.S. Supreme Court case *Plessy v. Ferguson*, the majority upheld the constitutionality of racial restrictions on intrastate train travel, thereby solidifying a doctrine of separate-but-equal that would rule the land for the next half century or so – the "or so" remaining hotly debated. The *Plessy* decision formally articulated social inequality as a natural design despite America's persistent civic myth articulated in Justice John Marshall Harlan's famous dissent: "There is no caste here."[1] In *Plessy*'s wake arose an elaborate apparatus of compulsory race segregation, including its pervasive icon: the Jim Crow sign. Elizabeth Abel argues, "By translating the theory of racial difference into the practice of segregation, the bits of writing tacked to walls across the nation opened a fault line between segregation's sociopolitical aims and its representational forms."[2] From this fault line erupts what we might call the literature of segregation and its core dilemma: how to represent compulsory race segregation without reinscribing it. To narrate the color line is to risk making it seem not only real but also inevitable or even natural – to make it imaginable. And yet ignoring Jim Crow seems hardly an option, given its fundamental influence on American life.

Generally, "Jim Crow" is shorthand for the diverse practices, customs, attitudes, and legal frameworks that arose in post-bellum America, especially the former slave-holding states, to undergird a regime of compulsory race segregation. The term originates from the minstrel stage, which in turn draws from African American folk traditions that blackface both loves and thieves, to use Eric Lott's famous formulation.[3] Thinking of Jim Crow as a distinct era of the late nineteenth through mid-twentieth centuries has the virtue of spotlighting restrictions on black political, economic, and social participation that were a prime target of the American civil rights movement, or in the parlance of the times, the black freedom struggle. That said, literary scholar Joycelyn Moody goes so far as to date compulsory segregation to the nation's founding and subsumes chattel slavery under that broader ontology.[4] Cultural historians, on the other hand, underscore the sheer ubiquity of cross-racial interaction in the Jim Crow South so that the familiar Whites Only signs do not so much enforce separation of the races as govern how and where they access the same space, such as restaurants with back entrances, adjacent drinking fountains, or department stores with separate changing rooms.[5] If such signs narrate life in Jim Crow America, what is the role of literary representations?

I frame this chapter as a dilemma of narrating Jim Crow to chart various literary responses to segregation rather than confer false coherence among diverse writings of the period under a singular category of "Jim Crow literature."[6] Such an aim incites debates about historical timelines, a problem to which I return in the conclusion. My main task is to track literary responses to what W. E. B. Du Bois famously deemed the problem of the color line. We can discern three intertwined tendencies: staging cross-racial encounters to probe the consequences of crossing the color line, turning away from the color line in what I call revolutionary indifference, and employing the speculative power of literature to imagine racial configurations beyond Jim Crow. The three responses share a goal: to fashion an aesthetic that can document injustices and black life under Jim Crow while also undermining the naturalized logic of racial inferiority. Of course, non-black writers also respond deliberately and often beautifully to segregation – William Faulkner is the most obvious example – but I choose to focus on the black literary tradition. In part, I am swayed by critics who examine how black writers wrest community, not just survival, out of Jim Crow and its racial terrorism.[7] I also defer thorny questions of what differentiates the anti-segregationist aesthetic of Du Bois, Carl Van Vechten, Ralph Ellison, and Harper Lee from the pro-segregationist literature of writers such as Thomas Dixon, whose Klan trilogy inspired the white supremacist classic film *Birth of a Nation*. This brief chapter charts a terrain of black literary responses to segregation so that others can map additional writers onto that cartography.

Staging Cross-Racial Encounters

The dominant response to Jim Crow is to stage encounters across the color line as a central hinge, especially in a protest mode. Most often, this results in pivotal scenes of violence, be it physical or psychological, interpersonal or on a massive scale. The most iconic encounter is the lynching, which famously drives Jean Toomer's *Cane* (1923), much of Richard Wright's fiction, James Baldwin's *Blues for Mister Charlie* (1964), and a diverse array of African American cultural productions, from Billie Holiday's "Strange Fruit" to Jacob Lawrence's paintings of the Great Migration. Lynching literature does more than merely document and protest racial terrorism. It narrates the internal lives, survival strategies, and kinship that Jim Crow engenders – or requires – in black communities. Koritha Mitchell, for instance, surveys lynching plays and finds that the actual violence so central to the plots goes curiously under-represented. "Their scripts," she argues, "spotlight instead the black home and the impact that the mob's outdoor activities have on the family."[8]

An exemplary lynching narrative is Wright's early 1935 short story "Big Boy Leaves Home," which features two cross-racial encounters, both fatal. In the story, a white woman happens upon four black male youth horse-playing in a swimming hole on white land, naked and vulnerable. Racial innocence evaporates when her white soldier boyfriend misreads the Edenic scene as one of sexual aggression, precipitating the deaths of two boys and the soldier himself. The lynching plot is set in motion. Before Big Boy escapes north in the false bottom of a community member's truck, we join him in witness to the lynching of his friend, Bobo. The sight is familiar from spectacle lynching photography: white mob, unspeakable cruelty and violence, bodily souvenirs, burnt black flesh. The vantage, however, is unique to literature: we can see the lynch mob lit brightly by the horrifying flames; they cannot see Big Boy amid the protective darkness of the hillside. With the story's publication in *Uncle Tom's Children*, Lawrence Jackson argues, "Wright broke new ground as the chronicler of black defiance and hostility toward malevolent white oppression."[9] Wright's early work, like much segregation literature, tends toward the naturalist mode, which presents characters as pure products of an environment and its social laws. In "How Bigger Was Born," Wright likens himself to a lab scientist and his characters to experimental subjects: plug in stimuli, see how they react.[10] The world's Big Boys and Bigger Thomases are the nation's creations, mere reflections of larger social designs.

The focus on violent cross-racial encounters is a necessary literary response to the pervasive terror of lynching and white mobs. Between 1882 and 1968, according to James Allen in *Without Sanctuary*, approximately 4,742 black men and women were lynched, especially in southern states and spiking in the 1910s and 1920s. Images of spectacle lynchings circulated on postcards and news photography to construct a narrative of the consequences of those who might cross the color line or in some way violate Jim Crow customs.[11] Lynching literature, on the other hand, Anne Rice argues, helps "raise political awareness, preserve the evidence of the slaughter, and commemorate those who died."[12] Further, lynching is only the most visible and ritualized of violence resulting from cross-racial encounters. In *Native Son*, Bigger Thomas unintentionally murders the young white heiress Mary Dalton, which, like Big Boy's cross-racial encounter, triggers a community-wide hunt, a northern corollary to the southern lynch mob. The basic plot structures are the same. Moreover, massive white violence toward African Americans is a literary staple, from Charles Chesnutt's fictionalized account of the Wilmington, North Carolina, massacre of 1898 in *The Marrow of Tradition* (1901) to the threat of racial terrorism in Karl Lindner's visit to the Youngers on behalf of the all-white community association in Lorraine Hansberry's *A Raisin in the Sun* (1959). The violence may be lopsided, but the consequences cross the color line. Birgit Brander Rasmussen argues, "Chesnutt not only condemns the racial terror that underpins a segregated state, but also warns his readers that such violence will backfire against white Americans."[13]

Beyond physical violence, the color line imparts psychological trauma, which literature is particularly adept at capturing. Perhaps the best example is Toni Morrison's 1970 novel *The Bluest Eye*, set in the segregated black community of 1940s Lorraine, Ohio. Morrison chronicles one young black girl's descent into madness in response to ruthlessly omnipresent messages of racial inferiority, even within her own home. More important is the narrator, Claudia MacTeer, who laments her community's failure to protect and love its own. As she tells it, "All of us – who knew her – felt so wholesome after we cleaned ourselves on her. We were so beautiful when we stood astride her ugliness."[14] Claudia models – belatedly – a key response to Jim Crow's psychological terrorism: reflect in order to refuse racial myths. James Baldwin shows us how to do so in his early essays, such as 1955's "Notes of Native Son" in which the black writer wrests hope from a legacy of bitterness. On the death of his father, Baldwin learns, "He had lived and died in an intolerable bitterness of spirit and it frightened me, as we drove him to the graveyard through those unquiet, ruined streets, to see how powerful and overflowing this bitterness could be and to realize that this bitterness was now mine."[15] For Baldwin, "to smash something is the ghetto's chronic need" so that an altercation between a black soldier and a white guy over a black woman, regardless of its truth, is "a lit match in a tin of gasoline."[16] Baldwin, too, succumbs when a waitress recites Jim Crow's script as she refuses him service. Baldwin's gut reaction is potentially fatal: he hurls a mug at her face, barely missing. In the end, what separates him from Bigger Thomas or Big Boy is his capacity for self-reflection. Still, Baldwin cautions, there is a little Bigger Thomas inside every black citizen of Jim Crow. Such threats may drive segregation literature as much as desires to reject Jim Crow.

Narratives of racial passing constitute another key fiction of the color line, most notably in Nella Larsen's 1929 novella *Passing*. The phenomenon was relatively common, especially in the North, as light-skinned black persons crossed into white society, often by simply omitting racial background. Those who passed accessed cultural and legal rights unavailable to Jim Crow's second-class citizens. That is why the inverse – whites passing as black – rarely occurred: it would require relinquishing privilege, as illustrated in *Black Like Me*, John Howard Griffin's infamous 1961 account of crossing the color line from white to black, with the help of some shoe polish and skin-darkening pills. Du Bois famously defines African American identity as "double consciousness," a sense of always looking at oneself through the eyes of others. In passing novels, we have a new line: those who have knowledge of racial identity and those who don't. The color line becomes a matter of how one is recognized, by whom, when, and where. M. Giulia Fabi explains, passing "turns what was once conceived of as natural opposition into a societal one."[17] Race becomes a category of knowledge, a figment, even if the stakes and consequences are profound. In short, the color line moves from the external world to interior life in modernist literature. Those with racial knowledge have interiority and depth, the ideal modern subject. Whiteness, on the other hand, becomes all surface and single-consciousness. In *Passing*, for instance, John Bellew knows nothing of his wife's Harlem childhood, ignorant of her kinship to a black community to which she desires to return, as if from the dead.

Jim Crow may parcel the world into tidy boxes of black and white, but the phenomenon of passing renders it a fiction. In fact, the *Plessy* case can be read as a refusal of the passing narrative. The bare facts of the case are less about advocating abolition of the color line per se and more about the right *not* to pass without forfeiting privilege. Plessy could have remained silent on the train reserved for white passengers, alone in the knowledge of his racial status. Plessy coordinated with the Comité des Citoyens of New Orleans to deliberately violate segregation laws so that when a ticket agent asked, he would make his racial status known – tell a Jim Crow story of himself. Thus Homer Plessy's racial status changed in that car irrespective of his skin color. In other words, some legally black people could ride the white car, but none could ride there as self-identified black people. Plessy's point and that of the passing narrative are the same: race is as much a narrative concept as a biological and legal one.

Neither lynching nor passing remains a widespread phenomenon in contemporary America, though their figurative shadows loom large.[18] So too, instances of violence are often deemed "modern-day lynchings" on the spectrum Koritha Mitchell calls "know-your-place aggression." This twin legacy informs contemporary literature, such as Mat Johnson's 2008 graphic novel *Incognegro*, which draws on the super-hero motif to craft a light-skinned reporter in 1920s New York who goes south and passes as a photographer's assistant to record names, occupations, and addresses of members of lynch mobs. Historically, lynchings were not often prosecuted on the legal fiction that the perpetrators were "persons unknown,"[19] despite considerable evidence and broad community participation. Johnson bases his protagonist on NAACP activist Walter White who documented lynching so that the nation could not deny its prevalence or barbarism. In *Passing*, Larsen's readers do not know Irene Redfield's race until it is revealed on the roof of the Drayton Hotel. In Johnson's world, however, we always know the protagonist's racial identity. This reflects the contemporary passing narrative generally, which Michele Elam traces from Danzy Senna's *Caucasia* (1998) to Colson Whitehead's *The Intuitionist* (1999) and Philip Roth's *The Human Stain* (2000). "These narratives of racial passing," Elam argues, "have risen seemingly from the dead not to bear witness to past issues but to testify in some of the fiercest debates about the viability of race in this 'beyond race' era."[20] If passing novels during the Jim Crow era destabilize the color line and lynching narratives protest its ferocious consequences, such stories now have a different function: to assert the continued relevance of race in a seemingly post-racial America.

Turning Away from the Color Line

While the dominant literary response to Jim Crow is to stage encounters across the color line, a second response is to turn away. We see this even in novels centrally located on the color line. For example, while the central act in Toni Morrison's *Beloved* occurs on the racial fault line – Sethe murders her own child to save her from a life as chattel – the narrative's gravitational center is the black community on the outskirts of Reconstruction-era Cincinnati. The whole point of the novel, in fact, is to create spaces off-limits to whites, whether 124 Bluestone Road or Baby Suggs's clearing. The infanticide results from a breach of such space. Hence Baby Suggs's refrain, "I'm saying they came in my yard."[21]

While the color line is profoundly influential, the main interests of some black writers simply lie elsewhere. An iconic example is Zora Neale Hurston's *Their Eyes Were Watching God*, which chronicles Janie's long march from the outskirts of a former plantation toward the all-black town of Eatonville and then the muck of the Everglades. Hurston finds customs, intrigue, joy, philosophy, and downright interestingness far from white culture, even if such cultural worlds are shaped by Jim Crow's designs. As a heroine, Janie is a far cry from Du Bois's talented tenth, Larsen's high-cultured passing women, and Wright's raised-fist protests of racial violence. Hurston dedicated her life to investigating black folk culture for the sake of documenting it, both as novelist and folklorist. She in turn trains us to read, understand, and celebrate black dialect and its "crayon enlargements of life."[22] For instance, we encounter neologisms – monstropolous, freezolity – with delight as we come to know their meaning. When we encounter them again, they are familiar, comforting, apt. We take our places on the porches of Eatonville, waiting for the next competition of "lies." Motivated by much more than a documentary impulse, Hurston embraces black folk culture in a full bear-hug.

What does turning away from the color line allow? When writers dim the glare of whiteness, we can better see intricacies, tensions, and subtle gradations within black communities independent of white culture. Hurston's cultural bear-hug is not without risk. "Through this logic, however," Leigh Anne Duck argues, "the novel displaces the enforced racial segregation of the South with the voluntary isolation of folkloric practices."[23] Segregation becomes an uncanny and folksy anachronism, Duck worries, not a site of contemporary protest. That is largely why contemporary reviewers dismissed the novel, including Wright's notorious 1937 review, "Between Laughter and Tears."[24] For Wright, Hurston dons literary blackface in a minstrel tradition that sells folksy renditions of black life to white audiences. He famously criticizes the book's humor, romance, and ever-delayed protest of systems of racial injustice. That is, white racism is not the focal point. On the other hand, for Hurston's advocates, the fanciful and folksy, rather than the mimetic realism of protest, may itself be a strategy. Cheryl Wall argues, "The will to adorn registers the freedom already achieved as it expresses the commitment to struggle for freedom yet denied."[25]

While Hurston sets up camp far from the color line, it is neither absent nor unremarked, only off on the horizon and not the central feature of black life. In the first two thirds of the novel, there are only two cross-racial encounters: white folks name young Janie "Alphabet" and a slave master violates Old Nanny. In the final third, we encounter more white people, still unnamed: the bossman, people on a bridge during the hurricane, and jurors and courtroom attendees in the penultimate chapter, after which Janie returns to Eatonville and its all-black world. We also meet other members of the black diaspora (Bahamians) and American Indians (Seminoles) who are on the muck with the black migrant workers.

Hurston's bear-hug joins a long line of portraits of black folk life, from Paul Laurence Dunbar's dialect poetry at the birth of Jim Crow to Langston Hughes's blues poetry during the Harlem Renaissance to Alice Walker's blockbuster 1983 novel *The Color Purple*, which was set in the Jim Crow South but reflects post–civil rights concerns. In contemporary literature, black writers frequently return to segregated southern communities to meditate on post–civil rights racial identity. A good example is Suzan-Lori Parks's 2003 novel *Getting Mother's Body*, which playfully reimagines William Faulkner's *As I Lay Dying* for a black family in rural Texas on the eve of the 1963 March on Washington. Another distinct manifestation of turning away from the color line is Afrocentrism, from free black David Walker's 1829 abolitionist appeal to the "Colored Citizens of the World" to the Black Arts Movement and beyond. Literary portrayals of the Jim Crow South in this vein produce often interesting ambivalence. For instance, in Wesley Brown's brilliantly playful account of black blackface minstrelsy in the 1994 novel *Darktown Strutters*, the black community begins to turn on the protagonist, Jim Crow, in his post-bellum career. He laments, "There was a time when the Jim Crow car was something special to colored folks."[26] For him, the Jim Crow car is a space of autonomy and self-determination as much as exclusion and injustice.

Such turns away from the color line risk accusations of Jim Crow nostalgia and demands that white supremacy be the object of explicit protest.[27] In fact, Hurston eventually provided something of a response to her detractors in the wry 1943 essay "Negroes without Self-Pity." Rather than dispute histories of oppression, she simply finds more interesting things to talk about. Hurston recounts a political meeting in which "Nobody mentioned slavery, Reconstruction, nor any such matter. It was a new and strange kind of Negro meeting – without tears of self-pity. It was a sign and symbol of something in the offing."[28] We might juxtapose this to Morrison's "rememory" in which Sethe cannot have a future without encountering her past, whether or not it means her well. Hurston counsels carefree forgetting, what I elsewhere call "revolutionary indifference." The best example is Sophia in Walker's *The Color Purple*. She ends the novel, I argue, "having completely detached her self-worth and ontology from white people."[29] If cross-racial violence seems inevitable in the protest mode, Sophia offers another option: don't give a damn about the white folks around you. That may not change the system, but it allows survival, and perhaps dignity, in a world bent on destroying it.

Imagining Other Racial Configurations

If compulsory race segregation is by definition limiting, writers can look elsewhere for alternate racial configurations, be it another place or even another time. Contemporary poet Kevin Young contends, "However we conceive of it, Elsewhere is central to the African American tradition."[30] Or, in the sardonic words of George Schuyler in the 1931 satirical novel *Black No More*, the United States offered three choices: "Either get out, get white or get along."[31] For some, "get out" is the most appealing option. We see this in the international settings of James Weldon Johnson's travels to Latin America in *Autobiography of an Ex-Colored Man*, the pan-Africanist expanse of Richard Wright's later work, and Baldwin's shift to a Parisian setting for his second novel *Giovanni's Room* and his own expatriate status, common among writers of the period. Ruth Blandón argues, "Transnational connections – whether real or fantastical – were a matter of psychological and emotional survival for African Americans who endured Jim Crow laws and segregation."[32] This may explain why in Larsen's *Passing*, a novel otherwise centered on the domestic color line, Irene's husband Brian wants to flee to Brazil, which he imagines as something of a nonracial utopia. Of course, race exists in Brazil and any locale, but black internationalist fiction illustrates that when African Americans map themselves onto new racial taxonomies, they occupy different – and often better – strata than the second-class citizenship of Jim Crow. Eve Dunbar argues that black writers of the period adopt regionalist sensibilities amid international frameworks to position the Jim Crow South as but one region in a global landscape.[33]

If black writers turn to transnational settings to help us imagine another country, that also takes the form of origin stories, such as Pauline Hopkins's *Of One Blood; Or, the Hidden Self*. The post-Reconstruction novel concerns Reuel Briggs, a light-skinned man passing as white and lacking racial loyalty despite America's one-drop rules of identity. This changes when, on an archaeological trip to Ethiopia, Reuel discovers his rightful place as descendant of Abyssinian royalty. Hopkins turns to African history before European conquest to recast her hero's station under Jim Crow in terms of class descent. For critic Jill Bergman, Reuel is a "motherless child" who must claim his slave mother's ancestry and, by extension, his mother county.[34] Still, the scenario pulls us out of the Jim Crow present as much as it returns to African heritage. For some, this is back-to-Africa escapism,[35] for others a pan-Africanist aesthetic, and for at least one critic, a post-racial fantasy.[36] Regardless, to unearth the "hidden self" requires leaving both the here *and* the now of Jim Crow America.

Writers may also opt for a speculative mode to imagine another country beyond Jim Crow. We see this especially in black science fiction from George Schuyler's satire of a raceless world in *Black No More* to Octavia Butler's speculative fiction and beyond. Where Hopkins uses an archaeological dig to access another place and time, Schuyler conjures another future through Dr. Crookman's sanitarium that turns black people white. Or Butler uses time travel to abruptly transport her 1970s protagonist, Dana, to meet her slave ancestors in *Kindred*. Finding herself on the Weylin plantation in antebellum Maryland, Dana meets not only her slave foremother but also the young white master who will become kin, too. The hard lesson is mutual dependence between black and white, master and slave, then and now. The seemingly liberated black woman is inextricability bound to history. Yet *Kindred* is as much about Jim Crow's contemporary valences in Dana's romance with her white husband, which become troublingly visible via the time travel conceit. For Isaiah Lavendar, science fiction's "estranged landscapes and powerful technologies extrapolate and model new racial formations in addition to old ones."[37] Black science fiction also underscores the difficulties and dangers of achieving such new formations.

The Prospect of Post-Racial Literature, a Long-Standing Fantasy

By the mid-twentieth century, especially following the 1954 *Brown v. Board* decision, segregation began to seem less a law of nature and more a series of deliberate policy decisions, social structures, and ideological stances. In the transition from de jure to de facto segregation, Jim Crow literature's primary aim shifted from denaturalizing racial logic to uncovering its legacies. Jim Crow has accrued a formidable shadow. It remains the go-to metaphor for racial inequality and its symbols litter the contemporary landscape – empty nooses, restrictive signs, minstrel faces, mammy memorabilia.[38] Jim Crow continues to explain other systems of racial inequality, such as disproportionate black incarceration rates in Michelle Alexander's influential study *The New Jim Crow*.[39] Nonetheless, by 2007, the Supreme Court effectively issued a death certificate to Jim Crow. In *Parents Involved in Community Schools v. Seattle School District No. 1*, a case involving voluntary school desegregation in Seattle and Louisville, Chief Justice John Roberts argued for the majority, "The way to stop discrimination on the basis of race is to stop discriminating on the basis of race." In Roberts's America, the mere acknowledgment of race perpetuates racism. Anti-racist activists and intellectuals, not to mention the Supreme Court minority, howled in protest at this equivocation. And yet the idea has taken hold: to speak of Jim Crow in a reputedly post-racial era is to conjure him from the dead.

So too, in *What Was African American Literature?* Kenneth Warren suggests the very idea of African American literature is "an imaginative response not merely to the lived reality but also to the legal fact of segregation."[40] With the formal end of Jim Crow, Warren asks, has the term African American literature lost its utility? The critical response has been impassioned as scholars are challenged to articulate with precision what connects writing by black people in the American context.[41] Literary critics continue to trace the extensive legacies of segregation-era writers, such as Lawrence Jackson's *The Indignant Generation,* Leigh Anne Duck's *The Nation's Region*, my own co-edited volume *Representing Segregation*, all building on such foundational work as Hazel Carby's *Reconstructing Womanhood* and Houston Baker's *Blues, Ideology, and Afro-American Literature*. Most of this work rejects any claim to a sharp end to segregation in order to explain racial inequality well after Jim Crow's official demise. Nonetheless, Warren's central observation holds: the Jim Crow regime, in its sheer pervasiveness, generated a degree of shared purpose that is unparalleled in American literary history. And it continues to shape what it means to be a black writer.

These are new versions of very old questions. The dilemma of narrating Jim Crow has long manifested in debates over whether one is a writer or a black writer. The question is something of a rite of passage. Hughes's famous 1926 essay "The Negro Artist and the Racial Mountain" is among the more famous entries in the tradition. The result is a long-standing dream of a post-racial literature driving African American literature from its very beginning, when the slave girl Phyllis Wheatley wrote lovely poems in the European style and appeared before Boston gentlemen to prove she could write such verse. Tucked in her small collection was "On Being Brought from Africa to America," the notoriously slippery signature poem by America's first published black poet. Some 150 years later, Harlem Renaissance writers defined themselves against "Old Negroes" who adhere to the color line and accept their racial self-inferiority, so the story goes, whereas the New Negro recognizes his own talent and beauty so that he, too, can sit at the grand table of literature. Hughes was responding to Schuyler's declaration in "The Negro-Art Hokum" that the idea of a "black writer" is a boondoggle. If race is a figment, Schuyler opined, then the idea of racial art is a marketplace invention, akin to African masks put on walls in gestures of racial pride. "The Aframerican is merely a lampblacked Anglo-Saxon," he argues. "Aside from color, which ranges from very dark brown to pink, your American Negro is just plain American."[42] In the end, for Schuyler, "color is incidental" and writing marketed as black is flavored with "a slight dash of racialistic seasoning."[43]

Hughes declares Schuyler's thinking nonsense, the real hokum. For Hughes, the desire to be a poet, rather than a negro poet, reflects internalized self-hatred, Jim Crow's worst legacy. The black writer must acknowledge race-specific histories, conditions, and – most important – cultures that Hughes finds so beautiful. And ugly, too. Loud, brash, glimmering, bright, in contrast to the big Nordic yawn of white standardization. Instead of yielding to the "desire to run away from his race," Hughes celebrates not the middle-class writer but rather the "low-down folks," the common people who laugh and shout and drink and holler and work a little. For Hughes, "they do not particularly care whether they are like white folks or anybody else."[44] By comparison, Warren's polemic nearly a century later looks downright tame. A better contemporary corollary is Amiri Baraka's scathing response to Charles Rowell's 2013 Norton anthology of African American poetry, *Angels of Ascent*. In one of his final essays, Baraka wields his signature dagger-sharp prose to lacerate the "bizarre collection" as mere "gobbledygook" professing a literary love that dare not speak its own name: race. With no sense of racial tradition and a none-too-subtle rejection of Black Arts, Baraka agues, "this is simply a list of poets Rowell likes. I cannot see any stylistic tendency that would render them a 'movement' or a coherent aesthetic."[45]

In all, debates about Jim Crow's legacy and timeline are heated, with many deeming any announced end premature, naïve, or reactionary. Trudier Harris, for instance, speaks of "attempted desegregation" to mark a historical shift while avoiding false declarations of resolution.[46] Perhaps it is a fool's errand to try to pin down a literary tradition of segregation, as much as it was for Wheatley and every writer thereafter to turn to literature to imagine a non-segregated world. It may be that the desire for a nonracial literature is what most characterizes black literary responses to Jim Crow and his cousins. Sometimes such desires are confident declarations, as when Du Bois avers in *The Souls of Black Folk*, "I sit with Shakespeare and he winces not."[47] More often such desires adopt the subjunctive mood of possibility, be it the alternate universes of Schuyler and Butler or the delicious irony of Colson Whitehead's application to be President Obama's first Secretary of Postracial Affairs.[48] Either way, we can think of the American civil rights movement as a concerted political attempt to realize the speculative aims of segregation literature. Such literature not only advocates that Homer Plessy may sit in any train car he pleases but it also imagines the kind of company he might wish to keep while riding there.

NOTES

1 See Brook Thomas, *Civic Myths: A Law-and-Literature Approach to Citizenship* (Chapel Hill: University of North Carolina, 2007), esp. pp. 5–13.

2 Elizabeth Abel, *Signs of the Times: The Visual Politics of Jim Crow* (Berkeley: University of California Press, 2010), p. 14.

3 Eric Lott, *Love and Theft: Blackface Minstrelsy and the American Working Class* (New York: Oxford University Press, 1995).

4 Joycelyn Moody, "Foreword," in *Representing Segregation: Toward an Aesthetics of Jim Crow, and Other Forms of Racial Division*, ed. Brian Norman and Piper Kendrix Williams (Albany: SUNY Press, 2010), pp. xi–xii.

5 Grace Elizabeth Hale, *Making Whiteness: The Culture of Segregation in the South, 1880–1940* (New York: Pantheon, 1998).

6 This chapter draws on my thinking in *Representing Segregation*, esp. pp. 3–9, co-written with Williams, and *Neo-Segregation Narratives: Jim Crow in Post–Civil Rights America* (Athens: University of Georgia Press, 2010), esp. pp. 9–14.

7 An exemplar is Koritha Mitchell's *Living with Lynching: African American Lynching Plays, Performance, and Citizenship, 1890–1930* (Urbana: University of Illinois Press, 2011).

8 Ibid., p. 2.

9 Lawrence P. Jackson, *The Indignant Generation: A Narrative History of African American Writers and Critics, 1934–1960* (Princeton, NJ: Princeton University Press, 2011), p. 109.

10 Richard Wright, "How 'Bigger' Was Born," in *Native Son* (New York: Harper and Row, 1989), pp. vii–xxxiv.

11 James Allen, *Without Sanctuary: Lynching Photography in America* (Santa Fe: Twin Palms, 2000).

12 Anne Rice, ed., *Witnessing Lynching* (New Brunswick, NJ: Rutgers University Press, 2003), p. 3.

13 Birgit Brander Rasmussen, "'Those That Do Violence Must Expect to Suffer': Disrupting Segregationist Fictions of Safety in Charles W. Chesnutt's *The Marrow of Tradition*," in *Representing Segregation*, ed. Norman and Williams, pp. 73–74.

14 Toni Morrison, *The Bluest Eye* (New York: Penguin, 1994), p. 205.

15 James Baldwin, *Notes of a Native Son* (Boston: Beacon, 1984), p. 129.

16 Ibid., pp. 144, 143.

17 M. Giulia Fabi, *Passing and the Rise of the African American Novel* (Urbana: University of Illinois Press, 2001), p. 5.

18 See Ashraf Rushdy, *The End of American Lynching* (New Brunswick, NJ: Rutgers University Press, 2012).

19 See Philip Dray, *At the Hands of Persons Unknown: The Lynching of Black America* (New York: Random House, 2002).

20 Michele Elam, *The Souls of Mixed Folk: Race, Politics, and Aesthetics in the New Millennium* (Stanford, CA: Stanford University Press, 2011), pp. 97–98.

21 Toni Morrison, *Beloved* (New York: Vintage, 2004), p. 211.

22 Ibid., p. 51. See Nellie McKay, "'Crayon Enlargements of Life: Zora Neale Hurston's *Their Eyes Were Watching God* as Autobiography," in *New Essays on Their Eyes Were Watching God*, ed. Michael Awkward (New York: Cambridge University Press, 1990), pp. 51–70.

23 Leigh Anne Duck, *The Nation's Region: Southern Modernism, Segregation, and U.S. Nationalism* (Athens: University of Georgia Press, 2006), p. 116.

24 Richard Wright, "Between Laughter and Tears," *New Masses*, October 5, 1937: 22–23.

25 Cheryl Wall, "On Freedom and the Will to Adorn: Debating Aesthetics and/as Ideology in African American Literature," in *Aesthetics and Ideology*, ed. George Levine (New Brunswick, NJ: Rutgers University Press, 1994), pp. 283–304.

26 Wesley Brown, *Darktown Strutters* (Amherst: University of Massachusetts Press, 2000), p. 133.

27 See Michelle R. Boyd, *Jim Crow Nostalgia* (Minneapolis: University of Minnesota Press, 2008).

28 Hurston, "Negroes without Self-Pity," in *Speech and Power: The African-American Essay and Its Cultural Content from Polemics to Pulpit*, vol. 2, ed. Gerald Early (Hopewell, NJ: Ecco Press, 1993), p. 300.

29 Norman, *Neo-Segregation Narratives*, p. 78.

30 Kevin Young, *The Grey Album: On the Blackness of Blackness* (Minneapolis: Graywolf Press, 2012), p. 53.

31 George Schuyler, *Black No More* (New York: Dover, 2011), p. 8.

32 Ruth Blandón, "'¿Qué Dice?': Latin America and the Transnational in James Weldon Johnson's *Autobiography of an Ex-Colored Man* and *Along This Way,*" in *Representing Segregation*, ed. Norman and Williams, p. 201.

33 Eve Dunbar, *Black Regions of the Imagination: African American Writers Between the Nation and the World* (Philadelphia: Temple University Press, 2013).

34 Jill Bergman, *The Motherless Child in the Novels of Pauline Hopkins* (Baton Rouge: Louisiana State University Press, 2010).

35 For example, Eric Sundquist, *To Wake the Nation: Race in the Making of American Literature* (Cambridge, MA: Harvard University Press, 1993), p. 569.

36 Melissa Asher Daniels, "The Limits of Literary Realism: *Of One Blood*'s Post-Racial Fantasy by Pauline Hopkins," *Callaloo* 36 (2013): 158–77.

37 Isaiah Lavender III, *Race in American Science Fiction* (Indianapolis: Indiana University Press, 2011), p. 19.

38 See John L. Jackson Jr., "Little Black Magic," in *Racial Americana* special issue of *South Atlantic Quarterly* 104 (2005): 393–402. See also my *Neo-Segregation Narratives*, esp., pp. 159–72.

39 Michelle Alexander, *The New Jim Crow: Mass Incarceration in the Age of Colorblindness* (New York: New Press, 2010).

40 Kenneth Warren, *What Was African American Literature?* (Cambridge, MA: Harvard University Press, 2011), p. 42.

41 See, for example, the "What Was African American Literature?" symposium in *PMLA* 128 (2013): 386–408.

42 George Schuyler, "The Negro Art Hokum," in *Speech and Power*, ed. Gerald Early, p. 86.

43 Ibid., p. 87.

44 Langston Hughes, "The Negro Artist and the Racial Mountain," in *Speech and Power*, ed. Gerald Early, p. 89.

45 Amiri Baraka, "A Post-Racial Anthology?" *Poetry* 202 (2013): 168.

46 Trudier Harris, "Smacked Upside the Head–Again," in *Representing Segregation*, ed. Norman and Williams, pp. 37–39.

47 W. E. B. Du Bois, *The Souls of Black Folk* (Oxford: Oxford University Press, 2008), p. 76.

48 Colson Whitehead, "The Year of Living Postracially," *New York Times* November 4, 1999. http://www.nytimes.com (accessed October 18, 2013).

3

GERSHUN AVILEZ

The Black Arts Movement

The literary period referred to as "Black Arts" occurs from about 1965 to 1975, at what is generally considered a transition point between the civil rights movement and the post–civil rights era. Its major players include the thinkers who shaped its aesthetics – Amiri Baraka/LeRoi Jones, Addison Gayle Jr., and Larry Neal; publishers Hoyt Fuller (*Negro Digest*), Haki Madhubuti/Don Lee (Third World Press), Dudley Randall (Broadside Press); and writers Ed Bullins, Lucille Clifton, Jayne Cortez, Henry Dumas, Etheridge Knight, Audre Lorde, and Sonia Sanchez. This nationwide surge in African American artistic productivity that became known as the "Black Arts Movement" gets started shortly after the passage of the Civil Rights Act of 1964 – which prohibited federal discrimination based on race, color, sex, creed, or nation of origin – and the Voting Rights Act of 1965 – which outlawed discriminatory voting practices. These documents marked a seeming victory for civil rights activism and suggested the possibility of a shift in African Americans' real and imagined relationship to the nation-state. Accordingly, the legislation had an undeniable impact on the world of African American cultural production.

This chapter examines the Black Arts Movement in the context of the shifting discourse of civil rights, and it positions the social reaction to legislative advances as crucial to understanding Black Arts aesthetic frameworks and institution building. The first section demonstrates how the concerted effort to move away from a rhetorical emphasis on reform toward one on revolution becomes a defining characteristic of Black Arts logics. The next section attends to the social history of the moment in examining how the perceived urgency of breaking away from traditional means of social change results in an ideological focus on metaphorical black nation building, meaning new forms of collective consciousness raising and social and political organizing. The final section offers a reading of a specific Black Arts text, Barry Beckham's 1972 novel *Runner Mack*, showing how Beckham uses disappointment with African American social and civic access – especially in regard to employment opportunities – as the framework for imagining revolution. This analysis suggests the ways in which artwork from the Black Arts period can function as a crucial lens for assessing civil rights legislation and its perceived social impact.

From Reform to Revolution

The Civil Rights Act sought to secure citizens access to the full social realm. Its provisions included banning voter registration requirements, prohibiting denial of access in public facilities, encouraging the desegregation of public schools, and prohibiting employment discrimination. It was an omnibus piece of legislation that attempted to bring together and strengthen earlier legislative attempts at disrupting social inequality, specifically the Civil Rights Acts of 1957 and 1960. Although the 1964 iteration and the Voting Rights Act of 1965 promised social change for African Americans in particular, this legislation was met with continued injustice and violence against black bodies.[1] Activists found that local governments failed to enforce the Voting Rights Act and that neither the Civil Rights Act nor the Voting Rights Act did much to impede the social abuse of black American citizens, as the 1966 shooting of James Meredith in Mississippi illustrated.[2] In addition, the 1965 social uprising that occurred in the Watts neighborhood of Los Angeles, California, stands as a testament not only to police mistreatment but also to the inevitable outcome of the stifling practices of segregation in U.S. society and the ongoing neglect and constriction of inner-city communities in the face of so-called legislative advances.[3] These social conditions led to the rise of black activist nationalist groups such as the Black Panther Party for Self Defense, whose members strove to protect and improve the conditions of their communities. Although achievements were met with setbacks, such hindrances spurred activism and radicalism. Accordingly, in the sociopolitical landscape, excitement was necessarily mixed with disappointment and happiness with frustration. This social situation provides the exact context for the emergence of the Black Arts Movement.

The periodical *Negro Digest* is a crucial resource for coming to terms with these circumstances because it reveals the relationship between civil rights discourse and the developing Black Arts Movement. The Johnson Publishing Company originally printed the magazine in 1942, and it ran until 1951. In 1961, Hoyt Fuller, a former newspaper journalist who had worked as the associate editor of the magazine *Ebony* until 1957, became the managing editor of the revived *Negro Digest*. Under Fuller's editorial leadership, the reconfigured periodical extensively explored the social and political situation of Black Americans in the United States.[4] For example, the opening article for the November 1961 issue concerns how the centennial of the Civil War reveals social attitudes about the struggles for civil rights. In 1966, in the wake of the civil rights legislations, the December issue is dedicated to the question "Black Power and the Civil Rights Crisis." The framing language of "crisis" indicates the rising sentiment that the promise of civil rights had still not been realized after the landmark 1964 act. The periodical was a platform for developing critical frameworks for talking about African American political and social situations. Importantly, Fuller also sought to make the magazine a prominent forum for the discussion of aesthetics and African American literature generally and the Black Arts Movement specifically. As the January 1968 issue illustrates, there are staged symposia with artists talking about questions of artistic value and the shifting terrain of aesthetics. Moreover, Fuller produces annual issues dedicated to poetry, fiction, and drama and solicits essays on aesthetics that appear year round.

Issues of the *Negro Digest* demonstrate not only a textual nexus between civil rights social critique and Black Arts artistic analysis, but they also reveal how theorizing during the Black Arts period can be understood as developing, in part, as a response to the civil rights predicament. One finds that creative writers were using the magazine as a forum for analyzing the social dilemmas of the 1960s. In a 1964 article entitled "What Does Non-Violence Mean?" LeRoi Jones insists, "In order for the Negro to achieve what I will call an 'equality of means,' that is, at birth to be able to benefit by everything of value in the society, of course, the society would have to change almost completely."[5] His point is that actual social equality would require a restructuring of the U.S. social realm, which goes beyond the ostensibly symbolic changes promised by further civil rights legislation. He goes on to say: "The point is, I think that the poor black realizes, at least instinctively, that no matter what deal goes down [in terms of civil rights legislation], i.e., no matter whose side [wins out] the 'Crackers' or the government, no help at all is being offered to him."[6] Fiction writer and regular contributor Anita Cornwell echoes this sentiment in 1965: "Voting-Rights Bill or no, many suns will set before the majority of all eligible Negroes are registered and voting in the South, and long before that comes to pass they will have learned what the northern Negro has always known – voting won't get you in there either.... *We shall overcome is merely a dream*" (4; emphasis in original).[7] Cornwell does not believe that pieces of legislation will necessarily do much to change the social situation of African Americans because a widespread investment in social inequality and racism will still exist at every level of U.S. society.

There is an older, larger problem that new legislation alone will do little to resolve. Cornwell's final comments reveal more than a suspicion of the possibility of legislation effecting change. She contends that "overcoming," or achieving social equality, is a wishful fantasy – no more than a fiction – thereby strategically undermining rhetoric that came to characterize civil rights movement activism up to that point. These essays (alongside many others) signal the shift in rhetoric from reform to revolution that would help to inspire the activism of the Black Power Movement and, importantly, the artistic projects of the Black Arts Movement.

In fact, the idea of reconfiguring the social realm as a whole is a central component of Black Aesthetic theorizations. A specific frustration with the social realm is the impetus for the formulation of aesthetic principles during the period of the Black Arts Movement. In his 1968 essay "Towards a Black Aesthetic," Hoyt Fuller writes, "The revolt is as palpable in letters as it is in the street…. Just as black intellectuals have rejected the NAACP, on the one hand, and the two major political parties, on the other, and gone off in search of new and more effective means and methods of seizing power, so revolutionary black writers have turned their backs on the old 'certainties' and struck out in new, if uncharted, directions."[8] Fuller recognizes a growing dissatisfaction with the familiar means of social change and connects (arguably even analogizes) this abandoning to the artistic critique and rejection of the "certainties" about cultural production that have led to a search for new ideas and methodologies. This linkage of the analysis of African Americans' civic situation to calls for new aesthetic practices subtends other critical discussions from the period. Addison Gayle's concept of the "cultural strangulation" of African American literature is a metaphor derived from an assessment of black Americans' civic confinement.[9] Larry Neal's insistence on a "radical reordering" of aesthetic describes an artistic strategy meant to parallel a radical reordering of the social realm beyond the reach of recent civil rights legislation. This idea is in line with Carolyn Gerald's insistence that the art of the 1960s was focused on "deliberate desecration and smashing of idols, the turning inside-out of symbols."[10] In other words, the descriptions of the artistic projects that populate the Black Arts period highlight an investment in reconstituting aesthetic practices and values. Accordingly, one can understand the formulation of a Black Aesthetic and the principles that the Black Arts Movement devised as artistic articulations of dissatisfaction and disappointments with the social sphere in terms of civil rights advancements. The recurring critique of dominant aesthetic values and methodologies act as civil rights complaints. The inadequacies of the U.S. civil rights situation for black Americans became the basis for imagining new aesthetic possibilities.[11]

Nation Building and the Modern Black Public Sphere

The social disappointment results in a turn to nationalist strategies, particularly the development of new black-controlled and black-operated organizations in the social and artistic realms. As opposed to evoking an unyielding confidence in the nation or a simple desire for an autonomous black state, nationalism – as advocated by black writers and activists at this historical moment – concerns primarily the possibility of black solidarity and the desire to redefine contemporary black identity and relationships.[12] Within nationalist frameworks, one finds thinkers fashioning both social and private identities in radical ways. In fact, Stokely Carmichael (later Kwame Ture) and Charles Johnson make it abundantly clear that the nationalist "black power" about which they write references the ability to (re)define oneself and the sociopolitical world one inhabits.[13] Reflecting a similar impulse, the primary goals of Ron Karenga's US organization (founded 1965) and the *Kawaida* movement were to cultivate African American cultural traditions and to shift black American consciousness from European models to African (or African-derived) ones.[14] Moreover, the speech "The Ballot or the Bullet" that Malcolm X delivered in Detroit, Michigan, in 1964 emphasizes the necessity of nationalism; he believed it could lead to the development of a "new political consciousness" and a social and personal reorientation of black Americans in the context of unending prejudice.[15] These examples demonstrate how the social, political, and cultural methods for addressing the desire for group redefinition and collective action in the face of injustice are all imagined as fitting under the rubric of nationalism.

The intensified investment in ideologies of nationalism that defined this moment encouraged the formation of black ideological and institutional spaces concerned with aesthetics. Cultural critic James Smethurst provides a detailed account of the development of such institutions throughout the United States in his social history *The Black Arts Movement*, which works to link together geographically distinct methods of organizing and artistic production. In 1965, LeRoi Jones announced the creation of the Black Arts Repertory Theatre/School (BARTS) in Harlem. Through this organization, Jones attempted to use creative expression to radicalize the poor of Harlem. Tom Dent and Kalamu ya Salaam helped to establish the important southern poetry and theater collective BLKARTSOUTH in 1968 in New Orleans; this community-oriented organization focused on developing a regional consciousness and supporting local artists alongside doing political work.[16] Don L. Lee (later Haki Madhubuti), Johari Amini, and Carolyn Rogers founded the Organization of Black American Culture (OBAC) in Chicago, in 1967, which was to become one of the longest surviving Black

Arts cultural organizations.[17] This period also witnessed the rise and development of black-owned and black-operated publishing houses and journals. In 1965, Dudley Randall founded Broadside Press in Detroit, and inspired, in part, by Randall's achievement, Lee, Amini, and Rodgers also began Third World Press in 1967 in Chicago. The Bay area *Journal of Black Poetry*, created in 1966 by editor Dingane Joe Goncalves, featured the work of young writers and became an important outlet for commenting on the national political scene. These organizations, and many others like them, represent an explicit fusion of cultural production and radical politics.

In part, what I am outlining here is the development of a modern black public sphere as a result of the post–civil rights sociopolitical environment. In his revision and critique of the concept of the public sphere as articulated by Jürgen Habermas, Houston Baker explains the concept of a black public sphere as a "new aesthetic consciousness" that has less to do with the exchange of arguments "in a realm between the family and the market" and more with "structurally and affectively transforming the founding notion of the bourgeoisie public sphere into an expressive and empowering self-fashioning."[18] This new consciousness that involves finding radical methods of expression and empowerment describes succinctly the Black Arts Movement as a response to civil rights frustrations. In fact, the Black Arts Movement, as a social phenomenon, symbolizes one of the best instances of the historical attempts at a black public sphere.

Again, this flourishing of organizations and institutions is fed by a renewed investment in the political ideology of black nationalism. This ideological framework is key to coming to terms with the modern black public sphere because of the rhetorical emphasis on nation building.[19] The active development of black organizations and the attempts to theorize aesthetic strategies sensitive to the lived experiences of African Americans represent metaphorical nation-building projects to protect the lives and foster the talents of a group of people who feel particularly disaffected by the ideologies and practices of their country. In the context of African Americans' reactions to and critiques of civil rights legislation and ongoing discrimination, the notion of the black public sphere becomes legible as a cultural and political necessity and as an extension of such nation building through the social imaginary. Accordingly, through the Black Arts Movement, as the cultural expression of this perceived need, one can track the movement from reaction against ineffectual legislative reform directly to innovations in and transformation of the world of cultural production.

Unfortunately, many of the collectives and projects that emerge during the Black Arts Movement do not last long in their original manifestations, and the movement itself is most often defined as being only about a decade in duration. It is difficult to pinpoint the "how" and "why" of the conclusion of this cultural movement and the endeavors that developed in and around it. It is more productive to think of this "conclusion" in terms of a transfer and transformation of energies as opposed to an absolute end. It is important to note that the social context for this shift is the rising conservatism in the early 1970s U.S. social world, particularly in regard to civil rights issues – marked by Richard Nixon's rise to power. Though allegedly a supporter of "black power" in the form of "black capitalism," Nixon criticized women on welfare, blamed the poor for their own poverty, and suggested nefarious links between the social movements of the 1960s and criminality and drug addiction. The overwhelming white support of Nixon represented a backlash from individuals who feared the spread of the social unrest in urban spaces and who felt that blacks were excessively benefiting from government aid. In addition, Nixon's conservative victory closely followed diligent attempts by the FBI's Counter Intelligence Program (COINTELPRO) to dismantle black activist organizations.[20] Accordingly, black activists faced new social and political pressures to rein in politically and socially radical sentiment. The 1974 National Black Political Convention's refusal to create an independent political party because of "red-baiting" effectively illustrates the outcome of such pressure.[21]

The eschewing of the realization of an independent black political party parallels and reflects the increasing desire of many activist and radicals to integrate themselves into the existing world of politics – in other words, to attempt reform from within. Martha Biondi and Matthew Countryman both characterize this historical moment by the movement from "protest" to "politics" among civil rights activists.[22] The social activism in which many blacks had participated (rallies, picketing, voter registrations, et cetera) ultimately created more opportunities within the U.S. public sphere, especially at the municipal and local government levels. Historian Robin D. G. Kelley explains that African Americans made significant progress in the electoral sphere during this time: "In 1969, 994 black men and 131 black women held public office nationwide; by 1975 the number of black elected officials grew to 2,973 men and 530 women. Black politicians won mayoral races in several major cities, including Los Angeles, Atlanta, New Orleans, Philadelphia, and Washington, D.C. By 1974, more than two hundred African Americans served as state legislators, and seventeen sat in Congress."[23] Thus, Black Arts period protests and campaigns ultimately altered the social and political terrain even as the movement as such waned.

Parallel to the movement into political offices, black activists and writers also found themselves entering the world of the academy at a much higher rate. Historically one can observe how black radical activism led to the increase of minority enrollment on college campuses and the advent of

Black Studies programs. As Fabio Rojas illustrates, the creation of the Black Studies department at San Francisco State College in 1969 was in part the result of Black Panther Jimmy Garrett (among others) enrolling at the institution to mobilize the black students and uncover the racist structures of the education system.[24] Accordingly, the social critique manifested in much of the Panthers' work also extended to the idea of the university and a university education. Some individuals, then, directed their actions wholly to transforming this site of power and educating themselves in the process.[25] In addition, Black Arts period writers such as Sonia Sanchez, Askia Touré, June Jordan, and Lucille Clifton took short- and long-term academic positions, transforming the political ideals driving their artistic production into radical pedagogies and revisionist curricula. In effect, colleges and universities began to attract some of the insurgent energy that had fed the revolutionary fervor of the Black Arts moment.

Nonetheless, if one examines the commentaries and social analyses of black public figures in the midst of these radical changes, it becomes readily apparent that there is a general reassessment of the efficacy and desirability of nationalistic frameworks as they had been espoused.[26] In other words, nationalist revolutionary discourses actually give rise to discussions of the limits of such thought and its implications. This consideration is a factor in the rise of black women's organizations in particular. The paradigmatic focus on nation building during the period of the Black Arts Movement also yields an abiding concern with investigating gender and sexual identity because of the persistent reliance upon patriarchal and heterosexist conceptions of black identity and collectivity.[27] This interest in questions of gender formation in relation to artistic production and activism encouraged the creation and proliferation of organizations and modes of analysis that went beyond the initially stated goals of the period. For instance, the National Black Feminist Organization and the Combahee River Collective each developed as a response to both (1) the widespread desire during the Black Arts moment to transform public conceptions of black gender identity and (2) the blatant racism that many women had experienced in some nationalist and activist organizations.[28] In the final analysis the paradigm of nation building helped to set in motion the kinds of social transformations that policy change sought to create.

Black Arts Literature as Civil Rights Literature

This chapter concludes with a consideration of how Black Arts Movement texts can shed light on the intricacies of civil rights as a social phenomenon.

Many texts from the Black Arts period respond to the ongoing dilemmas around African American citizenship and social access. These works include Amiri Baraka/LeRoi Jones's play *The Slave* (1965), Etheridge Knight's collection *Poems from Prison* (1968), Ed Bullins's play *Goin a' Buffalo* (1968), Lucille Clifton's poetry collection *Good Times* (1969), Sonia Sanchez's poetry collection *We a BaddDDD People* (1970), Jayne Cortez's poetry collection *Festivals and Funerals* (1971), and Henry Dumas's short fiction collection *Ark of Bones and Other Stories* (1974). Notwithstanding these important works, Barry Beckham's 1972 novel *Runner Mack* links together the major concerns of the Black Arts Movement and offers a particularly compelling assessment of the "civil rights crisis." Positioning this novel prominently in this discussion also makes it possible to consider how fiction writers explored Black Arts exigencies. Poetry and drama were the favored genres during the Black Arts Movement, but this prominence does not mean that fiction writers were not inspired by or involved in the aesthetic explorations that dominated the period. More important, Beckham's novel (1) illustrates a conceptual investment in revolution while casting aspersions on reform impulses and (2) traces a thwarted attempt at nation building.

Runner Mack is a surrealist novel that worries the line between dream and reality; in fact, the narrative content and structure reflect an investment in dreams.[29] The plot revolves around the disillusionment of twenty-year-old protagonist Henry Adams, whose one desire is to play baseball. This dream of becoming a professional (that is, salaried) baseball player structures all of protagonist Henry's actions in the narrative. The novel opens with his migrating north from Mississippi with his wife Beatrice to try to get recruited by the Stars' baseball team. Henry has faith that he will get selected to be on the team because of his undeniable talent: "I know I can make it. I can play. I can hit any pitcher they got. I can play better than them all" (38). He later insists to Beatrice, "this is the American pastime, they've got to be fair with me.... They have to judge me on my ability only" (81–82). These comments, which recur throughout the text, demonstrate Henry's belief that the professional world and U.S. society operate as meritocracies. He expects that the social world will be guided by the value of equality and will necessarily reward hard work. His dream of getting drafted onto the Stars team gets interconnected to the fundamental defining characteristics of U.S. democratic ideals.

Unfortunately, Henry's experience with the Stars transforms his dream into a nightmarish perversion of such ideals. After months of not hearing from the Stars' baseball management, Henry finally gets a letter alerting him of a tryout. While having Henry practice catching fly balls, the manager "Stumpy" throws a "hotball" (a ball rigged with electrical circuits) to Henry that electrocutes him.[30] The members of the team laugh at Henry, who has been knocked down by the shocking pain. The narrative leads the reader to suspect that Henry's race was the cause of this humiliation because of the way that characters in the novel talk about baseball as a white man's sport: "'Don't make no difference no more how good you are ... you still black'" (39). The purpose of the tryout has not been to exhibit Henry's skill but rather to make clear his powerlessness. The reader discovers that Stumpy – who is so small that he must be carried around on team members' shoulders – has the ability to decide both Henry's future and his bodily safety. Henry leaves the baseball field with a throbbing hand and still unemployed. Not only does the scene dismiss the idea of U.S. meritocracy as naïve, but it also showcases the seemingly total vulnerability of the black individual in the social world. As much of the early tension in the narrative revolves around Henry getting the chance to perform, the scene ultimately discredits the exact notion of "opportunity." The invitation to try out stands as merely an empty gesture as opposed to a genuine commitment to recognizing talent and reforming a profession that was historically exclusive.

As Wiley Lee Umphlett explains, Beckham's decision to write in the genre of popular sports fiction is significant because this genre has traditionally been racialized and middle-class focused so that black male writers have been largely excluded;[31] however, baseball as a subject is especially useful because the sport is rife with cultural meanings tied to national mythologies. Beckham purposefully chooses baseball as the vehicle for a metaphor of the desires for access and opportunity because of its specific social linkages to the United States' social imaginary and the country's conception of its social ideals. Cultural critic George Grella argues, "Baseball embodies some of the central preoccupations of the cultural fantasy we like to think of as the American Dream."[32] The dream motif allows for the presentation of the protagonist as a hopeful, naïve dreamer, but it also creates the opportunity for Beckham to transform hopeful expectations into nightmarish situations. However, Beckham actually relies on two interconnected metaphors that move from specific to general back to specific. The organized sport of baseball represents the idea of the American Dream, and the allusions to the American Dream of success in the context of the novel signify civil rights conceptions of social progress, access, and especially employment. These conjoined metaphors pivot around the possibilities for securing gainful employment, and at the heart of its narrative, *Runner Mack* is a novel about African American employment and economic stability in the wake of legislative reform.

Henry's inability to find a job materializes a socially constructed alienation from the body politic, which Beckham is at pains to link to collective lack of access for African American citizens. In a flashback, the reader discovers that Henry's father, a janitor and laborer, expresses interest in claiming social security in order to retire: "'I'm retiring. No more cleaning up those bathrooms in the bus station after next year. So I found out from my niece who's smart, got a good job up North – I told you about her – sent me a letter saying I should look into this social security thing. You know they been taking money out of my pay for fifteen years?'" (70). Unfortunately, his employers, who are surprised at his agitating "crazy" talk about social security, tell him that they forgot to send in the proper paper work to the government. Despite this "accidental" oversight, they insist that they would be happy to supply him with (menial) work for the rest of his life. In part, this conversation is important because an additional Social Security Act was passed in 1965, the same year as the Voting Rights Act. This act specifically created Medicare and Medicaid, but it also reinvigorated conversations about Social Security in general. However, this expansion of the program could not reach Henry's family. Importantly, it is not only Henry's father who emerges as incapable of benefiting from progressive legislation. Because he is without a baseball contract, Henry must search for work to provide for himself and his wife Beatrice. During an interview for a job at a manufacturing company, his height and weight are noted, and his teeth are checked, as is his penis. These examinations happen before he is offered the job and told that "you can go far – it all depends on you. Plenty of opportunities for our employees" (21). Yet, Henry quickly learns that there are no conceivable chances for promotion or advancement – his supervisor has held the same position for forty years. As most commentators on the novel have pointed out, the interview process itself mimics the protocols of a slave auction. More important, Beckham's reliance on these specific elements that are bookended by the promise of opportunity are a specific attempt to evoke and satirize the rhetoric of equal opportunity in employment that derived from the Civil Rights Act.[33] His father is unable to claim the resources that years of work have accrued, and Henry's experience first undermines the possibility of finding employment then mocks the idea that equality, non-discrimination, or achievement are any part of U.S. employment prospects. In short, the novel's focus on representing employment experiences works to suggest how official shifts in policies might do little to nothing to effect change. The employment situation of the African American characters in this novel becomes a reflection of their civic standing.

From this perspective, Beckham tracks a black disillusionment with the social world, and this idea reaches its fullest expression through the titular character: Runner Mack. This character befriends Henry in the army after the protagonist is unexpectedly drafted following his failed attempts to get a job. If Henry is the character who believes wholeheartedly – perhaps fool-hardily from the perspective of the narrative – in the civil rights narrative of progress, Runner Mack is his foil who refuses to accept this idea as truth and calls for the destruction of society. He is a social radical. In fact, he hatches a carefully crafted plan to blow up the White House, fully express-ing his commitment to actual revolutionary action. Throughout the narra-tive, Henry is often presented as naïve and credulous no matter how curious the events around him or conniving the people. Henry is taken with Runner Mack when he meets him in the army because Mack gives the impression of knowing and understanding the world in ways that have always eluded Henry: "Mack seemed to know things, had things to say, and Henry was sure he could learn something from him" (142). When Henry tells his new friend about the situation with the Stars, Mack immediately insists, "'Dude, can't you see they bullshittin you?'" Statements such as this one lead Henry to say, "I've been asleep all my life, a slumbering giant. I didn't know what was wrong with me and you [Mack] came along and named it" (145). Henry's life had been characterized by an inability to see or read signals carefully; Runner Mack offers Henry an awareness that he had not had before. He gives Henry a gift of knowledge or perception and inspiration to action. In effect, their relationship can be described as a veritable education of Henry Adams. This understanding demonstrates how Beckham is alluding to the historical figure of Henry Adams, the important historian and descendant of two U.S. presidents, actively throughout the narrative.[34] Like his namesake, Henry learns that his education thus far has not prepared him for the world he lives in. His faith in the democratic system begins to unravel because of Runner Mack's lessons in social radicalism.

In terms of the narrative structure, this friendship with Runner Mack stages the conceptual move from reform to revolution, which came to char-acterize the Black Arts Movement generally. What Runner calls for is revo-lution in the most absolute terms. This revolutionary destruction is imagined as being the only way to protect the country: "'We're takin' over the mutha-fuckin' country, goddammit. We gonna save it before those crazy muthafuck-ahs drive us all crazy'" (153). Disloyalty, however, prevents the men from realizing their plans. After elements of their scheme are leaked out, Mack tells Henry, "'anyone is capable of betraying you'" (174). This statement provides the frame for the end of the story. As both men wait in Washington, D.C. for their planned rally to begin so that their revolution can start, they find that (almost) no one shows up for it (203). In discussing the end of his novel in a 1974 interview, Barry Beckam explains, "I meant for the revolution to be taken seriously. In fact, revolution is a serious event in both my novel and [John A.] Williams's [*The Man Who Cried I Am*, 1968]. What happens, of course, is that it becomes both funny and sad. When push comes to shove, niggers just don't show up" (39).[35] The black community (and its supporters) cannot be depended on to participate in the exact revolutionary actions that would undermine and annihilate racist institutions and a discriminatory culture; in other words, they do not "show up" for each other. It is this realization – that the "niggers" would never appear and participate – that causes Runner Mack to hang himself in the bathroom at the end of the novel. Rather than reading this ending as a critique of revolutionary sentiment or the idea that revolutionary action is impossible, one can read the novel as providing a critique of half-hearted and insincere revolutionary action. The point is not that revolution is a pipe dream; it is real and realizable. That being said, the novel does not posit revolution as a certainty or a guarantee. The ending presents it as a possibility that requires work and collective commitment, which Runner Mack finds that his plan lacks in the end.

Ultimately, Beckham offers in narrative form the question that opens Sonia Sanchez's well-known 1970 poem "blk rhetoric": "who's gonna make all / that beautiful blk / rhetoric / mean something?"[36] Throughout the poem, Sanchez foregrounds a skeptical attitude about the widespread engagement of the political pressures for unity, yet the speaker of the poem does not cast aside collective action as an achievable goal. The poem offers a critique of those who devote themselves blindly to rhetoric alone and calls out for involvement and participation to provide substance to the language of revolution just as *Runner Mack* does later. The power of the novel is that it extends the sentiments of the provocative poem by providing a sustained critique of traditional civil rights reforms, thereby calling out for new methods, but it does so without naïvely presenting revolution as always-already achievable. Beckham's work demonstrates how for texts produced during the Black Arts period, revolution is a desperate desire, but it is also a sincere question. The text indicates that simply rejecting civil rights progress as insufficient only functions as a first move. The novel, like Sanchez's poem, also attempts to re-imagine the terms of black collective action vis-à-vis civil rights concerns. In the final analysis, *Runner Mack* provides insights on how the Black Arts Movement functions as a historical, rhetorical, and aesthetic response to legislative and policy change.

NOTES

1 The fact that the U.S. government saw fit to pass two more Civil Rights Acts (1968 and 1991) suggests that instruments of discrimination continued relatively unabated.

2 Peniel E. Joseph details the social repercussions of the act's passage in *Waiting 'Til the Midnight Hour* (New York: Henry Holt, 2006). James Meredith was

shot as he was walking from Memphis, Tennessee, to Jackson, Mississippi (220 miles), in order to challenge a social system that encouraged white supremacy and racial segregation. He called it his "march against fear." After Meredith was ambushed and shot, Martin Luther King Jr. (Southern Christian Leadership Conference), Floyd McKissick (Congress of Racial Equality), and Stokely Carmichael (Student Nonviolent Coordinating Committee) resumed the march. The event became an important moment in the civil rights movement and radicalized many individuals and groups, especially in the South.

3   For an examination of the situation in Watts, California, and the social climate that led to the insurgent course of events, see Gerald Horne, *The Fire this Time* (Charlottesville: University Press of Virginia, 1995).

4   See James Smethurst's discussion of Fuller in *The Black Arts Movement* (Chapel Hill: University of North Carolina Press, 2005).

5   LeRoi Jones, "What Does Nonviolence Mean?" *Negro Digest* 13.1 (1964): 6.

6   Ibid., 14.

7   See Anita Cornwell, "Why We May Never Overcome," *Negro Digest* 14.9 (1965).

8   See Hoyt Fuller, "Towards a Black Aesthetic," in *The Black Aesthetic*, ed. Addison Gayle (Garden City, NJ: Anchor Books, 1971), p. 3.

9   See Addison Gayle Jr., "Cultural Strangulation: Black Literature and the White Aesthetic," *Negro Digest* 18.9 (1969): 32–39.

10 See Carolyn Gerald, "The Black Writer and His Role," *Negro Digest* 18.3 (1969): 47.

11 Many of the contributions from Addison Gayle's anthology *The Black Aesthetic* – including Gayle's and Gerald's – come directly from the pages of *Negro Digest*, demonstrating the significance of this periodical to the articulation of the black aesthetic.

12 I make this point to clarify this period's call for nationalism as distinct from the black nationalism of the nineteenth century and from other discourses of nationalism that derive from an emphasis on the nation-state to the detriment of either local or transnational concerns. Wilson Jeremiah Moses explains the distinction between early black nationalism and modern black nationalism in *Classical Black Nationalism* (New York: New York University Press, 1996). Tommie Shelby's recent *We Who Are Dark* (Cambridge, MA: Belknap, 2005) provides an assessment of the contemporary significance of nationalist thought among African Americans, and he does so by theorizing nationalism in terms of identification and relationships and not simply commitments to the nation-state.

13 See Stokely Carmichael and Charles Johnson, *Black Power* (1967; New York: Vintage, 1992).

14 For discussions of Ron Karenga and *Kawaida*, see Amiri Baraka, *Kawaida Studies* (Chicago: Third World Press, 1972) and William L. Van Deburg, *New Day in Babylon* (Chicago: University of Chicago Press, 1992).

15 See George Breitman, ed., *Malcolm X Speaks: Selected Essays and Speeches* (New York: Grove Press, 1994).

16 The organization grew out of a workshop of the Free Southern Theatre, which was founded by John O'Neal, Doris Derby, and Gil Moses in Mississippi in 1963.

17 See Carmen Phelp's discussion of OBAC in *Visionary Women Writers* (Jackson: University of Mississippi Press, 2013).

18 See Houston Baker, "Critical Memory and the Black Public Sphere," *The Black
    Public Sphere* (Chicago: University of Chicago Press, 1995), p. 13. Jürgen
    Habermas introduced his conceptualization of the bourgeois public sphere in
    Structural Transformations of the Public Sphere (1962; Cambridge, MA: MIT
    Press, 1991). He understands the public sphere as a body of "private" – meaning
    not necessarily associated with the state – persons gathered together to discuss
    matters of common interest or "public concern"; this body uses "publicity" to
    hold the state accountable to society. Reconsiderations and critiques of his con-
    cept prove more attractive to thinkers in Ethnic Studies (among many other
    thinkers) than the original understanding, particularly because this body of
    "private" persons was made up of propertied white men. Although the con-
    cept was supposed to be inclusive, it always excluded certain identities. Nancy
    Fraser's reconceptualization and expansion of public sphere represents one of
    the reconsiderations of the concept that has been deployed often. She argues
    for the existence of "subaltern counterpublics," defined as "discursive arenas
    where members of subordinated social groups invent and circulate counterdis-
    courses to formulate oppositional interpretations of their identities, interests,
    and needs." Fraser insists that multiple public spheres exist simultaneously and
    that they rely on discursive measures comparable to those Habermas theorizes
    to accomplish their goals. See Fraser, "Re-thinking the Public Sphere," *Social
    Text* 25/26 (1990): 56–80.
19 Eddie Glaude Jr. offers a thoughtful analysis of the language of nation in the
    introductory essay "Black Power Revisited" to his edited volume *Is It Nation
    Time?* (Chicago: University of Chicago, 2002), pp. 1–21.
20 Amiri Baraka discusses COINTELPRO's involvement in the disintegration of
    the Black Arts Repertory Theatre and School in *Autobiography of LeRoi Jones/
    Amiri Baraka* (New York: Freundlich, 1984).
21 Harold Cruse would later characterize this publicized act as "a betrayal of the
    Black militant potential built up during the struggles of the Sixties" (127). See
    William Jelani Cobb, ed., *The Essential Harold Cruse* (New York: Palgrave
    2002).
22 See Martha Biondi's *To Stand and Fight* (Cambridge, MA: Harvard, 2003) and
    Matthew Countryman's *Up South* (Philadelphia: University of Pennsylvania
    Press, 2006).
23 See Kelley's chapter "Into the Fire" in *To Make Our World Anew*, Volume 2, ed.
    Robin D. G. Kelley and Earl Lewis (New York: Oxford University Press, 2000),
    esp. p. 280.
24 See Fabio Rojas, *From Black Power to Black Studies* (Baltimore, MD: Johns
    Hopkins University Press, 2007).
25 For histories of the Black Studies programs and discussions of the San Francisco
    State College case in particular, see Nathaniel Norment Jr.'s *The African
    American Studies Reader* (Durham, NC: Carolina Academic Press, 2001);
    Noliwe Rooks, *White Money, Black Power* (Boston: Beacon Press, 2006); James
    Edward Smethurst, *The Black Arts Movement*; and Fabio Rojas, *From Black
    Power to Black Studies*.
26 The events at the National Black Political Convention referenced earlier attest
    to such reconsideration. Amiri Baraka's abandoning of nationalist principles
    manifests the scrutinizing of this logic in ways that inform much social activism

and artistic production. Often considered to be one of the chief architects of black arts *and* the BPO, Baraka underwent a radical shift in his priorities in 1974 when he left nationalism behind to a become disciple of what he called "Marxism-Leninism-Mao Zedong" thought. Baraka's disappointment with newly elected black officials and the political lassitude of the representatives at important conferences and conventions made him feel as if nationalism served the black bourgeoisie and the elite of the white power structure primarily. He saw possibility for social change in the class-conscious ideologies to which he attached himself. More than signaling a drastic reinterpretation of his politics, Baraka's ideological reversal, as it is called, indicates an exploration of nationalism's limits. Jerry Gafio Watts provides a comprehensive discussion of Amiri Baraka and the ideological shifts that define his career in *Amiri Baraka* (New York: New York University Press, 2001).

27 Madhu Dubey provides an in-depth analysis of how patriarchal and masculinist understandings inform the work of this era in *Black Women Novelists and the Nationalist Aesthetic* (Bloomington: Indiana University Press, 1994).

28 For discussions of the rise and politics of these two organizations, see Kimberly Springer, *Still Lifting, Still Climbing* (New York: New York University Press, 1999) and Duchess Harris, "From Kennedy Commission to the Combahee Collective: Black Feminist Organizing, 1960–80," in *Sisters in the Struggle*, ed. Bettye Collier-Thomas and V. P. Franklin (New York: New York University Press, 2001).

29 Joe Weixlmann discusses at length the motifs of dreams and nightmares in "The Dream Turned 'Daymare': Barry Beckham's Runner Mack," *MELUS* 8.4 (1981): 93–103.

30 In an interview of Barry Beckham by Sanford Pinsker, a parallel is drawn between this moment of electrocution and the one that happens in the "Battle Royal" scene in Ralph Ellison's *Invisible Man*. See "About Runner Mack," *Black Images* 3 (1974): 35–41.

31 See Wiley Lee Umphlett, "The Black Man as Fictional Athlete," *Modern Fiction Studies* 33.1 (1987): 73–83.

32 George Grella, "Baseball and the American Dream," *The Massachusetts Review* 16.3 (Summer 1975): 268.

33 Phyllis Klotman discusses the parodying of the notion of "equal opportunity" in the novel in *Another Man Gone* (Port Washington, NY: Kennikat Press, 1977).

34 Barry Beckham explains that he actively used particular sections of Henry Adams's 1907 autobiography *The Education of Henry Adams* in constructing his narrative.

35 See Sanford Pinsker, "About Runner Mack."

36 See Sonia Sanchez, *We a BaddDDD People* (Detroit, MI: Broadside, 1970), p. 15.

4

NILGÜN ANADOLU-OKUR

Drama and Performance from Civil Rights to Black Arts

Devil wearying. Devil getting tired, trying to struggle with brother,
telling brother to slow down, brothers, some doing wild steps while
they building black blocks, ... a city dancing against the sun, gold
towers beat our eyes with sensuous natural harmonies.

Bloodrites, Amiri Baraka

I dedicate this chapter to the inexhaustible memory of Amiri Baraka
(1934–2014)

The drama of Africans' forceful migration and existence as an internal
colony under the control of the dominant white infrastructure in the United
States acts as the fundamental backdrop for protest discourse. By extension,
until the civil rights era, American theater owed its isolation and shortage
of original themes largely to the dearth of Africanist, feminist, womanist,
multiculturalist, gay, and lesbian voices. In *Playing in the Dark: Whiteness
and the Literary Imagination,* Toni Morrison argues that American literature more generally has sided with the oppressor: "clearly the preserve of
white male views, genius, and power, those views, genius and power are
without relationship to and removed from the overwhelming presence of
black people in the United States." Morrison further writes:

> For some time now I have been thinking about the validity or vulnerability of
> a certain set of assumptions conventionally accepted among literary histori-
> ans and critics and circulated as "knowledge." This knowledge holds that tra-
> ditional, canonical American Literature is free of, uninformed, and unshaped
> by the four-hundred-year-old presence of, first, Africans and then African
> Americans in the United States. It assumes that this presence – which shaped
> the body politic, the Constitution, and the entire history of the culture – has
> had no significant place or consequence in the origin and development of that
> culture's literature.[1]

Morrison's thinking forms a context for understanding how the development of theater and literature in the United States is linked with the colonial socioeconomic status of blacks. Blackness has been used as a means of justifying the subordination, marginalization, ridicule, oppression, and coercion of black artists who were not only entertainers but also the inspiration for ridicule and parody. After Emancipation and throughout Reconstruction, the relationship of control and suppression did not subside. Under Jim Crow, through the supply of unjustifiable stereotypes permeating the stage and popular culture – the "mammy," "Tom," "coon," "brute," "tragic mulatto," and "pickanniny" – racial oppression continued to intertwine in entertainment and in real life. While black people were dehumanized on stage they were prohibited from full participation in society. During the early decades of the twentieth century, racial antagonisms grew while race relations declined for the worst. For instance, during the summer of 1919 incidents of lynchings and white-on-black violence became so common across the country that it became known as "Red Summer."[2] Meanwhile, the entertainment industry took off – with theater in particular exploding into vaudeville, comedy, satire, Broadway, and local drama companies across the nation. This rise was built largely upon misrepresentations and deceptions about blacks and similarly estranged minorities, as well as new immigrants, reminiscent of the nineteenth century's popular entertainment, the minstrel show.

Largely absent from the examination of this history, and from critiques of subordination within the discipline of performance arts in the United States, is the analysis of the historical roots of protest and its consequent discourse in African American theater. The purpose of this essay is to trace those roots as they develop on the early twentieth-century stage, how they emerge full force during the 1960s and 1970s, and how they create lasting legacies for contemporary theater. It is likely no accident that traditions of protest discourse in performance art have gone under-studied until recently.[3] Even the contemporary world sees cultural products, including those originating from countercultural ideologies, transmitted to people in ways that fit prescribed roles. The process boils down divergent components into an indistinguishable mass of uniformity, an inferno feeding on negativity and separatism. In America the history of stereotypes has been advanced with racial intimidation on stage.

Amiri Baraka – the indefatigable spokesman for African American sociopolitical narrative throughout the post–civil rights era – is a key transitional figure for this subject. In the summer of 1960, Baraka, then LeRoi Jones, visited Fidel Castro's Cuba. On his return he wrote, "I carried so much back with me that I was never the same again.... It was not enough just to write, to feel, to think, one must act! One *could* act."[4] In the wake of Malcolm X's

1965 assassination, he was transformed. His decision to leave Greenwich Village (with due controversy) summoned changes in his personal life, and marked the end of his gradual transition from his so-called bohemian "Beat" period toward a "blacker," and separationist vision – his would-be center against white supremacy. Baraka asserted, clearly and shockingly, that until race and racial matters cease to plague human relations, there would be no reconciliation in the nation. Baraka's words spoke to a new discourse of liberation in African American literature, known as the "Black Arts Movement," that became evident in a variety of works: Baraka's own poetry, drama, and essays; critical studies by Larry Neal, Addison Gayle Jr., Hoyt Fuller, Julian Mayfield, Darwin T. Turner, John O'Neal, and James Stewart; poems by Sonia Sanchez and Haki Madhubuti; political treatises by Angela Davis; and dramaturgy by Charles Fuller and Ntozake Shange. The literary output of the Black Arts Movement, particularly the transition from the integrationist to the nationalist stage during the 1960s and 1970s, created a vibrant culture of performance and helped change attitudes about race in the United States.

The Formation of a Protest Discourse

The history of black theater in the United States is rife with contradictions. Negative stereotypes from the mid-nineteenth century continued to dominate the early twentieth-century stage. Successful vaudevillian Bert Williams (1894–1922) was forced to blacken his complexion and deepen the "cooning" effect of his voice through drawling and stammering. Similarly, stage and film persona Stepin' Fetchit (Lincoln Theodore Monroe Andrew Perry, 1902–1985) had to slur his perfect speech, walk as a clown, and indulge in outrageous buffoonery for white audiences who expected black minstrel show caricatures. It would take half a century for the black theater to honor its unsung pioneers, who spent their lives suffering in secret agony. Williams and Perry became the prototypical expressions of national parody as they tried, desperately, to fit the roles that were invented to destroy them. The starting point for understanding how and why discourse on black protest is connected to African counter-history lies in exposing the early preoccupation with the notion of biologically based "superiority" that generated racism. As cultural theorist Michel Foucault has argued, "The connection between racism and antirevolutionary discourse and politics in the West is not ... accidental."[5] Nor is it an accident that the culture of segregation under which men such as Williams and Perry lived and the minstrel show caricatures which proscribed their performances shared the name: "Jim Crow."

Conversely, early discussions of black theater should not be limited solely to analysis of stereotypes, because this era is characterized by stellar developments. In 1915 Anita Bush founded the first African American professional theater company, Harlem's Anita Bush Stock Company (later the Lafayette Players). The same year the interracial Playhouse Settlement (later the Karamu House) opened in Cleveland, Ohio. In 1925, poet and playwright Georgia Douglas Johnson founded the S Street Salon in Washington D.C., and in 1926, Garland Anderson's *Appearances* became the first full-length play by an African American on Broadway. A signal event of the period was Angelina Weld Grimké's 1916 *Rachel,* which opened in Washington, D.C, and New York City. The play is notable for several reasons: it was the precursor of anti-lynching plays, which spoke out about the ill effects of lynching on African American families; it portrayed African Americans in ways other than the commonly held stereotypical depictions; and, produced by the National Association for the Advancement of Colored People (NAACP) and staged by an all-black cast, it functioned as the first use of the African American stage for social protest.[6]

Such firsts were not the only developments. In the 1920s, W. E. B. Du Bois called forth a radical movement to address racial antagonisms and laid the groundwork for changing the white hegemonic power structure in the arts, literature, and theater. A significant event was the founding of the "Krigwa Little Theater," which began in 1925 in the basement of the New York Public Library's 135th Street branch. Du Bois defined the mission of this first internationally acclaimed black theater company as total commitment and service to black people. Du Bois's relationship to the NAACP as its founding director was extremely important for the development of black theater in general. After the turbulence caused by the events of 1919, where rates of white-on-black violence reached their twentieth-century peak, the Drama Committee of the NAACP took radical steps to address lynchings. The organization believed that theater had a social and communicative responsibility to educate, instruct, and inspire. Psychologically, if audiences were to be reminded of their humanity, social ills could possibly be purged. The NAACP's literary journal, the *Crisis,* organized literary contests and public performances to facilitate these goals. The *Crisis* Guild of Writers and Artists consisted of thirty artists, who participated in drama contests and published their essays, poems, and plays in the journal. The same group staged plays by Charles Burroughs, Eulalie Spence, Willis Richardson, Frank Wilson, and Georgia Douglas Johnson. In time CRIGWA, the acronym for the group, was inexplicably transformed to Krigwa.[7]

Under Du Bois and director Burroughs, the Krigwa Players went national with a focus on African American performers, audiences, and communities.

Their mission, as Du Bois described it, was to create a theater *by, for, near,* and *about* African American people.[8] The troupe's electrifying journey, which started in 1925 and continued until 1927, consisted of touring several cities and setting up branches in Washington, D.C., Baltimore, Philadelphia, and Cleveland. Their greatest success came with Spence's 1927 play, *Fool's Errand*, which placed second in Samuel French's Little Theatre Tournament. But the success also proved unfortunate, when Krigwa's New York membership questioned Du Bois over the earnings from Spence's *Errand*. Reportedly, Du Bois kept Spence's $250 award money for staging the play.[9] After the episode, Krigwa branches continued to perform outside New York, until the mid-1930s when the Little Theater movement itself quietly came to an end.

"My Time": Spreading the Discourse

The modern era of African American theater began during the late 1950s and early 1960s. The 1959 Broadway debut of Lorraine Hansberry's *A Raisin in the Sun* became a watershed event.[10] At age twenty-nine, Hansberry became the youngest, the fifth woman, and the only African American playwright to that time to win the New York Drama Critics Circle Award for the Best Play of the Year. With its powerful cast and talented director Lloyd Richards, the play opened the field for black commercial success on stage. Based on an African American family's long-standing aspiration to buy a house with inherited insurance money, *A Raisin in the Sun* was expected to induce compassion for the black freedom struggle in the American theatergoing public. A makeover for social healing between races would take time, and the road to eradicate racism was long – covered with the bumps of sociopolitical reform. But the play's financial success mobilized the Black Arts and theater scene, generating new prospects for profit.

At the helm of the play's achievement was its striking realism, as Hansberry focused on the lives of an everyday, working-class black family, the Youngers. An immediate effect was that many black writers began experimenting with drama. Another result was the proliferation of all-black casts, as plots relied on original themes derived from the black experience. Across the country, church groups, YMCAs, schools, and community groups aimed to entice both black and white audiences into their neighborhoods. Plays represented various aspects of black life, gradually moving away from Broadway's rigid norms, including the anxiety over box-office gains.

Whereas an entire nation was impressed with Hansberry's solo triumph, cast members Ossie Davis, Ruby Dee, Sidney Poitier, Claudia McNeil, Diana Sands, Lonne Elder III, Robert Hooks, Douglass Turner Ward, and director Richards were also instrumental in its success. The NAACP, through

Grimké and Krigwa, had produced plays with an all-black team, but prior to 1959, Broadway had not imagined that such a feat could draw audiences. Moreover, the play itself urged audiences to think *differently* about discrimination: it was not something that occurred only through negative racial stereotypes but also through structures of inclusion and exclusion. White systems of oppression made sure that no African American family before the Youngers bought a home in Clybourne Park and that no African American female before Hansberry became a Broadway success. As Woodie King and Ron Milner wrote, "Broadway does not want our blackness, wasn't designed or intended [for] ... any new strange forms inspired by that very blackness. She is a contented fat white cow."[11]

After the success of *A Raisin in the Sun*, black playwrights, actors, technicians, and workers began to collaborate on numerous other projects that represented African American life. Influential groups included Harlem's Black Arts Repertory Theatre/School (BARTS), which Baraka, Charles Patterson, William Patterson, Clarence Reed, and Johnny Moore opened in the spring of 1965. Also in New York, the Negro Ensemble Company and Barbara Ann Teer's National Black Theater opened for the 1967–1968 season, followed in 1970 by Woodie King Jr.'s New Federal Theater on Henry Street.

The Negro Ensemble Company (NEC) bears discussion here. The group's rise was orchestrated by a talented trio, namely, playwright Douglas Turner Ward, producer and actor Robert Hooks, and their manager Gerald S. Krone. Earlier, Ward (who was lead actor Sidney Poitier's understudy in *A Raisin in the Sun*) had a successful off-Broadway run with his 1965 plays *Happy Ending* and *A Day of Absence*. When Krone decided to start a training studio by knocking down the walls of his Greenwich Village apartment, the company's first permanent location was established. Promoting the *agency* of black professional artists, directors, and managers, the NEC aimed to increase the visibility and longevity of the first black-owned theater in the city. As Ward asserted, the NEC wanted to illuminate black life on stage. Until Hansberry's award-winning play, the American public had remained, to a larger extent, oblivious to black life and art. Ward explained:

> A theater concentrating primarily on themes of Negro life, but also resilient enough to incorporate and interpret the best of world drama – whatever the source. A theater of permanence, continuity, providing the necessary home-base for the Negro artist to launch a campaign to win his ignored brothers and sisters as constant witnesses to his endeavors ... so might the Negro, a most potential agent of vitality infuse life into the moribund corpus of American theater.[12]

Ward's ideas may have reflected his allegiance to the original premises established in 1925 by Du Bois. Yet beyond his Du Bois-oriented, and pacifist standpoint, a revolutionary attitude was already developing in black theater.

In 1972, African American playwrights could say, "Until quite recently so-called Negro plays were plays about Negroes written by whites to be viewed by a white audience.... It was about then that it was discovered, in a series of small community projects, that survival meant developing within the community."[13] King and Milner argued that this new discourse involving "total theater" had begun earlier in the 1960s. Separating themselves from former arguments of the civil rights era, new artists of the 1960s and 1970s called for a structural reorganization in black art and aesthetics, a theory that had its roots in the experiences of enslaved black masses. *A Raisin in the Sun*'s unprecedented success on Broadway in 1959 reflected, among other things, the desire to tell the truth about racial prejudice in the United States.

That desire for truth-telling reached new heights and took new forms during the mid-1960s, with the shock caused by the assassinations of President John F. Kennedy, Robert Kennedy, Medgar Evers, Malcolm X, and Martin Luther King Jr. With these events, black theater assumed a new character – where psychologically, aesthetically, and artistically, black actors could say, "our time has arrived." The 1960s' revolutionary spirit quickly transported black playwrights and their audiences to a new consciousness as they focused on the realities of a world that continued to change dramatically well into the 1970s. Black theater no longer needed a literal stage since the "stage" was everywhere, even the street corner: black theater had reached *home*. In King and Milner's words, this new theater would comprise "strange new forms inspired by ... blackness ... [about] the destruction of tradition and the traditional role of Negroes in white theater."[14] This was the dawn of what Baraka called "revolutionary theater," of black arts and its *movement*, the forward motion, and the *dynamo* of the fight for black freedom.[15] In describing this theater, he wrote:

> Plays that will split the heavens for us will be called, "the destruction of America." The heroes will be Crazy Horse, Denmark Vesey, Patrice Lumumba, but not history, not memory, not sad sentimental groping for a warmth in our despair. Revolutionary Theater should *force* change; it should *be* change. The Revolutionary Theater must EXPOSE! Show up the insides of these humans, look into black skulls. Because they have been trained to hate.[16]

Baraka's language reflects this theater's radical politics, which went hand-in-hand with radical aesthetics. The theater of liberation birthed original forms and genres that positioned themselves against conventional – white – artistic practices that intertwined with oppression.

During this time, the determination of black actors, playwrights, and directors, combined with originality of black themes and subject matters, gradually transported the Black Arts Movement into the heart of the American arts scene. The black public's responsiveness to black themes would steadily increase the number of plays that employed black actors, producers, and directors, continuing through the 1980s, 1990s, and beyond. In the 1970s, however, while the methods of subordination had changed, blacks remained oppressed and dominated by the white power structure. Revolutionary theater addressed all aspects of this racial inequality while it engaged the discourse of protest in new plays.[17]

Hansberry had actually constructed an invisible bridge between the arts and society. Walter Lee's decision not to leave the white neighborhood by refusing a buyout offer forced the audience to perceive challenges faced by the black family in a new light. Lena, as the resilient matriarch of the Younger family, set the model to build stronger family and communal ties. Beyond the theater, the social stage of human relations was preparing the nation for a reevaluation of intercultural dealings. The *New York Times* stated that "*A Raisin in the Sun* changed American theater forever."[18] Through its characters, cast, and themes of black liberation, the play helped to lay a foundation for the revolutionary theater that was to come.

Launching the "Total Theater"

Historian Peniel Joseph asserts that the civil rights and Black Power movements have similar origins. Both "occupy distinct branches [yet] they share roots in the same historical family."[19] I argue that what occurred after 1965 can be associated with the civil rights spirit, with the exception that its latter radical voice belongs to the Black Power ideology. The Black Power era – which contains the sweeping changes of the Black Arts Movement – is not necessarily rooted in the civil rights movement, as Joseph suggests. Some awareness might have stirred then, but historical and aesthetic practices differed significantly. Throughout the Black Arts Movement, black theater in particular distanced itself from the civil rights era's quiescent polemics and its discourse of liberal concessions.

Whereas the Voting Rights Act of 1965, and the Civil Rights Acts of 1964 and 1968 barred discrimination in the United States, they failed to expunge racism. The Black Arts Movement laid the groundwork for the creation of a new black consciousness through black agency advocated in arts, as in life. The world had become a public arena for black artists. They expressed, at every occasion, their certainty that the *amalgamation of* the artist, art – rooted in Africa – and society was crucial to educating black masses. Black audiences should be involved in the creation and representation of black art and aesthetics; this was the key element in maintaining an Africa-centered discourse. Black youth should be trained about the virtue of "moral earnestness" – the ability of acting with determination on the world despite the prevalence of white supremacy. Young black authors advanced the principle of "art for society's sake" as they worked with community groups on staging agit-prop, guerilla, and street theater. Disappointment with mainstream politics was translated into consummate inner dynamism, aspiring to serve black communities through artistic expression and communal learning.

Larry Neal and Amiri Baraka – who would collaborate to edit the foundational Black Arts anthology *Black Fire* (1968) – stood at the center of this grand project. Beginning in 1965, BARTS in Harlem and, later, Spirit House in Newark manifested Baraka's commitment to community-based programs and practices. Similarities abound between earlier groups such as Krigwa and the NEC and the Black Arts Movement's founding principles. Du Bois and his friends at Krigwa first defined premises such as conceptualization of an African-centered theater prioritizing black aesthetics. Later, Neal's theoretical assumptions heralded the transformation of African American theater into a self-governing entity outside the realm of a mainstream – one that systematically projected the majority's values as a consensus opposed to African American culture's tenets yet ironically and, ultimately, encompassing them.

On the other hand, Neal's point of separation from Ward's NEC lies in the role that the black cultural context played in a larger Black Arts Movement. Neal explains, "We began to listen carefully to Smokey Robinson, the Miracles, to Martha and the Vandellas."[20] The singer ought to be *one* with the song; through song, the black artist conveyed something of substance to the person on the street. "Dancing in the Street" and "Keep on Pushing"[21] were instantaneously considered revolutionary code-songs signaling, to black people, "to get out and do the dancing [the social protest] in the streets."[22] James Brown became the hero of young poets. Neal said they began to listen to the "music of the rhythm and blues people, soul music … and envied him [James Brown] and wished that [they] could do what he did."[23] "Feelin' good," as Brown asserted, became the aphorism for black liberation and set the tone for the upcoming discourse of transformation. The language reiterated the need for strong black role models and nationalist leaders and carried nuances from oral as well as written narratives of the past generations. Rhythm resonated with call and response, a way to speak to the unfolding drama of Africans' exclusion from American history.

The work of postcolonial memory as it was expressed in song, rhythm, and poetry became an exploration of culture for those who were once subjugated mentally, physically, and spiritually. Such cultural exploration was about deliberately reclaiming African epic memory, which had been stolen, ignored, and purposefully isolated from the mainstream. Addison Gayle Jr. referred to the reclaiming process as "de-Americanization." He asserted, "The problem of the de-Americanization of black people lies at the heart of the Black Aesthetic."[24] The discourse of protest was intended to counter the anti-revolutionary discourse of racism and those who believed it[25] – those who would see themselves situated in the upper echelons of society relative to blacks and black cultural expression.

As Larry Neal suggested, the Black Arts Movement narrative was based on the inseparable nature of black ethics and aesthetics. Gayle argued that African American people could be rescued from the "polluted mainstream of Americanism, which was often anti-African.... The black aesthetic is a corrective – a means of helping black people." Gayle further asserted that the important point is to inquire, "How far has the work gone in transforming an American Negro into an African-American or black man?"[26] African American art and aesthetics should be freed from integrationist politics, which adhered to a European-derived, and thus limited, standard of criticism in art, literature, and aesthetic taste. Artists and thinkers should enable African-based agency and its compelling oratory for self-definition; however, the co-optation of black art should not be allowed. Black aesthetics instead involved the "unraveling, raveling and collecting"[27] of a black narrative for blacks themselves. Houston A. Baker Jr. further explained the distinct characteristics of black aesthetics and art:

> [The] Sixties' revolutionary Black Aesthetic paradigm had distinctive perceptual and semantic ramifications ... which changed the meaning of both "black" and "aesthetic" in the American literary-critical universe of discourse so that these terms could continue to make "useful distinctions" in a world where works of Afro-American expressive art had come to be seen quite differently from the manner in which they were viewed by an older integrationist paradigm.[28]

A black aesthetic differs greatly, in other words, from a civil rights movement aesthetic. Neal defined the role of the black author of the post–civil rights era as follows:

> The task of the contemporary Black writer, as of any serious writer, is to project the accumulated weight of the world's aesthetic, intellectual, and historical

experience. To do so he must utilize his ability to the fullest, distilling his experience through the creative process into a form that best projects his personality and what he conceives to be the ethos of his national or ethnic group.[29]

The Black Arts Movement writer was the "de-Americanized" writer – a conduit of black culture for black people.

However, art and aesthetics as cultural elements could not explain the formation of the notion of protest in black society in the 1970s. The attitude of protest rose after a thorough detailing of negative responses from mainstream scholars, critics, and politicians following a series of wider sociopolitical crises that enveloped the nation. The controversial Black Panther Party for Self Defense was founded in 1966. On April 30, 1970, President Nixon announced the invasion of Cambodia, a provocative move in an already contentious Vietnam conflict. Political developments and foreign wars at remote geographies spurred widespread student protests, which were suppressed by police brutality. Anti-war protests that turned deadly at Kent State (May 4, 1970) and Jackson State (May 15, 1970), and the Watergate scandal (1972–1973), which ended Nixon's presidency, divided the nation in unprecedented ways. Distrust in government policies and openly expressed anti-war sentiments turned the United States into a country of social conflict and civil unrest that extended well beyond the black freedom struggle.

By the 1980s, the political and cultural divide duly affected theater, as protest and anger set a general tone for society. Rhythm and blues artists utilized familiar elements of black culture and made them accessible to the nation in order to restore "national liberation and nationhood."[30] Neal asserted that the main tenet of Black Power was the necessity for black people to define the world in their own terms.[31] Contrary to former policies adopted by the Little Theater Movement and the NEC, the emerging black arts catapulted the protest movement forward and demonstrated a new trend. It was clear that creative forms (such as poetry and music) and forceful discourses (such as critical essays and theoretical treatises) could engage black masses on aesthetic issues. Black identity and African themes energized activism and a radical outlook in art while community engagement promoted black political perspective among artists. James T. Stewart asserted, "The dilemma of the 'negro' artist is that ... he makes assumptions based on the wrong models ... white models. These are not only wrong, they are even antithetical to his existence."[32] The "non-white" models should correspond to black culture in aesthetic, moral, and spiritual terms, and aspire "to emancipate [black] minds from Western values and standards, create new definitions founded on his own culture."[33] The Black Arts Movement provided this emancipation.

On Hansberry's second play, *The Sign in Sidney Brustein's Window* (1964), James Baldwin remarked, "It is possible, that her plays attempt to say too much; but it is also exceedingly probable that they make so loud and uncomfortable a sound because of the surrounding silence; not many plays, presently, risk being accused of attempting to say too much!"[34] Black writers were expected to "make loud and uncomfortable sounds." Ultimately the mission of the black artist was to be a revolutionary, and LeRoi Jones/Amiri Baraka knew this firsthand. His revolutionary stance involved not only a geographical re-positioning, but a name change, and a personal sacrifice. After moving from Greenwich Village to Harlem in 1965, his charge was to be the engineer of "total theater," while Neal became its theoretician. The duo envisioned an evolution of black theater not in linear ascendancy of Aristotelian pragmatism, but in vertical explosions, as epic units thrust from Krigwa to the NEC, toward the BARTS. The continuity of a black cultural tradition – lyrical elements, manifest in song, rhythm, oral tradition, epic memory, and African polycentrism – were embedded within the historical consciousness of revolutionary black artists; they aimed at transcending Eurocentric negations in theme, plot, characterization, and style.

Revisiting History and Historicism

History has become for me a way of re-examining black people in the long journey of the United States.[35]

Lorraine Hansberry believed in the importance of truth-telling as she often mentioned her disapproval of white supremacist ideology with its adverse consequences for black people. "Adversity" meant lack of civil liberties, unfair treatment, and unrelenting discrimination. Her family's experience with "red lining," her father's struggle to defeat the odds of "owning a house of his own" in Chicago's Southside, and Mrs. Hansberry's anxiety over protecting her children from hostile neighbors served, first, as inspiration for *A Raisin in the Sun*, and later, as inspiration for future playwrights.[36] Ironically, the Hansberry house in Washington Park, which became the center of a fierce litigation battle in 1937, was granted "National Historic Site" status in 2010 by Chicago's City Council.

Clybourne Park, Bruce Norris's 2010 Pulitzer Prize-winning play, is set in the same Chicago neighborhood, only fifty years later. The premiere was in March 2013, a production by Boston's Speak Easy Stage Company at the Boston Center for the Arts. In 2012 a book titled *Reimagining* A Raisin in the Sun included four plays that jumped off from where *Raisin* ended.

Another spinoff play, *Beneatha's Place*, made its world premiere in May 2013 at Center Stage in Baltimore. *A Raisin in the Sun*'s steady revival, both on and off Broadway, exemplifies how African American discourse on emancipation is maintained and projected into the twenty-first century. Three plays in particular – *Dutchman* (1964), by Baraka, writing then as LeRoi Jones; Ntozake Shange's *for colored girls who have considered suicide/when the rainbow is enuf* (1976); and Charles Fuller's *Zooman and the Sign* (1980) – helped to propel that discourse forward. Baraka, Shange, and Fuller exemplify a discourse that emerged during the Black Arts Movement and specifically comments on black manhood, black womanhood, and black families.

Black theater has provided superlative enactments of emancipation and survival in order to deconstruct white supremacy. For instance, in *Dutchman*, Jones argued that the play is "about the difficulty of becoming a man in America."[37] On a subway train, which symbolically reenacts the infamous slave ship with an identical name, a ritualistic cycle continues relentlessly while Lula, the cruel temptress, murders *another* black man, who becomes, according to the playwright, the victim of his assimilationist fantasies. Highly symbolic and allegorical in texture, the play conjures "*la belle dame sans merci*" (Lula, Lilith, Lamia) and Clay as the "natural man," who evokes Adam, Jesus, and innocent black youth who are destined to be ruined either by white women or the racist tendencies of white America. Clay's descent begins after he is engaged in sharing an apple – the forbidden fruit – with Lula for the sake of a flirtatious talk. In the beginning Lula seems to dominate the entire act, but in the final scene Clay challenges all that Lula represents – the white mainstream, hypocritical intellectuals, oppressors, and integrationist fantasy. In a brilliant soliloquy, Clay transcends Eurocentric negations and a black middle-class mentality, which matches his looks. He *tells* the truth, *loud* and unrestrained; he speaks of his disappointment with white supremacists, and how they have scorned the black artist, including Charlie Parker and Bessie Smith, through stereotypical renditions. Lula reacts to the irony; *he is her destined prey* and his murder will end the sacramental ritual. Jones reinstates, in a revolutionary act, a drama of sacrilege in order to illustrate the inexorable consequences of integrationist fantasies for black men who pursue, or even dream, of interracial liaisons.[38]

During the Black Arts Movement, black theater tackled the dilemma of male characters battling against white supremacist ideology. In *The Price of the Ticket*, James Baldwin addressed the scrutiny against black actors on stage: "Until today, no one wants to hear their story, and the Negro performer is still in battle with the white man's image of the Negro – which the white man clings to in order not to be forced to revise his image of himself."[39] On a different note, Shange's choreopoem *for colored girls who have considered suicide/when the rainbow is enuf* is about seven women who have endured rape, loss, desertion, abortion, domestic violence, and death of a loved one. The women are named after the color of their dresses, such as the "Lady in Blue," or "Lady in Brown." Unfolding through a collage of themes and episodes based on a series of tragic events, the play focuses on the multidimensional reality of black women's experiences as they transition through youth, adulthood, motherhood, and a sisterhood that unites them in struggle. After opening in a California café in 1974, the play appeared off-Broadway and then on Broadway. It was ultimately adapted as a book and into a film, and nominated for Tony, Emmy, and Grammy awards.

Shange's play can be viewed as a theatrical tour de force both artistically and politically, particularly as the issues of its era relate to women's lives. The "choreopoem" – the term Shange coined for her work – blends music, dance, and poetic monologues into one dramatic performance. As the play opens, Shange's characters enact the "self-fulfilling prophecy syndrome" while they "reconstruct" stereotypes about black males and express disappointment. However, in the final scene, they unite in fostering understanding and tolerance toward each other. Healing comes as mutual support and encouragement while the women perform their stories and reorganize their own thoughts about developing new relationships with men, and with themselves. The ability of these women to speak the truth about their lives, as well as Shange's ability to cast that truth-telling as a choreopoem – a genre of her own invention – come directly from the Black Arts Movement's focus on new forms and, especially, new agency.

Although Shange's play is experimental, it draws primarily upon realism for its characters and its themes. Black theater is rarely based upon the supernatural or the mystical, with the exception of the allegory that writers such as Baraka employ and the magical realism seen in playwrights such as August Wilson. Like Hansberry and Shange, Charles Fuller – the recipient of the 1982 Pulitzer Prize for *A Soldier's Play* – employs realism. Like Hansberry, Baraka, and Shange, Fuller believes in telling the truth through his art. Fuller epitomizes the relationship between African agency and the realization of that ideal in the black experience. He resents those who comply with white American middle-class values that determine, ethnocentrically and epistemologically, *what kind of* truth is acceptable, or *how* it shall be told to the black community. He creates strong personalities portrayed in real-life situations, exhibiting accountability and responsibility, as well as displaying very human traits of good and evil. In the 1970s Fuller co-founded and co-directed the Afro-American Arts Theater in Philadelphia, and he also worked with the NEC. In line with Du Bois's enthusiasm to produce plays *about* and *for* black people, as well as Neal's and Baraka's commitment to moral earnestness, Fuller set out to write historic plays that depicted the humanity of black men and women in realistic situations. He wrote and staged for the NEC, from 1974 on, several plays including *The Brownsville Raid* (1976), *Zooman and the Sign* (1980), *A Soldier's Play* (1982), and a trilogy titled *Sally, Jonquil, Prince* (1988–1990). Fuller's plays helped the NEC to be fully recognized as the premier black theater company.[40] In Fuller's view, the fundamental thrust of drama should be events and personalities, ordinary citizens who operate as agents of black expression, race-pride, and self-determination in a multicultural world.

In 1980, Fuller's *Zooman and the Sign* opened in Theater Four of the NEC and brought him an Obie Award. The play depicted an estranged black couple, isolated from the community due to a breakdown of shared pride and identity. However, the play was not meant to be a disparate attack on black values and morality. Rather it aimed to unite the society against social ills that devastated its core values. Fuller's Catholic upbringing urged his characters to abide by the teachings of the Bible: to "purge the evil from among you" (Deuteronomy 24:8). Examining a segment of the African American urban life, Fuller highlights the plight of young Lester and the Tate family, who lost their child to a stray bullet fired by a character named Zooman. The community prefers to keep their silence about the murder, yet their indifference to crime is indicative of social disintegration in contemporary neighborhoods. As the parents struggle to come to grips with the death of their child, Zooman is shot. His lifeless body falls onto Titan Street, yet no one comes forward to claim it. Fear, inertia, and terror have taken hold of the neighborhood.

Fuller brilliantly captures the sad account of a modern-day dilemma as he demands that his audience examine the past in order to get ahead in the future. Human tragedy unearths a multiplicity of emotions and behavior patterns. Fuller often reenacts African American history mainly because of the way African Americans were depicted during the post-Emancipation era. "For me, *our* birth is the Emancipation," he writes, "Our relationship to this nation is fundamentally a post-1863 phenomenon." Fuller's plays thus advocate an inner search to overcome oppression. He explains:

> Part of dispelling that is to go back to where it started and dispel it forever from that place and time. Given the nature of the history and the facts, there's no denying it: these were real people. You have to start thinking differently about them, and about yourself in relationship to them. You begin to change at the root.[41]

Conclusions

This chapter has explored, from a multifaceted standpoint, discourses that spurred varied perspectives on the formation of black theater before and after the civil rights movement. Historical facts rooted in the predicaments that African peoples face on American soil illuminate the causes that hampered African Americans' claim to truth, freedom, and equal rights. Given the racial environment of the first fifty years of the twentieth century, it is almost understandable why predominantly white-owned theater and film corporations that controlled the vast majority of the entertainment industry would see it as profitable to sell a standardized pejorative image of blackness to the predominantly white consumers of Broadway and Hollywood. It should also stand to reason that having learned from the same cultural system as all other Westerners, generations of African Americans would internalize that system's resulting pathology. Individual black artists, it could be argued, shared some culpability in the American entertainment industry's design and transmittal of stereotypes. Still others fought back to create the seeds of a protest discourse.

During the 1970s the Black Arts Movement saw those seeds bear fruit. By the 1980s, a turning point had been reached. Black artists, actors, and writers had broken from subjugated knowledge perspectives, blatantly challenging the very foundations of the "universalist," "orientalist," and "colonialist" attitudes. Beginning with Lorraine Hansberry, the American civil rights debate audaciously entered performance arts, demonstrating a new concentration on Africa-centered ideologies as well as upholding a black historical consciousness. Whereas black arts emerged primarily as a post-1960s movement, art, aesthetics, drama, literature, and music were rapidly connected with an emerging black revolutionary ideology. While this move liberated African American arts and literature from the exclusion and elitism of "peripheral essentialism,"[42] its radical outlook and activist spirit generated controversy. A defining aspect of Black Arts was the constant negotiation of its roots as a transgressive social movement, not only as a medium for black literary and dramatic narratives but also as a long-standing theoretical discourse that facilitated a cultural leap from "American" to African and countercultural ideologies.

The rise of the Afrocentric idea in the late 1980s prompted an advancement of the Black Arts Movement and a discourse of the black experience, which had been preoccupied, since David Walker's *Appeal* (1829), and Frederick Douglass's *Narrative* (1845) with a single undergirding question: How have African people, across time and space, transmitted culture using literacy and spirituality in such precision over prolonged adversity? Clearly African cultural dispersal was rooted in an involuntary removal from Africa. Such discourse needs to be evaluated in the light of African agency as well. The three fundamental existential postures of agency – *affective* (feeling), *cognitive* (knowing), and *conative* (acting) – are interconnected in the discipline of Africology.[43] Protest discourse was shaped against the prevalence of Eurocentric negations as black artists prioritized the existence of African American agency. The idea of "total theater" meant the amalgamation of African theatrical forms with revolutionary styles and post-1960s principles to assert, in order to re-organize, the agency of the African American artist. An example can be observed in *Raisin,*[44] a musical adaptation, which found followers on Broadway both in 1973 and in 2013.

When Walter Younger's son Travis reaches adulthood, he is not expected to be as quiescent as his father. He is more likely to idolize Walker Vessels, from Amiri Baraka's 1964 play *The Slave*, or Baraka himself, who moved from his "private voice to the public voice" by publicly announcing his transformation from a Beat poet to a black revolutionary artist.[45] Unlike Bert Williams or "Stepin' Fetchit" Perry, Travis – his agency forged in the crucible of the Black Arts Movement – would not suffer silently: he would *feel, know*, and *act*. His sisters in Shange's choreopoem would speak their truths as well. Those who remained silent, as with Fuller's Tate family, would now do so in ways that spoke volumes.

NOTES

1 Toni Morrison, *Playing in the Dark: Whiteness and the Literary Imagination* (Cambridge, MA: Harvard University Press, 1992), pp. 4–5.

2 See Cameron McWhirter, *Red Summer: The Summer of 1919 and the Awakening of Black America* (New York: St. Martin's Griffin, 2012) and *Philip Dray, At the Hands of Persons Unknown: The Lynching of Black America* (New York: Modern Library, 2002), pp. 252–392.

3 More recent studies examine African American performance in inventive ways. See Soyica Diggs Colbert, *The African American Theatrical Body: Reception, Performance, and the Stage* (New York: Cambridge University Press, 2011); Koritha Mitchell, *Living with Lynching: African American Lynching Plays, Performance, and Citizenship, 1890–1930* (Champaign-Urbana: University of Illinois Press, 2012); and Lisa Woolfork, *Embodying Slavery in Contemporary Culture* (Champaign-Urbana: University of Illinois Press, 2008).

4 Amiri Baraka, *The Autobiography of LeRoi Jones/Amiri Baraka* (New York: Freundlich Books, 1984), pp. 165–66.

5 Michel Foucault, *"Society Must Be Defended": Lectures at the Collège de France, 1975–1976* (New York: Picador, 1997), pp. 80–81.

6 From 1916 to 1938 several theater companies opened in New York City. Some of these are the Negro Art Theater, Negro Experimental Theater, Ida Anderson Players, the Negro Players, Player's Guild, Acme Players, National Ethiopian

Art Theater, Aldridge Players, Alhambra Players, and Harlem Suitcase Theater, which was established by Langston Hughes. These groups were part of a larger Little Theatre Movement, which brought non-commercial – sometimes experimental and reform-minded – drama to cities and towns across the United States. On early black theater, see Jonathan Shandell, "The Negro Little Theatre Movement," in the *Cambridge Companion to African American Theatre*, ed. Harvey Young (New York: Cambridge University Press, 2012), pp. 103–17. On Grimké, specifically, see Kathy A. Perkins and Judith L. Stephens, eds., *Strange Fruit: Plays on Lynching by American Women* (Champaign-Urbana: University of Illinois Press, 1998), pp. 23–25.

7 W. E. B. Du Bois, "Krigwa Players Little Negro Theater," *Crisis* 32.3 (1926): 134. For more information on the NAACP's anti-lynching efforts, see Robert L. Zangrando, *The NAACP Crusade against Lynching, 1909–1950* (Philadelphia: Temple University Press, 1980).

8 Du Bois defined black theater and his objectives for a national theater movement as "*About Us, by Us, for Us, and near Us.*" W. E. B. Du Bois, "Krigwa Players," p. 134.

9 Anthony D. Hill, *Historical Dictionary of African American Theater* (Lanham. MD: Scarecrow Press, 2009), p. 298.

10 The play had 530 performances running from its first opening on Broadway on March 11, 1959, to June 25, 1960.

11 "Evolution of a People's Theater," Woodie King and Ron Milner, eds., *Black Drama Anthology* (New York: New American Library, 1972), p. x.

12 Douglas Turner Ward, "American Theater: For Whites Only?" *New York Times*, August 14, 1966: 1, 3.

13 King and Milner, "Evolution of a People's Theater," p. vii.

14 Ibid., p. viii.

15 LeRoi Jones/Amiri Baraka coined the term in his essay titled, "Revolutionary Theater," in *Home: Social Essays* (New York: William Morrow, 1966), pp. 210–11.

16 Ibid.

17 My study of Lorraine Hansberry, Larry Neal, Charles Fuller, and Amiri Baraka adds nuance to my understanding of how African American discourse on protest operates, exists at the intersections of culture and performance, and moves beyond the prevailing notions of cultural history, knowledge, and empowerment. See Nilgün Anadolu-Okur, *Contemporary African American Theater: Afrocentricity in the Works of Larry Neal, Amiri Baraka, and Charles Fuller* (New York: Taylor and Francis, 1997).

18 Frank Rich, "Theater: *Raisin in the Sun* Anniversary in Chicago," *New York Times*, October 5, 1983.

19 Peniel E. Joseph, *The Black Power Movement: Rethinking the Civil Rights-Black Power Era* (New York: Routledge, 2006), p. 4.

20 Larry Neal, "The Social Background of the Black Arts Movement," *Black Scholar* (January/February 1987): 11–22.

21 "Keep on Pushing," was written by David Henderson, and its title was taken from a hit recording "Summer, '64" by rhythm and blues trio Curtis Mayfield and the Impressions. The poem narrated the days of the Harlem riots in the summer of 1964. See "Keep on Pushing," in *Black Fire: An Anthology of*

Afro-American Writing, ed. LeRoi Jones and Larry Neal (New York: William Morrow, 1970), pp. 239–44. "Dancing in the Street," was written by William Stevenson, Ivy Jo Hunter, and Marvin Gaye. See Mark Kurlansky, *Ready for a Brand New Beat: How "Dancing in the Street" Became the Anthem for a Changing America* (New York: Penguin, 2013).

22 Neal, "The Social Background," p. 19.

23 Ibid.

24 Addison Gayle Jr., Introduction, *The Black Aesthetic* (Garden City, NY: Doubleday, 1971), p. xxi.

25 Foucault, *Society*, p. 81.

26 Gayle, Introduction, p. xxii.

27 Neal, "The Social Background," p. 22.

28 Houston A. Baker Jr., "Generational Shifts and the Recent Criticism of Afro-American Literature," *Black American Literature Forum* 15.1 (1981): 8.

29 Larry Neal, "The Black Contribution to American Letters, Part II: The Writer as Activist (1966 and After)," in *The Black American Reference Book*, ed. Mabel M. Smythe (Englewood Cliffs, NJ: Prentice Hall, 1976), p. 784.

30 Neal, "The Social Background," p. 19.

31 Neal, "The Black Arts Movement," pp. 257–74.

32 James T. Stewart, *"The Development of the Black Revolutionary Artist,"* in *Black Fire*, ed. Jones and Neal, pp. 3–10.

33 Ibid., p. 10.

34 James Baldwin, "Sweet Lorraine," *The Price of the Ticket: Collected Non-Fiction, 1948–1985* (New York: St. Martin's Press, 1985), pp. 443–47.

35 David Savran, ed., "Charles Fuller," in *Their Own Words: Contemporary American Playwrights* (New York: Theater Communications Group, 1988), pp. 72–83.

36 Lorraine Hansberry, Letter to the Editor, *New York Times*, April 23, 1964, in *To Be Young, Gifted and Black* (New York: Signet, 2011), p. 8.

37 Le Roi Jones, "American Sexual Reference: Black Male," in *Home: Social Essays* (New York: William Morrow, 1966), p. 188.

38 Anadolu-Okur, *Contemporary African American* Theater, pp. 106–14.

39 Baldwin, *The Price of the Ticket*, "On Catfish Row," pp. 178–81.

40 An exception to this praise is Baraka, who blamed both the NEC and Fuller for dismissing revolutionary plays. In an essay titled, "The Descent of Charlie Fuller into Pulitzerland and the Need for African American Institutions," Baraka challenged the NEC, its director Douglas Turner Ward, and Charles Fuller, which led, eventually, to further antagonizing the NEC against the Black Arts Movement. Baraka's claim was that the NEC was supported by the "bourgeoisie's money" – it was not as "revolutionary" as he thought it should be – and he believed that Ward and Fuller created a "polemical event" rather than a "theatrical event." He wrote: "They have created as political a theater as any in the Black Arts movement, only it is the politics of our enemies." See *Black Literature Criticism*, Vol. 2, ed. James P. Draper (Detroit: Gale Research, 1992), p. 825.

41 Savran, "Charles Fuller," p. 83.

42 With "peripheral essentialism," I refer to Eurocentric positions based upon exclusion and elitism, particularly of "othering," in order to "isolate" and "exclude"

other cultures' achievements. It is a hegemonic position legitimizing the peripherality of non-Western cultures; its origins lie in essentialism, and antagonizing of multidimensional perspectives beyond the West. For further exploration on this matter see Karl Popper, *Poverty of Historicism* (New York: Routledge, 1957).

43 Molefi Kete Asante, *The Afrocentric Idea* (Philadelphia: Temple University Press, 1987), p. 17

44 *Raisin*, a musical based on Lorraine Hansberry's play, opened on Broadway in 1973, and it won the Tony Award for the Best Musical. *A Raisin in the Sun* was revived on Broadway in 2004 and received a Tony Award nomination for Best Revival of a Play. Later in 2008 it was produced for television and won two NAACP image awards. In 2013 it was again staged on Broadway.

45 Neal, "The Social Background," p. 13.

5

JULIE BUCKNER ARMSTRONG

Civil Rights Movement Fiction

A December 2013 *Slate* article bemoans the popularity of Kathryn Stockett's 2009 novel *The Help* in teaching U.S. civil rights movement history. However, if one follows educator Gerald Graff's well-known suggestion to "teach the conflicts," few books may be better suited.[1] On one hand, both the novel and the film adapted from it are extremely popular. Set in Jackson, Mississippi, during the height of protests against segregation, *The Help* tells the story of Eugenia "Skeeter" Phelan, a white journalist who interviews black maids to get their perspective on race and work. Stockett's book has sold more than five million copies internationally. The hardback edition of *The Help* appeared more than 100 weeks on the *New York Times* bestseller list, and more than fifty weeks there in paperback and electronic versions. The film was nominated for multiple Academy Awards, with Octavia Spencer taking home the Best Supporting Actress Oscar for her role as Minny.[2] On the other hand, *The Help* has generated much controversy among academics. The journal *Southern Cultures* devoted a special issue to the topic after a panel at a 2011 conference provoked extensive audience response. The Association of Black Women Historians famously issued a public statement decrying *The Help*'s simplified presentations of domestic workers, civil rights history, and African American culture more generally. The group described the book and the film's exchange of "historical accuracy" for "entertainment" as "unacceptable."[3]

Granted, many reasons exist to like *The Help*: its engaging plot, emotionally resonant characters, and a realistically depicted setting that makes audiences feel connected to a historical moment (even though some scholars debate the accuracy of that history). *The Help* makes perfect sense for secondary school teachers, as *Slate* writer Jessica Roake observes. Stockett's writing is accessible, and the film divides easily into three forty-five-minute sections that mirror typical class time frames. *The Help* also offers a comforting drama that reinforces the patriotic values of many mainstream school districts. Roake writes, "*The Help*'s neat narrative enforces a noble idea of history: When a minority group peacefully demands full status and rights, the American people, as a whole, always come to understand that it is only right, proper, and American to treat people equally." *The Help* offers an easy story, easy to teach, Roake says.[4]

The same simplicity gets to those who object to *The Help* as civil rights pedagogy. The issue is a broader one of what movement story gets told and whose perspective frames it. For well over two decades, scholars and activists have challenged what is termed civil rights "consensus memory."[5] The point of that challenge is moving beyond conventional ways of summarizing the movement as a brief moment during the mid-twentieth century when national figures led a successful fight against legalized segregation. More nuanced histories get obscured when popular culture repeatedly reinforces a story that Julian Bond famously summarized as, "Rosa sat down, Martin stood up, and the white kids came down and saved the day."[6] Too often, works such as *To Kill a Mockingbird* (1960/1962), *Mississippi Burning* (1988), *Ghosts of Mississippi* (1996), and *The Help* frame the movement from what Suzanne Jones calls "Miss Daisy's perspective," where a "white character [becomes] the heroic savior of helpless black people."[7] These examples offer what one might describe as the Movement's "easy-bake narrative," after the well-known toy oven that debuted in 1963: mix together a black and white "best friend," toss in a villain, then – (as the original commercial jingle goes) "slide 'em in / slide 'em out / Easy-Bake Wow!" – *civil rights problem solved.*[8]

This chapter proposes multiple alternatives to the easy-bake narrative. I begin by defining and providing examples of different civil rights fictions. From there I describe typical plots and themes found in those fictions. My point is to generate a positive pedagogical loop: to educate this chapter's readers, who will in turn educate others to perpetuate more enriching civil rights stories. By "more enriching," I mean those that, as Christopher Metress explains, do not "appropriate the movement as a satisfying morality tale in a larger American progress narrative."[9] The civil rights movement was complex, turbulent, and often violent; many see it as a continuing struggle of unrealized dreams. When I say, "educate ... readers," I do not assume that each member of my audience is an educator. Some, in fact, may be students or average citizens in the United States or abroad. Consensus memories and their manifestations as easy-bake narratives circulate primarily in popular cultural forms. I hope to provide the tools so that anyone can analyze and respond more critically to those narratives rather than accept them as Truth. As any child who ever owned an Easy-Bake can tell you, the oven was great entertainment, but nothing ever came out as good as television portrayed it.

Definitions and Genres

Many reasons exist for pulling fiction into a discussion of the civil rights movement: to study the relationship between the arts and social change, to convey the feeling of being part of a transformational moment in time, to show how memories of that movement are culturally constructed, just to name a few. No matter how scholars and educators employ fictional resources, most agree that they possess an emotional or intellectual power that is different from documentary texts. Richard H. King and Margaret Whitt use fiction to engage readers more directly with past events. King states, "One of the best ways to establish a more immediate relation to the civil rights movement is to pay more attention to the fiction that has explicitly thematised the movement."[10] Christopher Metress and Barbara Melosh, conversely, describe fiction as a form of evidence. More than a device, some sort of key, used to unlock history's treasure chest, literature has its own "value" for "the production of social memory," Metress explains.[11] Because literary language traffics in the difficult, the hard-to-express, and the ineffable, Jacqueline Goldsby observes, fiction and related storytelling forms possess a "historicizing authority" that allows authors representational freedom they do not have with "conventional histories."[12] Fiction teaches things that history cannot.

Although civil rights scholars agree that fiction has a specific pedagogical or rhetorical power, little agreement exists over definitions. Many terms exist for categorizing works from and about the period. Describing them as "civil rights," "civil rights movement," "segregation," or "race relations" literature is not just an issue of academic hair-splitting. Each term refers to a particular history, set of artistic practices, and constellation of themes. Easy-bake narratives, like more complicated civil rights stories, can exist in almost any category. The particular story being told is the problem, not necessarily the definition under which a work falls. Categories often overlap; moreover, these ways of organizing transcend more traditional boundaries for teaching and marketing literature. Fiction from and about the civil rights movement is not necessarily African American or southern. It can be modern or postmodern, or make use of multiple generic conventions. This body of literature is much larger and more diverse than readers might expect from works about a specific historical moment. Many preconceptions about civil rights movement fiction originate with the easy-bake narratives that have dominated popular culture. Because they focus on one story and one storytelling perspective, they prevent readers from recognizing and valuing the variety that actually exists.

Take, for example, the differences between what Thomas Haddox calls the "white civil rights novel" and the "segregation narrative" as Brian Norman defines it. As Haddox explains, the white civil rights novel began appearing during the 1940s and includes works such as Lillian Smith's *Strange Fruit* (1944), William Faulkner's *Intruder in the Dust* (1948), Elizabeth Spencer's *Voice at the Back Door* (1956), Harper Lee's *To Kill a Mockingbird* (1960), Carson McCullers's *Clock without Hands* (1961), and Jesse Hill Ford's *Liberation of Lord Byron Jones* (1965). According to Haddox, these books share a particular regional and political point of view:

> All are set in small southern towns and their environs, all foreground the mores and politics of race relations, and all present these relations not as a metaphysical given (as earlier southern novels often did) but as a problem that requires attention.... [W]hite civil rights novels identify typically southern positions on race, place them in dialogue with each other, and attempt to adjudicate their competing claims.[13]

Although these novels emerged alongside significant civil rights developments, they do not necessarily discuss specific events, people, or places relevant to the historical movement. Addressing social change more generally, these works take political positions similar to one another: a liberal gradualism that, on one hand, does not condone the organized backlash of violence that took place against that movement, but, on the other hand, does not fully embrace radical transformation for African Americans – at least not any time soon.[14] At the end of *To Kill a Mockingbird*, Scout drifts off to sleep, peaceful in the assurance of her father Atticus that "Most people are [real nice] ... when you finally see them," and that nothing around her was altering visibly. Atticus "would be there all night, and he would be there when [she and her brother] waked up in the morning."[15] Easy-bake narratives have their roots in these novels, in the naïve belief that the world would be a better place if people could just learn to get along.

White civil rights novels differ markedly from segregation narratives, which Norman describes as responses "to the social and political institutions of compulsory race segregation." These works have their historical origins with the U.S. Supreme Court's legalized institution of Jim Crow in its 1896 *Plessy v. Ferguson* ruling. Segregation narratives, along with their more recent siblings, neo-segregation narratives, produced after the legal ending of Jim Crow, focus on the strategies that blacks use to negotiate difficult and sometimes dangerous racial lines, which can exist anywhere – not just the South.[16] The many examples include Frances E. W. Harper's *Iola Leroy* (1892), *Charles Chesnutt's Marrow of Tradition* (1901), James Weldon Johnson's *Autobiography of an Ex-Colored Man* (1912), Richard Wright's *Native Son* (1940), Ann Petry's *The Street* (1946), Ralph Ellison's *Invisible Man* (1952), Alice Walker's *The Color Purple* (1982), Wesley

Brown's *Darktown Strutters* (1994), Colson Whitehead's *The Intuitionist* (1999), and Suzan-Lori Parks's *Getting Mother's Body* (2003). A primary goal of these writers, Norman and Piper Kendrix Williams explain, is to expose or "to represent race segregation without necessarily reinscribing it."[17] The white civil rights novel *To Kill a Mockingbird* acknowledges Jim Crow: Scout and her brother Jem watch the trial of Tom Robinson, a black man falsely accused of raping a white woman, from the "colored" balcony and then later thwart a mob that attempts to lynch him. True to form, however, the book sees social progress as the product of white realization and redemption: Scout forces the mob into a change of heart when she politely asks a member about his son. Richard Wright, in his 1935 story "Big Boy Leaves Home," treats acts of witnessing and fending off a mob very differently from Lee. This segregation narrative follows a teenage protagonist as he watches his friend's lynching while in hiding and as he barely escapes the same fate.

In some instances, race-relations literature as Suzanne Jones describes it resembles Haddox's white civil rights novel or Norman's segregation narrative. For example, Connie May Fowler's *Sugar Cage* (1992) and Nanci Kincaid's *Crossing Blood* (1992) use the civil rights movement as a backdrop and share their southern forebears' focus on narratives of white redemption.[18] Ernest J. Gaines's *A Gathering of Old Men* (1983) and *A Lesson before Dying* (1993) show how blacks navigate the literal and figurative places of a supposedly post-segregation society. Jones explains that what marks novels such as Fowler's, Kincaid's, and Gaines's is their ability to "imagine new ways of racial knowing."[19] Race relations fiction set in the South since the 1960s draws upon a variety of strategies. Books such as Susan Choi's *The Foreign Student* (1998) and Monique Truong's *Bitter in the Mouth* (2010) render an ethnically diverse region no longer split along black-white lines but still wrestling with its controversial history. Writers such as Ellen Douglas in *Can't Quit You, Baby* (1988) and Madison Smartt Bell in *Soldier's Joy* (1989) interrogate whiteness and question stereotypical ideas that different groups have about one another. And in novels such as Toni Morrison's *Song of Solomon* (1977) and Bebe Moore Campbell's *Your Blues Ain't Like Mine* (1992), African American writers depict characters undertaking reverse migration narratives to understand their relationship to the past and to heal old wounds.

Several novels explore the violent backlash to the civil rights movement: Campbell addresses the 1955 murder of Emmett Till in Money, Mississippi; Morrison, the 1963 Birmingham, Alabama, church bombing that killed four girls; and Fowler, 1964 integration efforts in St. Augustine, Florida. Sharon Monteith distinguishes between fiction that is specifically about the civil rights movement ("civil rights organizations, voter registration and demonstrations, and activists in the African-American freedom struggle") and "fiction that locates 'civil rights' within a broad range of race relations."[20] This more focused definition, like the one Haddox employs, would categorize *To Kill a Mockingbird* as "civil rights" fiction and *The Help* – because it portrays people, places, organizations, and events – as "movement" fiction, even if some regard the latter as an "easy," "Miss Daisy" version.

Under the rubric of civil rights movement fiction, one might further distinguish works that look back (*Song of Solomon, Your Blues Ain't like Mine*) from those produced during the historical era itself: novels such as Junius Edwards's *If We Must Die* (1963) and John O. Killens's *'Sippi* (1967), or stories such as Eudora Welty's "Where Is the Voice Coming From?" (1963) and John Updike's "Marching through Boston" (1966). Monteith points out that many of these older works have gone under-examined because it has become a critical commonplace to think that "fictional responses to the movement were deferred." Alice Walker's *Meridian* (1976) and Rosellen Brown's *Civil Wars* (1984) are often cited among the first examples of movement fiction.[21] However, R. V. Cassill's 1958 story "The First Day of School," whose protagonist is a boy on desegregation's front lines, predates Walker's novel by almost two decades. The difference lies in how writers imaginatively render the movement. Those caught up in its transformations try to make sense of a racial landscape that may – or may not be – on the brink of radical change. Those looking back try to make connections between that world and the one they currently inhabit.[22]

Another critical assumption that Monteith unpacks and dismisses is that fictional responses to the civil rights movement always fall along racial lines – with black writers producing protest literature and white writers producing literature about moral choices (similar to the dynamic observed in Wright's "Big Boy Leaves Home" versus Lee's *To Kill a Mockingbird*).[23] By taking that assumption as a given, one misses the different genres, produced by writers of various ethnic backgrounds, that do not fit the binary. For example, humor gets overlooked as a means of addressing the movement, a "serious" topic. Although they appear less often, comic works do exist. Michael Thelwell's "Direct Action" (1963), Flannery O'Connor's "Everything that Rises Must Converge" (1965), and, more recently, Suzan-Lori Parks's *Getting Mother's Body* (2003) provide just a few examples. Thrillers – which depict investigations, trials, and the reporting of murders – also get overlooked. This form's popularity among writers is not a surprise given the era's many headline-making crimes. Texts from the period include Elliot Chaze's *Tiger in the Honeysuckle* (1965) and Jay Milner's *Incident at Ashton* (1961), while Lewis Nordan's *Wolf Whistle* (1993) and Elizabeth Nunez's *Beyond the Limbo Silence* (1998) serve as more current examples.

Both Nordan and Nunez employ elements of magical realism to tell their stories, with animals especially providing darkly comic perspectives on civil rights issues. Although some readers might expect, or want, literary representations of particular historical periods to rely primarily on realism, such is not always the case, past or present. Certainly works such as *'Sippi, Civil Wars*, and *Your Blues Ain't like Mine* render people, places, and events with a certain degree of accuracy even as these books take liberties with plot and character. However, works such as Alice Walker's "The First Day: After Brown" (1974) and Henry Dumas's "Fon" (1968) draw upon fable. Others, such as Julius Lester's *All Our Wounds Forgiven* (1994) and Charles Johnson's *Dreamer* (1998), both of which take on Martin Luther King's legacy, employ the imaginative twists of postmodernism. As Monteith explains: "The slippage between imagination and the facts that historical commentators work so assiduously to retrieve, becomes the creative wellspring for writers of fiction for whom strict allegiance to the facts may limit what they can do with them."[24] Creative writing tells stories that documentary writing does not.

Whether one defines a piece of writing as civil rights fiction, segregation, race relations, or movement literature is often a rhetorical matter. These categories exist in overlapping relationships. One could describe *Your Blues Ain't like Mine* as a work of race-relations literature because it takes steps toward racial healing in what some characters view as a post–civil rights age. Or, one might think of the novel as a civil rights movement text that considers how specific historical events shape the present in both overt and subtle ways. However, just because books cross boundaries of definition does not mean that each category is the same. Fictional representations emerge from particular perspectives. And those perspectives, in turn, emerge from a complex constellation of literary and historical forces. Easy-bake narratives such as *The Help*, which share a common source with the white civil rights novel *To Kill a Mockingbird*, will see discrimination against maids or the murder of Medgar Evers as an occasion for its protagonist to extend the hand of friendship across racial lines and expect a willing hand to be offered in return. Civil rights movement works as varied as *'Sippi, Meridian*, "Everything that Rises Must Converge," and "Where Is the Voice Coming From?" might look at different parties across racial lines to see whether their hands are open in peace, closed in fists, or aiming weapons. The historical connections, evidence, and lessons that each of these works provides are not independent from the frameworks used to describe them.

Plot, Theme, and Narrative

These works, in turn, perpetuate other frameworks through the narratives they create. One can consider the issue of narrative from different, disciplinary perspectives. Historians find the consensus narrative problematic because it obscures more accurate and nuanced ways of looking at the civil rights movement. Focusing on a southern geography, for example, gives the impression that "movement" did not occur in places north and west, or that local events had no connections to global ones. The emphasis on charismatic national leaders such as Martin Luther King and Malcolm X leaves out grassroots efforts, women, and students. Looking only at events within a certain range of years (say, from the 1954 *Brown v. Board of Education* decision to the 1965 Voting Rights Act) neglects what happened before (such as the work of labor unions or the legal precedent building that went into *Brown*) and after (Black Power or current attempts to maintain civil rights gains).

Literary scholars see the consensus narrative as a "plot," or story, that provides only one way of arranging events in order to create meaning or "theme." Easy-bake narratives such as *The Help* draw in audiences who like the comfort of familiar stories and themes – and not just about civil rights. The book offers a well-known tale where good, Skeeter, triumphs over an evil that gets its due: Hilly Holbrook loses social status, gaining the nickname "Two Slice Hilly," after eating Minny's supposedly chocolate pie. A wise figure, Aibeleen, assists the heroine on her quest for knowledge without claiming too much for herself. Clownish figures (Minny, Celia) provide comic relief in an otherwise serious story. Such plots, so familiar that they come to writers and readers alike unconsciously – the damsel in distress, battling a monster, rags to riches, the orphan finds the perfect home – underlie fairy tales, myths, novels, and even social policy. Like the civil rights movement consensus memory, any plot is a construction: a way of organizing story elements into a coherent pattern toward a desired end.

Plots become so familiar, or comforting, that people forget they are fabrications and accept them as established truths. They settle into what Jacqueline Goldsby calls "narrative molds" that structure ways of thinking so completely that seeing beyond them becomes difficult.[25] Gwendolyn Brooks points to this danger in her long poem, "A Bronzeville Mother Loiters in Mississippi, Meanwhile, a Mississippi Mother Burns Bacon" (1960), written in response to the 1955 murder of fourteen-year-old Emmett Till, killed for allegedly whistling at a woman named Carolyn Bryant. Here, the Mississippi Mother of the poem's title has imagined herself as the damsel in distress, "Pursued / By the Dark Villain. Rescued by the Fine Prince."[26] As she looks back on the night in question, she cannot make the story pieces fit together. The Dark Villain "should have been older, perhaps"; he should have been more menacing. When the Fine Prince comes down for breakfast, and begins acting villainous himself – ultimately hitting his own child – the Mississippi Mother's illusions fall from her eyes. The Prince kisses her, but she hears "no hoof-beat of the horse and saw no flash of the shining steel." The romantic narrative that controls her life is shattered when she realizes its cost to her, her children, and ultimately the "Dark Villain," also a child himself. The poem is an imaginative tour de force for Brooks, an African American poet known for her poignant depiction of Chicago's South Side, where Till and his mother resided. Brooks takes the white woman's perspective in "A Bronzeville Mother" to get beneath the psyche of a woman whose word is so powerful that it can prefigure Till's death, showing the destructive influence of narrative molds upon individuals, families, and ultimately society itself. Till's murder resonated outward from its local setting to become a collective trauma felt nationwide.[27]

Stories of damsels in distress and fine princes to the rescue do not excuse the violence against Till. But they help to explain the mindset of women like Carolyn Bryant, and men like her husband Roy and her brother-in-law J. W. Milam who perpetrated that violence, as well as the mindset of a community that initially stood behind them and a jury that found the men not guilty of murder. The Jim Crow South of the 1950s accepted as fact that black males were dark villains who threatened white females who needed noble white males to save them. Civil rights movement fiction – at its best – operates by shattering narrative orthodoxies. As Brooks observes in her poem, when the Mississippi Mother begins to realize that her worldview does not hold up, she knows "that her composition / Had disintegrated. That, although the pattern prevailed / The breaks were everywhere. That she could think / Of no thread capable of the necessary / Sew-work." Civil rights movement fiction – at its worst – provides the threads that keep the familiar compositions stitched in place. The many fictions written during and about the movement, for all the variety in plot and character their different forms suggest – provide a surprising thematic consistency. This statement does not imply that most fictions deploy familiar narratives, but that a work's power lies in its ability to show the piecework in comforting stories.

A primary goal of movement-related fiction is exposing structures of white supremacy and privilege. In *Your Blues Ain't like Mine* Campbell uses the "Honorable Men of Hopewell" to show the interconnected, long-lasting relationship between money, race, and power. The Honorable Men, whose roots in the town extend back to the slave-holding South, continue to manipulate property taxes, the local education system, regional economic health, and even medical care so that they win and everyone else – including poor whites and all blacks – loses. In two key scenes from the novel, Campbell shows how important justice and business decisions are made among local power brokers rather than through legal or equitable processes. The Honorable Men, not the court system, decide how the Cox brothers will be punished for Armstrong Todd's murder. After the men break ground on a new industry, it operates just as its name suggests: the New Plantation Catfish Farm and Processing Plant. Campbell is not alone in illustrating that when white men meet in smoky rooms, those who get left out wind up in trouble. Civil rights fiction has relied upon this trope for at least a century – in Harper's *Iola Leroy*, Chesnutt's *Marrow of Tradition*, and Johnson's *Autobiography of an Ex-Colored Man* and many more works. McCullers's *Clock without Hands* has a committee draw straws to see who will bomb Sherman Pew's house after he blatantly oversteps Jim Crow's boundaries. At multiple points throughout *'Sippi*, Killens follows the workings of a town's White Citizens Council, which – as in Campbell's novel, includes its "honorable men." They, too, draw straws to see who will kill Reverend Purdy, the "preaching nigger" they see as responsible for local movement-related efforts. Purdy, highly attuned to white supremacy's machinations, meets its resulting trouble with a posse of black men carrying guns.

That a white man calls to warn Purdy ahead of time, and that the preacher shows up with protection, both point to a related element of movement fiction. Texts challenge structures of white supremacy not only by revealing them but also by undermining the binary oppositions that support them. Civil rights fictions have their share of stock characters: the good white, the evil police officer, the brutish white, the segregationist, the black Christ figure, and the militant yet non-violent black.[28] In novels such as *'Sippi* and *Meridian*, authors work against simple equations of white with evil (or, in other cases, heroism) and black with saintliness (or, when paired with the white hero, in need of salvation). These books cross racial lines in multiple ways: blacks and whites work together, become friends, have sex, and argue over issues large and small. *'Sippi*'s Charles Othello and Carrie Louise, and *Meridian*'s Truman and Lynne thus become complex figures rather than caricatures. Other works, especially Howard Cruse's graphic narrative *Stuck Rubber Baby* (1995), show how the fight to end legalized segregation intersects with other social movements. Here Cruse unsettles binary equations of civil rights with "black" and gay with "white" through protagonist Toland Polk's encounters with other characters who refuse neat classifications.[29]

Some fictions, however, dive deeply into caricature to see what it reveals. James Baldwin's "Going to Meet the Man" (1965) uses the "evil police officer" to probe connections between racial and sexual violence. The protagonist of this story whips himself into a frenzy of arousal by recalling a lynching he had seen as a boy. In "Where Is the Voice Coming From?" Eudora Welty ominously, and with surprising accuracy, profiled Medgar Evers's assassin long before Byron de la Beckwith was arrested. The "voice," in this case, is not so much that of a psychopath acting alone but one of a segregationist acting on his society's worst thoughts. Killens's Carrie Louise, although not exactly a caricature, does embody many stereotypes of the spoiled white girl of privilege. Carrie fancies herself enlightened as she travels back and forth between the Mississippi Delta and New York. It takes much convincing from her black radical college roommate, and from Charles Othello, before she begins educating herself about race. The novel leaves open the question of whether Carrie – or any white person – can learn the necessary lessons.

Texts that examine notions of white supremacy and privilege sometimes consider the role of region in those structures. Whether or not a work describes racism as a "southern" or a "national" problem depends on when it was written. In *The Nation's Region*, Leigh Ann Duck explains that before the 1920s, books about the American South did not usually appear on bestseller lists. During the 1930s, two "Souths" emerged in film and literature to place the region in the forefront of popular imagination: the plantation romance, which idealized the slave-holding past as a "privileged site of a coherent and binding white culture," and a "'problem South' ... in need of economic and social reform."[30] Two widely known examples are both set in Georgia: Margaret Mitchell's celebratory, and highly popular, *Gone With the Wind* (1936), made into an Oscar-winning film; and Lillian Smith's "white civil rights novel," *Strange Fruit*, which faced bans in some states because of its interracial romance and lynching violence. Many representations of the civil rights movement, in fiction and film, continue equating racism with region. Rare is a story such as John Updike's 1966 "Marching through Boston," where characters participate in an anti-segregation march and Martin Luther King hovers in the background. As Duck explains, "regionalism masks national participation in racism."[31] Equating white supremacy and privilege with one region often acts as a way of denying its existence in other locations. More contemporary texts often try to disrupt that equation. Norman points out that "as the segregation narrative evolves in a post–civil rights era, the distinction [between the region and nation] becomes less important than that between de jure and de facto modes of segregation" – as in the earlier Updike story.[32]

Concepts such as race, region, and nation ultimately intersect with ideals that activists in the civil rights movement fought to make real for all Americans: equality, freedom, and justice. Literary representations of that movement do not specifically define those broad concepts as often as they pose questions about the most effective methods of achieving them: non-violence, more aggressive tactics, or armed self-defense. Black men with guns keep watch in Anthony Grooms's "Negro Progress" (1994) as well as Killens's *'Sippi*. The earliest representations of the movement focus on non-violent direct action, but authors create dramatic tension by using other emotions. In a 1968 story by James W. Thompson, the protagonist retains his composure on his first day integrating a school, while other students call him names, throw eggs at him, and trip him. Retaliation remains present in his thoughts, however. When the final school bell rings, he considers a boy who taunted him in history class, consoling himself with the reminder that gives the story its title, "See what tomorrow brings."[33] Retribution is a key theme of both Alice Walker's *Meridian* and Toni Morrison's *Song of Solomon*. In the latter, the character Guitar belongs to a black vigilante group called the Seven Days. Because he is the "Sunday Man," Guitar is tasked with bombing a white church after a deadly bombing of a black church in Birmingham. Meridian, the title character of Walker's novel, struggles with the idea of taking a life. When her radical friends push her to say whether or not she could kill for the movement, she remains noncommittal. Later, at a church memorial for a boy who died from racist violence, she feels a change of heart. Context is everything for Meridian: "Only in a church surrounded by the righteous guardians of the people's memories could she even approach the concept of retaliatory murder."[34]

For Meridian Hill and characters like her, movement-related events lead to political awakenings. Margaret Earley Whitt observes that in many short stories, particular events have "a permanent effect ... reshaping the way characters view their environments. If the character lives, the event becomes a turning point, a vision for a better world."[35] Carlton Wilkes, the main character of "Negro Progress," wavers throughout the story about participating in direct action. From a privileged background, Carlton distances himself from the protests in downtown Birmingham, begging his fiancée Salena to avoid the danger and elope with him to Paris. Carlton's moment of truth comes when Salena's neighbor Mr. Shannon – a member of the community's "self-defense" team – talks him into attending a march. Ever the reluctant protestor, Carlton runs the moment he sees firemen turn on their hoses. Still, he gets sprayed, the blast pounding him to the ground. The story ends with Carlton having met his worst fear and turning again, not to run, but to stumble toward Salena, throughout the story a mainstay of doing the right thing. Grooms's longer movement work, *Bombingham* (2001), takes a more pessimistic view of political awakenings. The protagonist of this novel, Walter Burke, must write a post-battlefield letter from Vietnam to the parents of his friend and fallen comrade. He finds himself unable to do so because the task takes him back to his Birmingham childhood, where he lost another friend, this time to racist violence. Christopher Metress points out how novels such as *Bombingham* deconstruct easier narratives of civil rights progress. "Grooms' novel," he writes, "seeks to make visible a different civil rights legacy from Birmingham, one that casts the events of that summer of a series of dark yesterdays that failed to produce the perfect union of a brighter tomorrow."[36]

A related question that some scholars raise is the relationship between an author's race and the treatment of progress narratives or political awakening themes. In "Politics and Fictional Representation," Richard H. King addresses what he says is "the rarely spoken suspicion that white writers are incapable of doing justice to the African-American experience." King specifically discusses William Styron's controversial 1967 novel, *The Confessions of Nat Turner*, which prompted a full book of negative criticism, *William Styron's Nat Turner: Ten Black Writers Respond* (1968). Certainly, as King explains, arguments that white writers cannot fairly represent different perspectives on controversial historical events are founded themselves upon controversial ideas rather than facts – most notably essentialist notions of race and mistaken beliefs in a homogeneous "African American" experience.[37] Sharon Monteith, on the other hand, demonstrates that whether the white writers of 1990s fiction that she reads *can* equitably represent cross-racial perspectives is beside the point; the fact is they usually *don't*. Instead, they have begun to fall into a predictable, "easy-bake" pattern, where the writer uses interracial friendship as a lens for envisioning social change. The authors Monteith examines, who represent white female characters' reactions to Martin Luther King, "risk appropriating the black women characters they create as secondary or auxiliary to their white protagonists." Of the examples Monteith studies – *Sugar Cage, Crossing Blood*, and *Can't Quit You Baby* – only the latter novel questions the trope to any extent. By comparison, she explains, there is no "paradigm in which black characters created by black writers achieve a politicized sense of self and become aware of the nexus of race and power as the result of a single intimate engagement with a white counterpart."[38] The opposite usually occurs. *'Sippi, Meridian*, and *Your Blues Ain't like Mine* show how movement-related events directly intrude upon the cross-racial friendships of, respectively, Charles Othello and Carrie Louise, Meridian and Lynne, and Ida and Lily – the latter never making it past the railroad tracks that mark their respective "sides" of town.

If some movement fictions consider the difficulty people had establishing and maintaining friendships, others look at the toll that a political life exacted on those involved and on their loved ones. *Meridian*, as Richard H. King explains, may provide the most detailed examination of "the various motivations propelling activists into the movement, and the complexities of living a political life in it, as well as how people, whose life had been devoted to the movement, functioned after it had run its course."[39] Meridian herself is, at different times, a one-woman community organizer, physically ill, mentally unstable, a visionary, unsure of herself, and the glue that binds together a small band of long-term, committed activists. Truman, her friend and one-time lover, is equally complex. He worships black women and sleeps with white ones. He strays from Meridian and the cause, but ultimately comes back to take up where she left off. Lynne, Meridian's friend and Truman's lover as well, stereotypes those around her and ultimately becomes a stereotype herself – the suburban Jewish girl who joined other white kids during Freedom Summer to "save the day." Brown's *Civil Wars* is significant for the way it explores post-movement life for those white activists. Teddy and Jessie were fully alive during the movement, but what do they do with their lives once activism no longer keeps them active? Teddy's sister and brother-in-law are killed in an accident, and the couple must raise their children along with their own, forcing the family to reckon with their past, present, and, future. Other books, such as Brown's *Half a Heart* (2001) and Danzy Senna's *Caucasia* (1998) trace the impact of the past upon the present lives of movement participants' children.

The movement legacy is another area where competing narratives emerge. One such narrative, related to notions of progress and friendship, involves reconciliation and healing. Ideals of reconciliation, intrinsic to the work of non-violent direct action, are based on peaceful conflict resolution. The goal is not repairing an earlier (and non-existent) time of harmony but looking forward to a future time of "beloved community" which recognizes, and uses as the basis of social action, the human dignity of all individuals. *Your Blues Ain't like Mine* provides an example of this philosophy in action. The opposite of reconciliation – violence and retribution – leads to the cycles of domestic violence readers see in the Cox family, and to the racist violence Floyd Cox enacts on Armstrong Todd. When, at the novel's end, individuals begin working across the lines that divide them they not only transform themselves but also their whole community, which has lived with decades-long wounds. Lily Cox questions her daughter Doreen about working with African Americans like Ida to unionize the catfish plant. Doreen admits that she harbors prejudice, but those "feelings just ain't practical when you work at the New Plantation."[40] Other novels point to the difficulty of healing. In *Bombingham*, Walter finally writes a letter, albeit an imaginary one, and the connection he finds between individuals involves suffering. What is the difference "between Birmingham and Da Nang?" he asks. "But just below the surface – or maybe just on top of it, visible to those who would see it, invisible to those who would not – is the incontrovertible proof that the world is a tumultuous place and every soul in it suffers."[41] For the beloved community to exist, it must recognize this fact and root itself in compassion.

How, or whether, one heals from the past may inevitably lead to a statement William Faulkner made in his 1950 *Requiem for a Nun*: "The past is never dead. It's not even past."[42] Many contemporary works suggest that racial cooperation and healing may be difficult because, even if a civil rights *movement* took place during the 1950s and 1960s, civil rights *goals* have still not been reached. As Suzanne Jones points out, a growing number of southern writers "represent race relations as being closer to Booker T. Washington's 1890s promise of economic cooperation but social separation" than to any dreams Martin Luther King had during the 1960s. In the authors that Jones examines – including Josephine Humphreys, Tom Wolfe, Toni Cade Bambara, Christine Wiltz, Elizabeth Spencer, and Randall Kenan – dividing lines read like the grids of an infamous redlining map, used to mark who can live in which parts of town. Bambara's *These Bones Are Not My Child* (1999), based on the Atlanta child murders of 1979–1981, shows that separate still clearly means "unequal."[43] In his work on segregation narratives, Norman uses the term "temporal dysphoria" to describe how "we encounter Jim Crow *today* when we think – and know! – he should be *then*."[44] Literature, as well as the life it represents, offers many examples of an unfinished movement and a risen Jim Crow. Aaron McGruder, Reginald Hudlin, and Kyle Baker's graphic novel *Birth of a Nation* (2005) offers biting politic satire prompted by beliefs that Florida disenfranchised African American and Hispanic voters during the 2000 U.S. presidential elections. More personal, Amina Gautier's "Dance for Me" features a girl who is the only African American in her class at an exclusive Manhattan preparatory school. Highly conscious about fitting in, she winds up conforming to the worst of her peers' stereotypes. Unlike the protagonist of Thompson's "See What Tomorrow Brings," this young woman integrates without the National Guard's protection, dancing through a minefield of race, economics, gender, and sexuality. Temporal dysphoria can feel, as Trudier Harris states in the title of an essay, like being "Smacked Upside the Head – Again."[45]

Civil rights fiction includes both the stories audiences want to read and the stories that get written. Sometimes that fiction lifts the spirit and sometimes, as Monteith points out, it "can be a tough and dispiriting read."[46] The historical events themselves record humans acting out roles that often seem larger than life in dramas that resonate across local, national, and international lines. It stands to reason, then, that fictional representations of those events show us ourselves: at our best, our worst, and struggling to muddle through when choices are not clear. Some of us come to these stories seeking familiarity: narratives of comfort – like the toys and treats we remember from childhood. Some of us seek to explore new territory: how the past guides us to what we might become. Civil rights fiction is yet one more rendering of what James Baldwin heard in the blues: "For, while the tale of how we suffer, and how we are delighted, and how we may triumph is never new, it always must be heard. There isn't any other tale to tell, it's the only light we've got in all this darkness."[47]

NOTES

1 Jessica Roake, "Not Helpful: Making Kids Read *The Help* Is Not the Way to Teach Them about the Civil Rights Struggle," *Slate,* December 2, 2013, http://www.slate.com/articles/life/education/2013/12/teachers_assigning_the_help_to_teach_jim_crow_and_civil_rights_aren_t_teaching.html; Gerald Graff, *Beyond the Culture Wars: How Teaching the Conflicts Can Revitalize American Education* (New York: W.W. Norton, 1993).

2 Best Sellers, *New York Times,* http://www.nytimes.com/best-sellers-books/2011-04-03/hardcover-fiction/list.html, http://www.nytimes.com/best-sellers-books/2012-04-08/combined-print-and-e-book-fiction/list.html (accessed June 9, 2014); Nominees and Winners for the 84th Academy Awards, http://www.oscars.org/awards/academyawards/84/nominees.html (accessed June 9, 2014).

3 Association of Black Women Historians, "Open Statement to Fans of *The Help,*" http://www.abwh.org/index.php?option=com_content&view=article&id=2:open-statement-the-help" (accessed June 10, 2014); Harry L. Watson, "The Front Porch," *Southern Cultures* 20.1 (Spring 2014): 1–6.

4 Roake, "Not Helpful."

5 Renee C. Romano and Leigh Raiford, eds., *The Civil Rights Movement in American Memory* (Athens: University of Georgia Press, 2006), pp. xiv–xv.

6 Julian Bond, qtd. in Wesley Hogan, "Freedom Now! SNCC Galvanizes the New Left," in *Rebellion in Black and White: Southern Student Activism in the 1960s,* ed. Robert Cohen and David J. Snyder (Baltimore, MD: Johns Hopkins University Press, 2013), p. 43.

7 Suzanne Jones, "The Divided Reception of *The Help,*" *Southern Cultures* 20.1 (Spring 2014): 12. Worth noting, in this essay Jones shows how responses to the book and film do not fall along expected black/white, academic/popular lines. The paradigm that Jones points out has a long history in southern fiction as

Sharon Monteith has traced in *Advancing Sisterhood? Interracial Friendships in Contemporary Southern Fiction* (Athens: University of Georgia Press, 2000) and in southern cinema, as Allison Graham has examined in *Framing the South: Hollywood, Television, and Race during the Civil Rights Struggle* (Baltimore, MD: Johns Hopkins University Press, 2004).

8   Toymaker Kenner introduced the Easy-Bake Oven in 1963, in a version that used 100-watt incandescent bulbs. Hasbro later bought out Kenner and continues to produce Easy-Bake using microwave technology. See Easy-Bake Oven Commercial, 1963, https://www.youtube.com/watch?v=XcYoghee5Sc (accessed June 10, 2014). Credit for the "easy-bake" metaphor goes to Thomas Hallock.

9   Christopher Metress, "Making Civil Rights Harder: Literature, Memory, and the Black Freedom Struggle," *Southern Literary Journal* 40.2 (Spring 2008): 148.

10   Richard H. King, "Politics and Fictional Representation: The Case of the Civil Rights Movement," in *The Making of Martin Luther King and the Civil Rights Movement*, ed. Brian Ward and Tony Badger (New York: Washington Square Press, 1996), p. 163. See also Margaret Earley Whitt, Introduction, *Short Stories of the Civil Rights Movement* (Athens: University of Georgia Press, 2006), pp. ix–xviii, and "Using the Civil Rights Movement to Practice Activism in the Classroom," *PMLA* 124 (2009): 856–63.

11   Barbara Melosh, "Historical Memory in Fiction: The Civil Rights Movement in Three Novels," *Radical History Review* 40 (Winter 1988): **p.** 14 especially; Christopher Metress, "Making Civil Rights Harder: Literature, Memory, and the Black Freedom Struggle," *Southern Literary Journal* 40.2 (Spring 2008): 140.

12   Jacqueline Goldsby, *Spectacular Secret: Lynching in American Life and Literature* (Chicago: University of Chicago Press, 2006), pp. 34–35.

13   Christopher Metress's essay in this volume describes the genre by way of Lettie Hamlett Rogers's *Birthright* (1957) and Elliot Chaze's *Tiger in the Honeysuckle* (1965). Thomas F. Haddox, "Elizabeth Spencer, the White Civil Rights Novel, and the Postsouthern," *MLQ: Modern Language Quarterly* 65.4 (December 2004): 561.

14   Ibid., pp. 563–64.

15   Harper Lee, *To Kill a Mockingbird* (New York: HarperCollins, 2014), p. 323.

16   Brian Norman, *Neo-Segregation Narratives: Jim Crow in Post–Civil Rights American Literature* (Athens: University of Georgia Press, 2010), pp. 3, 7; Brian Norman and Piper Kendrix Williams, Introduction, in *Representing Segregation: Toward an Aesthetics of Living Jim Crow, and Other Forms of Racial Division*, ed. Brian Norman and Piper Kendrix Williams (Albany: State University of New York Press, 2010), p. 3. For more detailed discussion of the ways Jim Crow narratives work, see Brian Norman's chapter in this volume.

17   Norman and Williams, *Representing Segregation*, p. 1.

18   On this point see Monteith, *Advancing Sisterhood?*, and "The 1960s Echo On: Images of Martin Luther King Jr. as Deployed by White Writers of Contemporary Fiction," in Media, Culture, and the African American Freedom Struggle, ed. Brian Ward (Gainesville: University of Florida Press, 2001), pp. 264–67.

19   Suzanne Jones, *Race Mixing: Southern Fiction since the 1960s* (Baltimore, MD: Johns Hopkins University Press, 2006), p. 3.

20 Sharon Monteith, "Civil Rights Fiction," in *The Cambridge Companion to the Literature of the American South*, ed. Sharon Monteith (Cambridge: Cambridge University Press, 2013), p. 161.

21 Ibid. See also Richard H. King, "The Civil Rights Debate," in *A Companion to the Literature and Culture of the American South*, ed. Richard Gray and Owen Robinson (Malden, MA: Blackwell, 2004), p. 233.

22 In *Neo-Segregation Narratives*, Brian Norman explains that these works are as much about the present as the past. Like civil rights movement texts that look back retrospectively, neo-segregation narratives "arise at the moment when segregation is perceived as having a past, even if it has not fully passed" (13). The point here is not to draw a fine line of distinction between two definitions. A movement text, in general, deals more specifically with people, places, and events, while a neo-segregation narrative is a broader category that focuses on representing Jim Crow in its past and present forms. Again, much overlap exists.

23 Monteith, p. 161. See Zoe Trodd's chapter in this volume for a discussion of protest literature.

24 Sharon Monteith, "Revisiting the 1960s in Contemporary Fiction: "where do we go from here?" in *Gender and the Civil Rights Movement*, ed. Peter Ling and Sharon Monteith (New Brunswick, NJ: Rutgers University Press, 2004), p. 230.

25 Goldsby, p. 9.

26 Gwendolyn Brooks, "A Bronzeville Mother Loiters in Mississippi, Meanwhile, a Mississippi Mother Burns Bacon," *Selected Poems* (New York: HarperPerennial, 2006).

27 See Christopher Metress, ed., *The Lynching of Emmett Till: A Documentary Narrative* (Charlottesville: University of Virginia Press, 2002); and Harriet Pollack and Christopher Metress, eds., *Emmett Till in Literary Memory and Imagination* (Baton Rouge: Louisiana State University Press, 2008).

28 See Floyd Watkins, *The Death of Art: Black and White in the Recent Southern Novel* (Macon, GA: Mercer University Press, 1970).

29 I am grateful to Robert J. Patterson's contribution to this volume for making me conscious of this binary.

30 Leigh Anne Duck, *The Nation's Region: Southern Modernism, Segregation, and U.S. Nationalism* (Athens: University of Georgia Press, 2006), p. 20.

31 Ibid., p. 33.

32 Norman, *Neo-Segregation Narratives*, p. 8.

33 James W. Thompson (Abba Elethea), "See What Tomorrow Brings," in Whitt, *Short Stories*," p. 10.

34 Alice Walker, *Meridian* (New York: Harcourt Brace, 1976), p. 205

35 Whitt, Introduction, *Short Stories*, p. xiii.

36 Metress, "Making Civil Rights Harder," p. 144.

37 King, "Politics and Fictional Representations," pp. 165–68.

38 Sharon Monteith, "The 1960s Echo On: Images of Martin Luther King Jr. as Deployed by White Writers of Contemporary Fiction," in *Media, Culture, and the African American Freedom Struggle*, ed. Brian Ward (Gainesville: University Press of Florida, 2001), pp. 264–67.

39 King, "Politics and Fictional Representations," p. 172.

40 Bebe Moore Campbell, *Your Blues Ain't like Mine* (New York: Ballantine, 1992), p. 290.

41 Anthony Grooms, *Bombingham* (New York: Free Press, 2001), p. 302.
42 William Faulkner, *Requiem for a Nun* (New York: Vintage, 2012), p. 73.
43 Jones, *Race Mixing*, pp. 244–45.
44 Norman, *Neo-Segregation Narratives*, p. 154, emphasis in original.
45 Harris, "Smacked Upside the Head – Again"; Norman and Williams, *Representing Jim Crow*, pp. 37–39. The idea of "integrating without the National Guard" comes from Sharon Holland, quoted in Koritha Mitchell, "Love in Action: Noting Similarities between Lynching Then & Anti-LGBT Violence Now," *Callaloo* 36.3 (2013). 689.
46 Monteith, "Civil Rights Fiction," p. 160.
47 James Baldwin, "Sonny's Blues," in *Going to Meet the Man* (New York: Vintage, 1995), p. 139.

6

CHRISTOPHER METRESS

The White Southern Novel and the Civil Rights Movement

Responding to the publication of Eudora Welty's "Where Is the Voice Coming From?" in the July 6, 1963, issue of the *New Yorker*, Flannery O'Connor warned her friend Betty Hester against addressing the civil rights movement in fiction. "The more you think about it [Welty's story] the less satisfactory it gets. What I hate most is its being in the *The New Yorker* and all the stupid Yankee liberals smacking their lips over typical life in the dear old dirty Southland. The topical is poison." Fully aware that she too had once succumbed to the temptation of the topical, O'Connor quickly added, "I got away with it in 'Everything That Rises,' but only because I say a plague on everyone's house as far as the race business goes."[1] Exactly how O'Connor's 1962 story cast a "plague on everyone's house" is a matter for some debate, as is O'Connor's own record on engaging, or failing to engage, the demands of the civil rights movement and the "race business." What is clear, however, is that O'Connor's white southern contemporaries did not heed her warning against the topical. In hundreds of novels, stories, poems, and plays, white southern writers of the 1950s and 1960s made the civil rights movement the central focus of their work. Surprisingly, however, this literary output has yet to receive the full attention it deserves.

In particular, critics have largely neglected the wide range of novels white southern writers produced during this period. This neglect may be in part because major figures such as William Faulkner, Robert Penn Warren, Walker Percy, and William Styron avoided the movement in their fiction: although each engaged the issue of civil rights as an essayist, editorialist, historian, or public intellectual – and each continued to reflect deeply on race in his fiction – none produced a literary work grounded in the day-to-day activities of the movement (a few scenes from *The Last Gentleman* notwithstanding). Other major writers, such as Welty, O'Connor, and Carson McCullers, did address the poisonously topical challenges of the movement in their fiction, and they too could not avoid making significant personal and public choices about how to respond to the powerful forces that were reshaping the South.

However, their fictional engagements with the movement were few and limited. For the most part, it was left to a series of lesser-known or emerging white southern writers to fully embrace the challenge. Some of those writers, such as Elizabeth Spencer, William Bradford Huie, Shirley Ann Grau, and Jesse Hill Ford, produced significant works that garnered a wide readership, while many others, such as Lettie Hamlett Rogers, Ann Fairbairn, William F. McIlwain, Philip Alston Stone, Ben Haas, Francis Irby Gwaltney, and Leon Odell Griffith have largely been forgotten. While several recent critics have written insightfully about civil rights novels produced by white southerners during the movement,[2] the field still lacks a more comprehensive analysis, one that can help literary historians assess the full scope and impact of the movement on fiction of the 1950s and 1960s. Such an assessment assumes that O'Connor's warning about the poisonous nature of the topical was beside the point – the topical was there; it demanded attention; and many white southern writers responded. The civil rights movement forced the white South to undergo its most significant social and structural reconfiguration since the Civil War, and white southern novelists of that era have left us a rich legacy for understanding how that reconfiguration played out during a time when the direction and success of the movement was still uncertain.

In his 1990 essay "Politics and Fictional Understanding: The Case of the Civil Rights Movement," Richard King wagered that "fiction – like history – delivers, in Raymond Carver's words, some 'news of the world'; that it has cognitive, as opposed to simply aesthetic, self-referential value; and that historical understanding may be enhanced – though never automatically – by a fictional working-through of historical phenomena."[3] The two earliest critics to address the impact of the civil rights movement on white southern fiction had deep reservations about how well that fiction enhanced our historical understanding of the region's shifting racial dynamics. In the opening pages of his 1970 study *The Death of Art: Black and White in the Recent Southern Novel,* Floyd Watkins noted, "The best Southern literature was written in the few decades after World War I, but the Southern Renaissance is now ending."[4] For Watkins, the fault lay less with a diminution of talent than with a turn in current events. "The troublesome issues of our time may in part be responsible for the decline," Watkins speculated. "It has been more than fifteen years now since the Supreme Court made its decision to end racial segregation in schools. Since then a social revolution has begun with race as the issue, and Southern white novelists have become deeply involved in the controversies" (1–2). With special animus toward such works as Ben Haas's *Look Away, Look Away* (1964), Jesse Hill Ford's *The Liberation of Lord Byron Jones* (1965), Douglas Kiker's *The Southerner* (1957), and

Eliott Chaze's *Tiger in the Honeysuckle* (1965), Watkins bemoans that fact that "In the hands of the Southern white author, the [post-*Brown*] novel has become a weapon turned against his own race" (2). As a result, the region's literature has degenerated into "propaganda" full of "anti-Southern, pro-black, anti-white hostilities and sympathies," and the only remedy is for southern writers to reject "emotionalized melodrama" and to stop writing novels designed "to exploit the marketplace" (65). According to Watkins, "the great novels about the struggles between white and black in the modern South remain to be written," and in those works "the reader will not be able to tell whether the novelist is a white man or black man, and possibly the fiction will be neither liberal nor conservative" (65). To achieve this, the white southern writer must reject "fictitious sociology" (64) and "write profoundly about the human heart" (65).

In *Civil Rights in Recent Southern Fiction* (1969), James McBride Dabbs is tentatively more generous than Watkins in his assessment of the South's emerging civil rights fiction.[5] For instance, he praises Elizabeth Spencer's *The Voice at the Back Door* for its "success in combining ... the old racial accommodation and the new racial conflict" (29), signals out Haas's *Look Away, Look Away* for providing "in one believable story the double South ... of racial antagonism and ... of racial affection" (117), and even has kind words for O'Connor's "Everything that Rises Must Converge" which, although the story seems to be written "to prove that [the civil rights movement] doesn't amount to much," still manages to capture the essential truth that "beneath the political causes there are non-political depths, where each of us must walk in private, facing God – or the abyss" (62). Against such praise, however, Dabbs expresses some strong reservations about how certain novels are depicting the South. Acknowledging that Huie's *The Klansman* is "an ugly story, made uglier by the knowledge that there is raw truth" in its depiction of the racial and sexual violence, Dabbs critiques the novel for having white characters who "are too simply and darkly drawn," and for overemphasizing the South as "racially divided" (106). The same is true of Ford's *The Liberation of Lord Byron Jones*, which Watkins considered a work so replete with "white atrocities" that it encourages the reader "to hope the Negroes will wreak a terrible vengeance on the whites who wronged them" (29). Dabbs is not as critical, but he does call out the novel for failing to depict the region's "complex network of positive white-black relationships" (111). Dabbs suggests that the "passing years of the civil rights struggle have polarized the opposition, so that in more senses than one everything is black and white" (113), making it "more difficult than ever ... to sense the positive interracial relationships, and doubly difficult for the writer of fiction to incorporate them in his stories" (113). Perhaps this is why Ford omitted such relationships in his flawed novel and produced a "study of Southern extremism" that "is not always convincing" (113).

Despite his occasional admiration for those white southern writers who gave "creative shape" (143) to the movement in their fiction, Dabbs reaches a conclusion about the "topical" similar to both Watkins and O'Connor. In a brief final paragraph, he notes that "the best-known and best-established writers tend to be less involved than others in … [the] topical matters" of the "sit-ins, marches, and boycotts" that have been "massive and widespread" throughout the South. Rather than seeing this as a matter of the best-known and best-established writers failing to engage the demands of the historical moment, Dabbs praises these writers for "moving toward the position of the poet: away from the transitory problems of life and toward the enduring" (143). Although he does not, like Watkins, dismiss "the transitory problems of life" as "fictitious sociology," or, like O'Connor, deem them "poisonous," Dabbs characterizes those problems as "grievances" (143). The best literature, however, turns away from "grievances and toward griefs" (143). Grievances can be "remedied" (143), but griefs "have to be borne" (143). For Dabbs, the task of the southern writer in the era of the civil rights movement is not to propose reforms. Instead, in this world where "men have become so conscious of remediable grievances that they forget their irremediable griefs," the southern novelist must concentrate on those griefs, "to recognize them, and name them, and help us to bear them" (144). The topical may not be poison, but the best-known and best-established writers do not let it distract them from that which truly endures.

These early assessments by Watkins and Dabbs provide a valuable, albeit limited, insight into the emergence of the white southern movement novel as a rich and distinct genre within southern literature. To begin to understand that genre more fully in this essay, a few definitions and demarcations are necessary. First, a matter of terminology: I employ the term "white southern movement novel" as opposed to the "white civil rights novel," a term coined by Thomas F. Haddox in 2004. According to Haddox,

> During the 1940's, around the time that Allen Tate looked back at the recent achievements of the southern renascence and gloomily opined that such literary riches would not come again, a new kind of southern novel – what I will call the white civil rights novel – began to appear. For several decades a steady stream of these novels, including Lillian Smith's *Strange Fruit* (1944), William Faulkner's *Intruder in the Dust* (1948), Elizabeth Spencer's *Voice at the Back Door* (1956), Harper Lee's *To Kill a Mockingbird* (1960), Carson McCullers's *Clock without Hands* (1961), and Jesse Hill Ford's *Liberation of Lord Byron Jones* (1965), would attract critical attention and, often, popular success. These novels are easy to identify as a group: all are set in small

southern towns and their environs, all foreground the mores and politics of race relations, and all present these relations not as a metaphysical given (as earlier southern novels often did) but as a problem that requires attention. Like the nineteenth-century "condition of England" novels, which weigh possible responses to the social upheaval caused by industrialization, white civil rights novels identify typically southern positions on race, place them in dialogue with each other, and attempt to adjudicate their competing claims.[6]

In many ways, what I identify as the "white southern movement novel" shares much in common with Haddox's "white civil rights novel." There are, however, important differences that must be maintained.[7] For instance, while both types of novels "foreground the mores and politics of race relations, and present these relations not as a metaphysical given (as earlier southern novels often did) but as a problem that requires attention," the "white southern movement novel" foregrounds these mores and politics in the context of a black-led freedom struggle that emerged in the wake of *Brown v. Board* and lasted throughout most of the following decade. Although critics such as Jacqueline Dowd Hall have recently urged historians to embrace the idea of "a long civil rights movement" that does not isolate the freedom struggle of the 1950s and 1960s from its foundations in the "the liberal and radical milieu of the late 1930s" and World War II, there is still merit in acknowledging that a distinct African American civil rights movement did emerge in the mid-1950s, a movement that was clearly understood by the white South as a sustained national drama led by an identifiable group of black leaders and drawing wide support from the federal government, the national media, and a substantial portion of the American people outside the region.[8] Employing the term "white southern movement novel" is an attempt to preserve the integrity of that distinct movement and to focus attention on how white southern writers responded not so much to changing race relations in the South but to changing race relations in the South in a very specific national context. Moreover, noting the existence of a white southern movement novel that is distinct from the white civil rights novel acknowledges that there is something qualitatively different about the racial dynamics at play in works such as *Strange Fruit* (1944) and *Intruder in the Dust* (1948) and later novels such as Carter Brook Jones's *The White Band* (1959) and Elise Sanguinetti's *The Last of the Whitfields* (1962). All of these books are "white civil rights novels," but only the last two must engage the issue of civil rights in the context of a black-led national civil rights movement with wide media support and the threat of strong federal government intervention. If, as Haddox rightly claims, white civil rights novels "identify typically southern positions on race, place them in dialogue with each other, and attempt to adjudicate their competing claims," Jones and Sanguinetti are adjudicating a set of competing claims that are much different from those negotiated by Smith and Faulkner in the 1940s. Making this kind of distinction is essential to understanding how a set of particular historical circumstances in the mid-1950s not only shifted the discussion of civil rights in the South but also altered its literary landscape. For many white southern writers before the 1950s, the civil rights of African Americans were indeed a "problem that required attention"; with the coming of a national movement that took shape in the wake of the *Brown* decision, however, the nature of that "problem" changed, and the attention it required made for a different kind of white civil rights novel, one with its own particular challenges and opportunities.

As a distinct genre, the white southern movement novel of the 1950s and 1960s developed a set of core concerns, dilemmas, tropes, and narrative strategies. For some critics, like Watkins, these shared qualities mark what is wrong with the genre: "When a similar cast of characters is repeated in many novels, obviously something other than the imaginations of good writers is in control.... [The] same types of personae appear over and over. Characters fall into patterns designed to convey social messages" (5). According to Watkins, some of those character types include "the solitary good white man" (5); the "Christ–like" Negro (18); the "militant" Negro who is "nonviolent" and "admirable" (21); the "brute white" (27); the "evil policemen" who are "freakish ... symbols of depravity" (44); and, not least of all, "segregationist Southerners" of all stripes who are defined by their "Unprovoked hatred of Negroes, violence, crime, and sexual aberrations" (53). In his assessment of the white civil rights novel more than three decades later, Haddox concurred, with qualification: "If it is an exaggeration [for Watkins] to suggest that the white characters in these novels are mostly villains and the black characters saints, his larger point stands: all the characters are essentially stock figures" (566). There is some truth in this, as evidenced by how these novels were often marketed to the public. For instance, on the back cover of the 1963 paperback original *Tear Gas and Hungry Dogs* by William Sloan, we find a large banner headline proclaiming "THE SIGHT AND SOUND AND SMELL OF HATRED," followed by a list of characters straight from central casting:

The **Bigots**, ridden with fear, shouting obscene slogs of illiterate intolerance ...

The **Agitators**, organizing and inciting and fanning the smoldering flames of angry resentment ...

The **Night-Riders**, shooting and lynching and burning fiery crosses across the troubled land ...

The **Demonstrators**, chanting hymns and locking arms, heedlessly marching to equality or death ... [9]

There is no denying that the genre over-traffics in certain character types and relies on recurrent story arcs and plot twists, and any assessment of the white southern movement novel must acknowledge this. However, it must also be noted that the best novels in the genre work creatively within this larger formulaic framework and manage to speak with complexity and depth about the challenges facing the South in the changing historical moment. In fact, many of most accomplished novels in this genre use those formulaic expectations to their advantage – aligning themselves closely with anticipated tropes, these novels are often able to assert better their own originality, pushing against patterns and reconstituting tired conventions. This is exactly the case that Haddox makes for *The Voice at the Back Door*. Noting that Spencer's 1956 novel is populated by "characters who are formulaic, predictable, and often laughable," Haddox shows how Spencer manages, at times, to wield those characters "ironically" (568). This sense of irony re-employs rather than rejects the formulaic, allowing the novelist to reframe the inherited tropes of the genre. For instance, in crafting certain "obligatory scenes," Spencer "shows how well she knows the standard moves and winks at us as she makes them" (573). The result is a novel that self-consciously traffics in clichés while "engag[ing] issues of race with utter seriousness and ... great courage" (658). Moreover, Spencer is able to create at least one character who is not formulaic or predictable, Beckwith Dozer, a black man at the heart of the novel whose "actions and motives remain obscure," who is "neither a grinning Sambo nor a potential rapist nor even a man of unassailable dignity, like Lucas Beauchamp in Faulkner's *Go Down, Moses*" (573). According to Haddox, there are multiple ways of reading Dozer's incomprehensibility, but one way may be "the historical circumstances surrounding the novel's appearance in 1956" (577):

> The civil rights movement had begun to reveal that many African Americans were no longer content to enact the roles established for them in the South. African American men in particular had long been figured as threats (in the specter of the black rapist, for instance), but the new, nonviolent forms of activism failed to lend themselves to caricature. It may have been that in these changed conditions the truest threats to white hegemony were the unpredictability and inconsistency, rather than the possible violence, of African Americans. (577–78)

While few works in the genre are as intentionally parodic as Spencer's "postsouthern novel" (566), Haddox's reading offers a valuable example of how to negotiate the undeniably formulaic, and perhaps unavoidably formulaic, qualities of the white southern movement novel: the changed circumstances of the historical moment make stock characters and plots unavoidable, yet at the same time those changed circumstances provide the very unpredictability that can generate new ways to image race relations in the South. Therefore, rather than asking these novels to be wholly original in character, plot, setting, and circumstance, we are perhaps better served to appreciate how the best writers in the genre deploy those conventions both to clarify and to complicate the tensions of the day, as well as to assess in the heat of the uncertain moment the region's capacity and promise for change.

To make a case for reading the white southern movement novel in close relationship to the very tropes that appear to make it formulaic (instead of continuing to dismiss the genre as irredeemably formulaic), I turn in the remaining pages of this chapter to a close reading of two neglected novels: Lettie Hamlett Rogers's *Birthright* (1957) and Elliot Chaze's *Tiger in the Honeysuckle* (1965).[10] Separated by nearly a decade, the novels differ radically in scope and temperament, and the historical situations they depict show the movement at different points of development on the national stage. However, both novels are creatively engaged with the trope of white racial conversion.[11] As a sub-genre of the larger white civil rights novel, the white southern movement novel inherits one of its precursor's core narrative preoccupations – how capable are southern whites of being "converted" on the "race issue"? As Fred Hobson established in his influential 1999 study *But Now I See: The White Southern Racial Conversion Narrative*, a new "form of southern self-expression" emerged in the 1940s and reached its height in the years during and following the civil rights movement.[12] In this new form of southern narrative, "the authors, all products of and willing participants in a harsh, segregated society, confess racial wrongdoings and are 'converted,' in varying degrees, from racism to something approaching racial enlightenment" (2). Noting the similarities between these twentieth-century conversion narratives and their nineteenth-century counterparts – the slave narratives – Hobson urges us to see the white southern racial conversion tale as a "freedom narrative" in which the authors "escape a kind of bondage, flee from the slavery of a closed society ... into the liberty of free association, free expression, brotherhood, sisterhood – and freedom from racial guilt" (5). Focused mainly on memoirs, Hobson does acknowledge "that any treatment of southern racial conversion could certainly include fiction as well" (5–6), and we should not be surprised that a good many white southern movement novels are positioned, either in whole or in part, as "freedom narratives" preoccupied with how their characters negotiate their bondage to the region's racial mores. Some of the best novels in the genre are astutely aware of this positioning and resist being dismissed as predictable narratives predetermined by the inherited trope of redemptive conversion. A close reading of *Birthright* and *Tiger in the Honeysuckle* will bear this out and, I hope, stimulate an interest in how other works in the genre recast their own potentially "poisonous" tropes, managing to appear utterly conventional while speaking with great seriousness about the most important issues of the day.

In *Birthright*, Seth Erwin, a handsome, well-respected preacher and Chamber of Commerce Man of the Year, must decide if he will risk his standing in the town of Peegram by supporting a nascent NAACP petition to desegregate the schools. The novel opens on May 13, 1955, nearly one year to the day after the *Brown* decision, and one day following the death of Seth's nephew, the young Roy Hibbard, who was killed during a baseball game when a line drive hit him in the stands. A few days earlier, Roy had supported his schoolteacher, Martha Lylerly, who was fired when she told her students she supported integration. Roy's support for her came in the form of the assertion in class that, when he grows up, he will "be for liberty and justice for all, black and white ... *I'll be like my dad*" (44). His classmates, as well as the whole town, understood the allusion. Several months before, Roy's father Harry had attempted to deed some of his family land to Jim Erwin, a black man. Harry and Jim were long-time fishing buddies, but their friendship caused no particular tension in town since it extended no further than fishing. Jim might have been known as an "agitator and a radical who didn't know his 'place,'" but Harry "knew nothing about any of this firsthand and did not care to" (180). Harry, then, was no racial liberal; in fact, as a young man he was a "Peegram hero," a local football star and college All-American beloved by everyone. His motives for selling the land to Jim came mainly from a power conflict with his wife, Carrie, a domineering woman who, through a series of careful business investments, owned most of the town. When Harry decided to sell his land to Jim, Carrie checked her husband, causing Jim to be fired from his janitor's job at the high school and run out of town. Harry's neighbors responded with equal fury to "the worst piece of insolence since the days of Reconstruction" (190). At a Rotary luncheon three days after his decision, the same men "who had been slapping him on the back since he was knee-high to a grasshopper; who had yelled their throats raw for him in the ball park and stadium" (192), now refused to speak to him. Finding himself unable to break free of his wife's power and abandoned by his friends, Harry killed himself, unsuccessfully masking the suicide as a boating accident.

The challenge for Seth Erwin is how he will respond to the events of the past year. Harry was not only Seth's best childhood friend and college roommate, but also his brother-in-law (Carrie is Seth's sister). When Harry decided to deed his land to Jim, Seth opposed him, asking his friend why he had "to pick *the race issue* to fight [his] most intimate and personal battles around?" (197). "You have been untrue," Seth insisted. "– not just to a woman, but to a whole tradition, a whole manner of life" (199). Moreover, Seth is on the school board, and he votes with the segregationists to terminate Martha Lyerly's contract just days before Roy is killed at the baseball game. Now, in the wake of this turmoil, Jim has returned to town after a year's absence, sent by the NAACP to challenge the town's continued resistance to integration. Jim wants Seth's support, an alliance complicated by the fact that Jim is also Seth's unacknowledged stepbrother (from the union of Seth's father and Sarah, the family's cook and Jim's mother). Although Seth seems an unlikely ally of the NAACP, we do get glimpses earlier in the novel that Seth is attracted to rebellion and unorthodoxy, tempting us to believe he may be ripe for racial conversion. As a young seminary student poring over his readings in library, Seth enjoyed defacing his books, fantasizing that he would "make his magnificent contribution to truth by traveling all over the world, from great library to great library, inscribing the great and solemn books with obscenities for posterity to come upon and reckon with" (60). We learn quickly, however, that his "obscenities" are merely "word games," "striking through [words like] *age-old*, inserting *old-age*, and feeling tremendous gratification" (60). Moreover, his rebellion does not emerge from beyond the library walls, for he graduates "first in his class, and formally designated, in the final exercises, as the seminary's great white hope" (60). His success is due, in large part, to the fact that "Never once had Seth raised his voice in doubt or disagreement with the professor of dogmatic theology ... or any professor whatsoever" (61).

When Jim returns to Peegram, this is exactly what he is asking Seth to do, raise his voice in disagreement with the South's racial orthodoxy, and to do so in ways that will require systemic changes in race relations. Earlier in the novel, a few months before Jim's return, Martha issued the same challenge, daring Seth to "take the segregation issue to the pulpit ... with the church as strong as it is in the South, desegregation couldn't lose" (110). At the time, however, Seth will have none of this, countering that there are "certain ironclad prejudices you can't run counter to" (111). Now, three weeks after Martha has left town, Seth appears to have experienced a racial conversion. However, Rogers's novel quickly problematizes that conversion. It is true that Seth preaches "a full-dress sermon on the topic of, and in favor of, desegregation and integration" (275) just four days after the Supreme Court reaffirms the *Brown* decision. But in a curious twist on the racial conversion narrative, it is clear he had not intended to deliver such a sermon, "Proved by the fact that there was not one mention of desegregation in the sermon notes he prepared so carefully in advance ... [on the topic of] 'Solitude and Self-Realization'" (275). The irony is not lost upon Seth: "As it was, his sermon had been inspired – terrific – superb. He had very little memory of its particulars, but he had the strong suspicion that it was one of his best. As the final twist of the knife, here he was, doubtless about to be crucified for his stand, when in point of fact he did not believe in that stand which he had now so irrevocably and publicly proclaimed!" (276). Not only is Seth not converted, but when he thinks about all of the massive resistance that has been generated by the first *Brown* decision and will be generated with even greater furor in the wake of *Brown II*, Seth bemoans that the "Court's way was not only not the right way but the way of retrenchment and regression and grievous trouble" (278). In fact, none of it seems to make any sense to Seth – when he thinks of how he has been raised "chapter and verse" to believe that "Our Creator segregated man," he "sets this sort of thing against the Court and the NAACP sort of thing ... [and wants] to wash his hands of the whole business" (279–80).

Jim insists that Seth not wash his hands, that he take seriously the words of his sermon and translate those words into deeds (that he opt to be the crucified Christ, not the clean-handed Pilate). First, Jim asks to Seth to recommend him for the janitor's job at First Baptist Church, and perhaps open the doors of that white church to black worshippers. Second, Jim asks Seth to use his position as a member of the school board to support an NAACP petition to enroll Jim's son in town's white school. When Seth insists that Jim is fighting things the wrong way, Jim tells Seth that he takes Seth's sermon from the other day "as a sign that – you have regrets" (200). It is clear that Seth does, but he does not know how to translate those regrets into action. He insists again that Jim's way is the wrong way, and that he will block Jim's attempts to immediately integrate his church and the school. When pushed to say what he will support, Seth falls back on gradualism, telling Jim that "there will have to be a great deal more spadework – lessons in how to deal with hate – *sermons*" (292). But words are not good enough for Jim: he knows that Seth's gradualism is a way to avoid structural changes, and he presses Seth to commit to real action. Finally, Seth agrees to sign the NAACP petition as long as Jim gives him a year to work it through the school board and garner support by appealing "to the best in people rather than waving the red flag at the worst in them" (294). Seth's position remains gradualist, but when he tells his powerful sister Carrie he will be siding with Jim and the forces of integration, he has at least moved beyond words.

What the novel leaves unanswered, but has raised so enticingly, is the question of Seth's racial conversion. The white southern movement novel has many concerns, none more important than how – and whether – structural change will take place in the South. Although *Birthright* gives us a strong black character seeking agency through collective active (the

NAACP), the novel does not, like other works such as Haas's *Look Away, Look Away*, provide an in-depth look at the black community as a force for positive change. In this way, the novel is more closely aligned with the politics that Haddox identifies as essential to the white civil rights novel, a mitigated liberalism that not only treats "political change as the sum of individual changes of the heart rather than as a systemic transformation of policies achievable by collective action," but also insists on representing the white South "as an organic 'community' [that] must painstakingly work out its own salvation without interference from the outside" (563). Such novels, by definition, must embrace the trope of white racial conversion. In creating a character like Seth (an admired preacher with a repressed unorthodox streak), Rogers calls to mind the trope and its attendant anticipations; however, by novel's end she has refused to allow her readers to position *Birthright* comfortably and securely within the "freedom narrative" tradition of white racial conversion. Seth has moved from words to action, that is clear, but those actions may or may not be the result of racial enlightenment. In fact, in the immediate aftermath of his declaration to Carrie that he will push for integration, Seth stands alone on a sidewalk outside of her house, "forgetting where he was and ought to be going" (305). "My God, My God," Seth thinks, using the language of the forsaken rather than the converted. "He wanted to turn around and go back in" (305). He does not, but he is left envisaging the "frightful mess" that lies ahead and wondering if he is "going to be able to take it" (305). It is true that, following Watkins and Haddox, we can find any number of stock figures and predictable tropes in *Birthright*; what is more interesting, perhaps, is how at key moments Rogers refuses to be predictable in the handling of those figures and tropes.[13] The result is a 1957 novel that anticipates structural change in the South, but does not require white conversion at the starting point. Rather, in its own modest way, the novel suggests that the white South need not wait for the certainty of conversion to see its way forward when confusion, allied to action, might do.

In his 1965 novel *Tiger in the Honeysuckle*, Elliot Chaze also engages the trope of white racial conversion, but his handling of the convention shows not only how the genre is adjusting itself to the ever-changing topical realities of the movement, but also how it is doing so with an increased sense of self-awareness and sophistication. The novel opens with civil rights activists from across the nation descending on a mid-sized, fictional city in Mississippi called Catherine. At stake is a successful voter registration drive, and the novel's protagonist, Chris Haines, is a forty-three-year-old reporter for the *Catherine Call* whose sympathies rest more with the city than with the activists. When we first see him, he is ribbing a reporter from the *Detroit*

Daily Sentinel: "How come when we had the flood last year none of you one-world, one-race lads came down to help the Negroes? I never laid eyes on [the] NAACP or SNCC or COFO during the flood.... I didn't see a god-damned thing about it on TV or in *Time* or *Newsweek*" (3). For Haines, the voter registration drive smacks of hypocrisy, and he sees the black protestors as "professional agitators" (6) trained by national civil rights organizations to promote a more insidious agenda than voting rights. We are not surprised, then, that local law enforcement officials watching the march with Haines agree to alert him to any inside information they have because "You're our boy, Chris, you know that" (7).

However, Haines is less their boy than they think. It is true that he tells a northern journalist that "[I am] rooting for [my] team: I was born white and I'm *for* the whites" (10), but his coverage of the registration drive is compromised by the fact that its leader is a local black man named Carver Compton, Haines's childhood playmate. Of course, like all such playmates in the Deep South, they have gone their separate ways, and despite his sympathies, Haines now views Compton with suspicion. At a church rally on the evening following the march, Haines listens to Compton address the protestors. Although he is "irritated to realize he was moved" (12) by some of Compton's anecdotes, Haines understands the whole address as a "classic case of demagoguery" (11), a "thoroughly professional job of heating and cooling and reheating," of "delivering the facts, or what [Compton] reported to be the facts" (12). However, when his editor chastises Haines's "middle-of-the-road" (19) coverage of the rally, the reporter objects that he does not "like [blacks] much individually, or collectively," but "the bastards ought to be allowed to vote" (19). Yet he tempers his sympathy for the movement when he insists that in his coverage he is "not trying to be completely fair.... I back away from [the black man] even more than I used to because it's gotten to be so damned fashionable to feel sorry for them. I despise people who feel a certain way just because they read that's the way they ought to feel" (20).

Protestations aside, Haines is not backing away completely from the cause of the black man, and as the novel progresses he moves in fits and starts toward racial conversion. When Compton is arrested on bogus assault charges that will surely land him in prison for many years, Haines agrees to testify in Compton's defense. He understands how this decision will affect his position in town, and he begins to resist his own conversion. "Certainly he was no professional martyr," he muses, "the professional-martyr market was jammed to overflowing without him, southerners who turned against their own kind so they could wallow in the admiration of northerners and a few southern liberals, or clean up the cash writing brave pieces for the slick magazines" (72). Still, when in the case preceding Compton's trial he watches the local judge give five white fraternity boys from Ole Miss minor probation for a series of robberies, Haines refuses to laugh it off with the others during a recess. When the "judge smiled at him and beckoned ... [Haines] arose and walked to the bench, willing himself not to react in the old pattern. There had to be a starting place. This was as good as any" (102).

After he testifies on Compton's behalf, most of the city turns on him and he is asked to take a vacation from the newspaper. However, although the city believes he no longer defends the "southern way of life," Haines is not so certain he has rejected the old pattern, nor is he convinced he has been converted to something new. When a Justice Department official tells Haines, "I get the word you're with us," Haines insists, "I'm not with anybody.... I think qualified niggers should be allowed to vote and that's the size of it" (172). Despite such protests, Haines is clearly being pulled into sympathy with the movement. His disgust with "the relentless hypocrisy of the intellectual southerner," coupled with his growing attraction to one of the black civil rights workers, has Haines questioning his own confident bigotry: "How much parental propaganda and plain general bullshit did you have to swallow ..." Haines asks, "before you could sit on a city bus and watch a pregnant Negro woman stagger to the back end [of a bus] with an armload of bundles" and never think to help her (184–85). As he looks back at the hatred he has imbibed as a white southerner, he concludes, "It was enough to make you puke if you reviewed carefully the filth and hypocrisy that had been pumped through your head in forty-odd years" (191). Although Haines will occasionally resist the full implications of racial conversion, Chaze makes it clear a conversion has occurred. During a race riot in the black section of town, Haines defends an injured black woman against a mob of white racists, and a few days later he quits the newspaper, refusing to tell the owner that he is "a believer in the Southern Heritage" (245). As Haines sees it, "If you subtracted the racial situation, there was no friendlier bunch of people on the face of the earth than the people of Catherine. But, of course, you couldn't subtract it. The disease was in terminal stage, inoperable" (248).

Whereas Rogers's twist on the conversion narrative is to leave the conversion ambiguous – and thereby to question whether it is necessary for progress on race – Chaze empties the trope of its power to move the converted into "the liberty of free association, free expression, brotherhood, [and] sisterhood" that Hobson claims is indicative of the genre. Instead, the converted white southerner in *Tiger in the Honeysuckle* is thrust into loneliness and despair. Urging himself one afternoon to "Drink [yet] another drink" and wondering what for, Haines concludes, "For nothing. A lot of things are worse than nothing, drink another drink. *Drink to … your liberation*" (274, italics added). Instead of finding solace or strength in his newfound sympathies, he feels only loss, concluding that "Perhaps the most terrible thing about the human equation … was the fact that a man lived anxiously all of the days of his life.… It was fear from start to finish, anxiety was the timid word for it" (278). Even when he manages to muster enough care to attend one more civil rights rally at the local black church at the end of the novel, he questions the progress that will be brought about by the movement, even if it does convert men like him, who had learned to "contradict everything [they'd] ever been taught to believe in."

> [He] had no illusions about the Negro blossoming graciously into full citizenship, abruptly laying aside the suspicion and hostility of centuries as soon as the battle was done. If ever it was done.… The black man … [had] been hungry too long to play patty-cake. It was going to be a nerve-wracking mess, complete with hackles and blood, a miserable and enervating struggle for adjustment. (299)

Haines's disenchantment and self-doubt are striking, but what is more striking still is what he decides to do next. As he listens to the singing of the protesters, Haines pieces together a series of conversations from the last few weeks and concludes that Klansmen have planted a bomb in the church. Not wanting to cause a panic, he searches for the bomb by himself, finally discovering it in the church basement. Unable to defuse the mechanism, Haines crawls out a basement window and sprints away from the church, hoping to toss the bomb into a nearby storm sewer. But as he runs "dizzily, squinting against the sweat and the glare of [a] street light," he feels something slam "the front of him as if he had hit a wall of stone and fire and there were lights, orange, pink, and blue.… He was lifted high and then he fell, the falling very soft and curved and silent" (303).

In a sophisticated final chapter, Chaze continues to empty the white racial conversion narrative of its transformational power. At first, this is not easy to see because the death of a white martyr appears to have rekindled the spirit of the local movement. Having dwindled at one point to only nine marchers, the demonstrations have been revitalized, for "the day after the bombing, the [march] was as massive as it had been at the beginning." It is tempting to read this revitalization as affirming the inspirational power of white racial conversion; however, Chaze constructs this chapter in ways that mitigate against, even undermine, such a reading. The chapter opens, for instance, in words that repeat, nearly verbatim, the first few lines of the novel. Whereas the novel opens with, "There they were, marching in the cold rain in front of the Courthouse, a hundred and twenty-five of them, young and old, white and black, most of them Negroes of school age. Across the street from the Courthouse the front doors of Sears were locked and clerks breathed against the glass, staring out at the demonstrators in the hurt and puzzled manner of a person who gazes at a boil that has come to a head" (1), the final chapter opens with, "There they were, marching in the warm rain in front of the Courthouse, a hundred and thirty of them, young and old, white and black. Across the street from the Courthouse in the front of Sears five police riot squadmen stood in yellows slickers, plastic helmets shining, staring from beneath their visors in the hurt and puzzled manner of a person who gazes at a boil that has come to a head" (304). These repetitions, combined with seven other repetitions that mark this brief two-page chapter, suggest that Chaze is problematizing a redemptive reading of Haines's death. Such a redemptive reading may be possible, but the repetitions seduce us into a more cynical interpretation of the novel's narrative arc: the more things change, the more they remain the same – and white racial conversion, although it can happen, provides no assurance that we are moving toward a beloved community of free association, free expression, brotherhood, sisterhood – and freedom from racial guilt. In fact, it provides no assurance of movement at all.

When Flannery O'Connor warned her friend Betty Hester that the topical was poison, she was referring not only to a very specific topic (the civil rights movement) but also to how that topic was likely to play out on the page (as "typical life in the dear old dirty Southland"). On the one hand, O'Connor was right. Could southern writers depict the civil rights movement in action without portraying their dear old homeland as anything other than dirty with bigots and agitators, night-riders and demonstrators? Probably not. And could they do so without falling into patterns so repetitive as to become, in the hands of the least among them, "formulaic, predictable, and often laughable." Again, probably not. But this is to miss the point. Even so astute a historian as C. Vann Woodward had to confess that the movement was like a "drama [that] unfolded on a familiar stage, with scenes deploying old settings." It played out, just as the "First Reconstruction" had, with a "cast of characters [who] mouthed the old lines and rattled the old stage swords," and with plotlines that repeated "the inevitable confrontations: North with South, black with white, federal power with states rights ... true believer with skeptic, Northern missionary with harsh reality, Southern paternalist with alienated beneficiary."[14] Fortunately, many of O'Connor's peers ignored her warning – instead, they embraced the challenge to say something meaningful, even prophetic, about the inevitable confrontations taking place all around them, no matter how often the cast of characters kept mouthing the same old lines and rattling the same old swords. In the end, the civil rights movement did not poison southern fiction of the 1950s and 1960s. If we are looking for poison, perhaps we – not the topical – are its source. From the beginning, too many critics believed that the white southern novelists of the civil rights movement had nothing to teach us, that their works were propaganda not art, their characters oversimplified not complex, their tropes tired, their plots conventional, their insights mundane. But maybe it was not, as Watkins proclaimed, "the art of fiction ... [that] died in novels about race since the Supreme Court decision of 1954." Perhaps it was the art of reading them.

NOTES

1 Flannery O'Connor, Letter to "A," September 1, 1963, *Habits of Being: The Letters of Flannery O'Connor*, ed. Sally Fitzgerald (New York: Farrar, Straus and Giroux), p. 357.
2 See Thomas F. Haddox, "Elizabeth Spencer, the White Civil Rights Novel, and the Postsouthern," *MLQ: Modern Language Quarterly* 65.4 (December 2004): 561–81; Suzanne Jones, *Race Mixing: Southern Fiction since the Sixties* (Baltimore, MD: Johns Hopkins University Press, 2004); Riché Richardson, "'The Birth of a Nation'hood': Lessons from Thomas Dixon and D. W. Griffith to William Bradford Huie and *The Klansman*, O. J. Simpson's First Movie," *Mississippi Quarterly* 56.1 (Winter 2002–2003): 3–31; Sharon Monteith, "'The 1960s Echo On': Images of Martin Luther King Jr. as Deployed by White Writers of Contemporary Fiction," *Media, Culture, and the Modern African American Freedom Struggle*, ed. Brian Ward (Gainesville: University Press of Florida, 2002); and Monteith, "Civil Rights Fiction," *The Cambridge Companion to the Literature of the American South*, ed. Sharon Monteith (New York: Cambridge University Press, 2013), pp. 159–73. More attention has been paid to white southern movement novels written after the movement than during the movement, such as Ellen Douglass's *The Rock Cried Out* (1979), Rosellen Brown's *Civil* Wars (1984), Butler's *Jujitsu for Christ* (1986), and Lewis Nordan's *Wolf Whistle* (1993). However, those novels, although part of a more expansive understanding of the genre, fall outside the purview of this chapter. As the full genre becomes more theorized, these later novels may emerge as "neo-white southern movement novels," much along the lines that Brian Norman has argued for "neo-segregation narratives," which are "post–civil rights" stories that offer "contemporary fictional accounts, often historiographic, of Jim Crow," but do so while their authors "write from a post–civil rights era and its inclusive, multi-cultural sensibilities while their characters inhabit the terrain of compulsory race segregation." Brian Norman, *Neo-Segregation Narratives: Jim Crow in Post–Civil Rights American Literature* (Athens: University of Georgia Press, 2010), p. 3. It is interesting to note that the two most-studied white novels about race written during the movement, Harper Lee's *To Kill a Mockingbird* (1960) and William Styron's *Confessions of Nat Turner* (1968), do not take place during the movement. Whether they can be considered "movement novels" is a

matter for debate. For a discussion of Lee's novel as such, see Eric J. Sundquist, "Blues for Atticus Finch: Scottsboro, *Brown*, and Harper Lee," in *The South as an American Problem*, ed. Larry J. Griffin and Don H. Doyle (Athens: University of Georgia Press, 1995), pp. 181–209.

3   Richard H. King, "Politics and Fictional Representation: The Case of the Civil Rights Movement," *The Making of Martin Luther King and the Civil Rights Movement*, ed. Brian Ward and Anthony Badger (New York: New York University Press, 1996), pp. 162–78.

4   Floyd Watkins, *The Death of Art: Black and White in the Recent Southern Novel* (Macon, GA: Mercer University Press, 1970), p. 1. Subsequent page number references given in text.

5   James McBride Dabbs, *Civil Rights in Recent Southern Fiction* (Atlanta: Southern Regional Council, 1969). Page number references given in text.

6   Haddox, "Elizabeth Spencer," p. 561. Subsequent page number references given in text.

7   In "Civil Rights Fiction," Monteith makes a similar distinction, albeit less explicitly than I do. Acknowledging Haddox "as one of the few critics to formulate how the 'white civil rights novel' understands civil rights as a theme" (163), Monteith nonetheless limits the focus of her essay on "civil rights fiction" to "literature that focuses on the Movement – stories about civil rights organizations, voter registration and demonstration, and activists in the African–American freedom struggle." She does so because this type of literature "differs from fiction that locates 'civil rights' within the broad theme of race relations" (161). Thus, although she retains "civil rights fiction" to describe the genre she is demarcating, we both agree that movement narratives differ in kind from more general civil rights narratives.

8   On the "long civil rights movement," see Jacquelyn Dowd Hall, "The Long Civil Rights Movement and the Political Uses of the Past," *Journal of American History* 91.4 (2005): 1233–63. For critics who defend maintaining the uniqueness of the "short civil rights movement," see Steven F. Lawson, "The Long Origins of the Short Civil Rights Movement," *Freedom Rights: New Perspectives on the Civil Rights Movement*, eds. John Dittmer and Danielle McGuire (Lexington: University of Kentucky Press, 2011), pp. 9–37; Sundiata Cha-Jua and Clarence Lang, "The 'Long Movement' as Vampire: Temporal and Spatial Fallacies in Recent Black Freedom Studies," *Journal of African American History* 92.2 (Spring 2007): 265–88; and King, *Civil Rights and the Idea of Freedom* (Athens: University of Georgia Press, 1996).

9   William Sloan, *Tear Gas and Hungry Dogs* (New York: Midwood-Tower, 1963).

10   Lettie Hamlett Rogers, *Birthright* (New York: Simon and Schuster, 1957); Elliot Chaze, *Tiger in the Honeysuckle* (New York: Scribners, 1965). Page number references given in text.

11   Haddox makes a similar connection to this trope in his essay.

12   Fred Hobson, *But Now I See: The White Southern Racial Conversion Narrative* (Baton Rouge: Louisiana State University Press, 1999), p. 1. Subsequent page number references given in text.

13   In a review of the novel in *Phylon*, James W. Byrd argued, "To do justice to this book in a short review is difficult. It would be easy to write a critical

review about certain triteness in plot and subplot, as well as obscurity in style. On the other hand, it would be even easier to write a review praising it as a novel about social justice, with some fine uses of satire, symbolism, and stream-of-consciousness. But to combine the two views honestly is a difficult job" (312). "Conflict, Prejudice and Hope in the South," *Phylon* 18.3 (1957): 312–13.

14 C. Vann Woodward, "What Happened to the Civil Rights Movement?" *Harper's* (January 1967): 29–37.

7

SHARON MONTEITH

Civil Rights Movement Film

Fiction writers have been cautious about how best to explore the African American freedom struggle and the politics of segregation in the civil rights South. Eudora Welty grappled with the aesthetic choices involved in writing political fiction in her essay "Must the Writer Crusade?" (1965), even as she created two of the most evocative civil rights stories in "Where Is the Voice Coming From?" (1963) and "The Demonstrators" (1966). Ralph Ellison expressed the idea that "revolutionary social political movements move much too rapidly to be treated as the subjects for literature in themselves."[1] Writers on both sides of the civil rights barricades found very different ways to tell stories of changing race relations in the 1950s and 1960s South, sometimes in quiet novels like Madison Jones's *A Cry of Absence* (1971) but more often in loud pulp fictions, while journalists turned what they witnessed on the civil rights beat into thrillers. The civil rights movement contained all the elements to inspire creative writers: courage in the face of violence, conflict in the face of social change, a moment in history when an old order fell. But many serious writers are wary of the subject when so much racial violence couched as massive resistance is such recent history. As Jack Butler observed in the 1990s, "There's still a lot of sheriffs out there with cowboy hats, big fat bellies and mirror shades, but try getting away with using one as a character." More soberly, he confided, "I do not see how we can afford to forget that there are murderers who have never come to trial walking the streets of the New South, some of them wearing badges still. The question for writers is how we observe these things, with what new manner of awareness."[2]

Stock character types proliferate, especially in cinema: the segregationist sheriff and his deputies; Klansmen and violent "rednecks"; corrupt politicians and planter-style patriarchs; and civil rights organizers conceived solely and erroneously as northern "outside agitators" fighting against white conservators of "our way of life." This typology is most familiar from fiction films, although it was a staple of 1950s pulp fictions and still finds its way into contemporary fiction, despite Butler's warning. It is a simplification of racial politics that elides the African American communities and civil rights organizations that forged social change.[3] More prevalent still are comforting feel-good dramas in which resolution and racial reconciliation are privileged over political struggle, and cross-racial friendship is featured, like Kathryn Stockett's bestselling novel *The Help* (2009) which Julie Armstrong, in her chapter for this volume, evokes as a typical "easy-bake" civil rights narrative: "mix together a black and white 'best friend,' toss in a villain, then – (as the original commercial jingle goes) 'slide 'em in / slide 'em out / Easy-Bake Wow!' – civil rights problem solved."[4]

When contemporary filmmakers turn to civil rights as a theme, all too often they risk underestimating audiences. Time and again the celluloid civil rights story is told as if for the first time – if it is really told at all. What changes is the lens through which the story is told: the point of view of young white "Skeeter" Phelan (Emma Stone) beginning to comprehend the deleterious effects of segregation on the lives of black maids in 1960s Mississippi because they agree to let her write about them, in the 2011 film adaptation of *The Help*; or of Cecil Gaines (Forest Whitaker), who serves eight presidents assiduously in *The Butler* (2013) and struggles with his allegiance to the civil rights cause when his son Louis (David Oyelowo) becomes an activist. In *The Butler* civil rights activism forms a subplot while in *The Help* it is little more than period texture. *The Help* isn't really "about" civil rights, despite the fact that both novel and film have been described and marketed as such. Fred Zollo, a producer with a long and difficult experience of bringing civil rights stories to audiences, with *Mississippi Burning* (1988) and *Ghosts of Mississippi* (1996), is quoted as observing that *The Help* is "hardly a civil rights film at all," and when *The Help* is located within scholarship on civil rights cinema, the verdict is similar.[5]

The Help and *The Butler* are representative in that the movement era is usually depicted in morality tales in movies, African Americans still feature in service roles, and the protagonist comes to consciousness of the need for social change rather than campaigning to achieve it. This is a successful formula as box-office figures show, with *The Help*'s $55,000,000 budget achieving a worldwide gross of $210,708,112 on cinema release, before DVD sales and streaming figures are added, and *The Butler*'s $57,000,000 commitment achieving $167,743,114 to date.[6] While box office receipts and consumer choice are not reliable gauges of the state of the nation, big budget films as well as more personal projects, like the Michelle Pfeiffer-backed *Love Field* (1992), typically translate large and complex historical and political issues into domestic situations. That is the case even when the situation is the assassination of John F. Kennedy in *Love Field*, or the setting is the

White House in *The Butler*, with Presidents Truman to Johnson struggling to balance attention to voting blocs behind segregationist politicians with escalating pressure to commit to federal legislation on civil rights.

Filmmakers find other means to ensure that audiences leave the theater with a light didactic dusting of "civil rights history," usually contrived as a series of flashpoints in a montage of television news footage. The burning of the bus in Anniston, Alabama, that temporarily stopped the Freedom Rides in 1961; the first attempt to cross the bridge at Selma when marchers were beaten and gassed in March 1965; the assassination of Martin Luther King in April 1968 and scenes of demonstrations in the streets stand in for more a complex understanding of what the civil rights movement was then and what it means now. The era is collapsed into television news sound bites that can be inserted into movies quickly and efficiently. This is one reason that the domestic context looms so large. In the film of Stockett's novel, "the help" find ways to watch civil rights demonstrations on television and listen to breaking news on the radio, specifically the report of the murder of NAACP leader Medgar Evers, in Jackson on June 12, 1963. Louis's activist role is so over-determined in *The Butler* that, as David Denby observes, it verges on parody because he is never allowed to miss "a history-making scene."[7] He is, it appears, the Forrest Gump of the contemporary civil rights fiction film.[8] Louis seems to be a member of all the major civil rights organizations simultaneously: he is present at the 1960 sit-ins and on a bus for the Freedom Rides; he is in Memphis when King is assassinated, and in Oakland to attend the first Black Panther rallies. He is a cipher for a political shift from an integrationist to a black nationalist agenda (in reality a complex series of political positions that did not neatly follow such a linear trajectory). Louis's story is told with an economy of style – with economy in this context also risking attenuation and commodification. Cliché is the risk and often the result when the same montage of widely used archival clips is the sole form of historical exposition and the standard authentication in civil rights cinema. Another risk is that audiences – not only those who lived through the 1960s but also younger generations knowledgeable about the rich and varied history of the civil rights era – will become desensitized by the same signature scenes operating as a familiar shorthand. Despite persistent reminders in montage sequences that civil rights was a heroic struggle and that social change did not come easily, the overriding message for audiences is that the "problem" was contained and, indeed, resolved in the 1960s – at least in the lives of the characters who carry the stories.

Character-led dramas, like *The Butler* inspired by Eugene Allen's service in the White House from 1952 to 1986, echo earlier films, including those for which memoirs and histories rather than fictions are source texts. Such films promote a single point of view to create what has ubiquitously come to be known as a "usable past." *The Butler* may be read in that continuum although, notably, it stands out as a result of its African American director and protagonist, while *The Help* is merely one in a long line of racial conversion narratives, a familiar paradigm in which white women protagonists are the focalizers of coming-of-age-in-the-era-of-civil-rights tales, like *Heart of Dixie*, the 1989 adaptation of Anne River Siddons's novel *Heartbreak Hotel* (1976), *The Long Walk Home* (1990), and *Love Field*. Such films function in a postmodern imaginary as socially symbolic texts in which issues that could not be resolved in the civil rights era find temporary resolution in narrative space, as when Lurene (Michelle Pfeiffer) waits for Paul (Dennis Haybert) at the end of *Love Field*, with the implication that they will live happily, and even easily together in 1964, despite interracial relationships being subject to Jim Crow laws and illegal in most southern states until overturned by the Supreme Court in the *Loving* decision of 1967.

By telling very particular stories, some films made in the 1980s and 1990s did succeed in conveying the intensity, and something of the complexity, of precise moments in civil rights history. *Crisis at Central High* (1981) was based on Elizabeth Huckaby's journals during the 1957 Little Rock school crisis in which, as a result of translating the *Brown v. Board* decision into reality in her school, she found her position changing from a conservative moderate who had neglected to address separate and unequal schools even as an educator, to a more active supporter of racial integration. *The Long Walk Home* is a beautifully realized period recreation of the Montgomery Bus Boycott, but it pushes the black boycotters to the background by foregrounding a white protagonist in Miriam (Sissie Spacek). Her development from upholder of the racial status quo ("The rest of the world around you is living that way so you just don't question it") to a determined supporter of the boycott provides the narrative impetus for the film. Novelist Reynolds Price once confided, "Now when I see [documentary] films of the flocking brave faces, black and white, of the early civil rights movement … I'm more than sorry that my face is missing."[9] In the 1980s and 1990s, fiction films began to insert the missing faces of white moderates into the celluloid civil rights story and, as a consequence, African Americans were carefully contained in auxiliary roles.

This is not to say that attempts were not made to depict African Americans in the movement, or indeed civil rights organizations on screen – but television rather than cinema carried the day. In 1978, ten years after he died, the made-for-television biopic *King* was released with Paul Winfield in the lead role. Abby Mann's six-hour biography was an epic project that aired in three episodes on NBC, but it provoked a barrage of complaints from members of the Southern Christian Leadership Conference (SCLC), arguing that the role white lawyer Stanley Levinson played in Dr. King's life and politics was exaggerated by Mann, and that King's decisiveness, as well as the significance of his associates in SCLC, was downplayed or elided. These debates, which took place in the press, were indicative of two main anxieties for African American viewers and critics: that whites not be presented as leading or influencing the movement – an issue that would still be debated fiercely a decade later over the film *Mississippi Burning* – and that icons such as Dr. King not only be portrayed as the heroes they were but also as steadfast and unwavering. By depicting discussion, doubt, and division within SCLC, the worry was that Mann's film risked undermining what SCLC had achieved for mainstream audiences for whom this film would be the first popular representation of the organization. The impossible tension between the "easy-bake" formula and realistic political representation inherent in such debates also aggravated hesitancy on the part of production companies and film directors.

Embarrassment at Home and Propaganda Abroad

Television's market leadership in civil rights drama is underlined in Elayne Rapping's assertion that "more than any other fictional form," TV movies "call on us to think and act as citizens in a public social sphere."[10] Television films like *The Autobiography of Miss Jane Pittman* (1973), and *For Us the Living* (1983), based on Medgar Evers's life and his wife Myrlie Evers's memoir, and series such as *Roots: The Next Generations* (1979) located the civil rights movement within the long struggle for freedom. But when cinema (re)connected with the history of the racially segregated South, the push was toward closure on the struggle for racial justice. The nostalgic sensibility that infuses the majority of fiction films literally whitewashes the civil rights era. This was made painfully apparent in the furor over *Mississippi Burning* (1988), Hollywood's first big budget civil rights movie. Former activists and spokespeople including NAACP Executive Director Benjamin Hooks and Coretta Scott King decried the film's distortion of history in representing the heroics of white FBI agents over courageous black southerners and civil rights organizers – and over the story of the brave young activists whose murders the FBI were charged with investigating. Scott King called it "Hollywood's latest perversion" of the civil rights era, and Barbara Reynolds in *USA Today* summarized the problem of what Armstrong now calls an "easy-bake" narrative: "Unless Hollywood cookie-cutters stop stamping out more films like 'Mississippi Burning,' they'll reduce real life black heroes to pitiful bit players in their own drama."[11] Controversy put paid to Academy acclaim for *Mississippi Burning*. Although the film was nominated for Oscars in seven categories – including for best director and best picture – it won only one award for cinematography. When Alan Parker came to direct *Mississippi Burning* it was from Chris Gerolmo's script, based on Don Whitehead's *Attack on Terror* (1970), which had already been made for television in 1975. But Parker underestimated the increasing investment activists and historians had in getting civil rights history right, especially in the Reagan era.

Studying film history for how civil rights movies fared in previous decades would have helped Parker very little in 1988. Hollywood had steered wide of the movement until *Mississippi Burning*. Film historian Thomas Cripps posits that "events provided Eisenhower with an opening to act boldly in using federal powers to hold open the schools of Little Rock, far earlier than they provided Hollywood with a crisis it could understand well enough to formulate into politically engaging or even informative movies."[12] However, Hollywood's understanding of the situation and any desire to turn it into political cinema were secondary to its fear of political repercussions and box-office failure. In 1966, while adapting Jesse Hill Ford's novel *The Liberation of Lord Byron Jones* (1965) for the screen, Stirling Silliphant admitted that civil rights was "a subject which has big studios more than slightly wary," even with Columbia Pictures on board and veteran William Wyler to direct. Adapting a source text like Ford's controversial novel was, Silliphant felt, a leap of faith for a studio: "the very rich Negro of the title ... is cuckolded by a white man and, as a man cherishing his dignity, demands that his white lawyer get him a divorce – an action that uncovers a barrel of civil rights fish in a Southern town that is enough to scare a senator or a studio chief."[13] Lack of attention to civil rights was underpinned by film production companies assuming that the issues at hand would have only minority audience appeal as "Negro material."

At the same time, many African American commentators were also insistent about the ways in which cinema audiences were racially differentiated when it came to civil rights themes. In his essays on film culture collected in *The Devil Finds Work* (1976), James Baldwin described Harlem moviegoers reacting with loud outrage during a screening of *The Defiant Ones* (1958) when escaped prisoner Noah (Sidney Poitier) decides to remain with his former nemesis Joker (Tony Curtis) in the final frames and leaps from the train that would carry him away to freedom to hold an injured Joker in his arms as prison officers close in. When the audience yelled for him to get back on the train, Baldwin decided that the deus ex machina was intended to delude white Americans into believing they were not resented by black Americans. Similarly, in an essay that charged Hollywood with being "the most Anti-Negro influence in the nation," John O. Killens was scathing about *Band of Angels* (1959), the film based on Robert Penn Warren's novel:

> In one particular scene, Clark Gable, who was Sidney Poitier's good massa, was coming from New Orleans via the Mississippi River back to his plantation. As the boat neared the shore, all of his happy faithful slaves were gathered there singing a song of welcome to old massa. White people in the theatre were weeping, some slyly, some unashamedly, at the touching scene, when suddenly my friend and I erupted with laughter because we thought that surely, in the time of Montgomery and Little Rock, this must have been put into the film for comic relief.[14]

Even when Hollywood made films billed as exposés of lynching – a rite of racial terrorism closely associated with massive resistance to civil rights initiatives in the South – criticism of white supremacy was studiously avoided. In *Storm Warning* (1950), the lead characters are all white, including the northern journalist investigating the Ku Klux Klan who is dragged from the jail and lynched. The film's tagline "Behind their cowardly hoods they hide a thousand vicious crimes" is made all the more ironic in a film that hides racial terrorism so completely.

Outside of the United States, however, cinematic critiques of white supremacy were becoming a sub-genre in themselves. Soviet propaganda films fixated on U.S. race relations. In 1932, Langston Hughes and novelist Dorothy West traveled to the Soviet Union with twenty other African American actors and consultants to work on a film that would be set in Birmingham, Alabama, with the title "Black and White." As Hughes reveals in his memoir, the screenplay was "so interwoven with major and minor impossibilities and improbabilities that it would have seemed like a burlesque on the screen."[15] Hughes reworked the screenplay while in Russia but, in the end, the decision not to proceed was made because the Soviet film industry felt the film "could not do justice to the oppressed and segregated Negroes of the world." Hughes was struck by the realization that politics rather than finance was dictating the terms, and touched by a demonstration in support of the Scottsboro Boys at the Park of Rest and Culture in Moscow. "I guess it's the red that makes the difference. I'll be glad when Chicago gets that way, and Birmingham," he wrote with bitter irony.[16] If "Black and White" was never made, other films were, like *The Circus* (1937), for example, in which a white American mother of a biracial child is subjected to racism in the United States and escapes to Russia for a better life.

European cinema was almost equally condemning of America's flouting of civil rights, with French films in particular reconfiguring southern race relations, and Richard Wright a major influence on both writers and filmmakers. Wright agreed to act as consultant for the 1952 film version of Jean Paul Sartre's *La Putain Respecteuse* (1946), and Boris Vian's pulp novel *J'Irai Cracher sur Vos Tombes* (1946) was a grotesque pastiche of the segregated southern culture Wright depicted. Michel Gast's 1959 adaptation of Vian's novel was a sensationalist culmination of America's civil rights problems in the French imaginary, with Mexican publicity declaring, "Only the French cinema has dared to present the horrible problem of discrimination" and a Memphis exhibitor facing charges for screening the exploitation movie. Despite its implausible visualization of the South – shot as it was on location in France and Italy – its strident critique hit home and the city's film censors feared that it depicted the "questionable morals of a southern town, supposedly Memphis." In fact, only the word "Memphis" uttered once in heavily accented French signals any possible correlation with the actual Southern city.[17]

In U.S. film culture there were many ways of containing the politics while entertaining the audience. Films that examined civil rights struggles in any guise at all were typically reviewed as "melodrama" or "social problem pictures." Genre classification and review culture did not, of course, dictate public response, but they could lead the terms of audience engagement and reception, and they certainly indicated that influential film reviewers rarely correlated southern cinema with racial politics. The indexing used by the American Film Institute Catalog is indicative, with *The Liberation of L.B. Jones* (1970) classified as melodrama and cross-referenced under the headings "Negroes," "Police," "Lawyers," "Undertakers," "Mistresses," "Mayors," "Revenge," "Race Relations," "Miscegenation," "Divorce," "Infidelity," "Murder," "Castration," "Lawsuits," and finally "Tennessee."[18] The terms are elliptical at best. *Nothing But a Man* (1964) was described by contemporary reviewers simply as a "small-town" movie even though Malcolm X reputedly described it as the most important movie ever made about the black experience in America. Indeed, *New York Times* reviewer Bosley Crowther, eschewing *Nothing But a Man*'s materialist depiction of Korean War veteran Duff Anderson (Ivan Dixon) and his failure to find an economic foothold in the segregated South, succeeded in obscuring its politics altogether: "On the surface and in the present climate, it might seem a drama of race relations in the South, and in a couple of sharp exchanges of the hero with arrogant white men, the ugly face of imminent racial conflict shows. But essentially it is a drama of the emotional adjustment of a man to the age-old problem of earning a livelihood [*sic*], supporting a family and maintaining his dignity."[19] On the film's re-release in 1997, Roger Ebert's assessment could not have been more different from conservative Crowther's: he celebrated *Nothing But a Man* as remarkable for *not* having employed the liberal pieties of the period and for failing to reassure white audiences that "all stories have happy endings."[20] By the end of the 1990s, after a clutch of comforting dramas, its re-release was an intervention in the field.

Mapping and defining the civil rights fiction film entails revisiting brave low-budget movies that were unappreciated on release or safely folded into other cinema categories to undercut their impact as political cinema. It also involves reading backward through film history to uncover the occasions when civil rights challenges were thwarted by self-censorship of producers or directors, or depicted only in subplots.

Almost-Films and Civil Rights Subplots

Even moguls like Howard Hughes were wary of storylines that lay outside the pale of the Hollywood dream factory. In 1943, Hughes imagined a project in which Hattie McDaniel would play Harriet Tubman in a "sure-enough *Gone With the Wind* that shows how slavery was wiped out and how courageous Negro men and women helped to wipe it out." When in the same year Langston Hughes asked "Is Hollywood Fair to Negroes?" the unlikelihood of Howard Hughes's project ever being made would be the evidence he used to prove it was not.[21] In the United States, politically aware artists and writers often failed to bring to the screen the civil rights stories they hoped to tell and had to find other cultural forms in which to tell them. Duke Ellington collaborated with Hollywood film writers on *Jump for Joy* (1941). In 1972 he recalled the project as "an attempt to correct the race situation in the USA through a form of theatrical propaganda," designed to "eliminate the stereotyped image that had been exploited by Hollywood and Broadway, and say things that would make the audience think."[22] Perhaps the best-known song in this musical critique of Hollywood, before the show suffered piecemeal censorship, was "Uncle Tom's Cabin Is a Drive-in Now." The lyrics proclaimed: "Jemima don't work no more for RKO / She's slinging hash for Uncle Tom and coinin' dough / Just turn on your headlights, and she'll take a bow / 'Cause Uncle Tom's Cabin is a drive-in now."

A byproduct of Hollywood's disinclination to address such topics was a proliferation of exploitation and "drive-in" movies that manipulated civil rights as sensationalism, as discussed later. But one film idea that never made it to the screen exemplifies the problems inherent in translating a vicious racist murder into a feature film. In 1960, William Bradford Huie would celebrate the liberalization of the film industry's self-censorship and tell the *New York Times* that United Artists was interested in financing his 1957 story "Wolf Whistle." Based on the investigative journalism he carried out around the horrific racist murder of fourteen-year-old Emmett Till in the Mississippi Delta in 1955, Huie had already created an exploitation film title and called his story a "true crime original."[23] In a "Note" to the first version of his screenplay, he declared, "the film aims to present the race-sex conflict so realistically that it can almost physically involve every viewer. One character or another will voice the attitudes of every viewer.... The Murder consumes the entire Third Act and must be so real that viewers can feel the blows."[24]

In the midst of the third act Big Matt (based on J. W. "Big" Milam who confessed the murder to Huie) is striking Bobo (Till) with the barrel of his gun. At this point, Huie interjects with a signal to potential producer Louis de Rochemont and United Artists: "these scenes will be perhaps the most brutal ever shown on the screen: race-sex hate – raw and in the dark. The viewer must be made to FEEL the obscenities and the blows" (104). The murder is comprised of graphic scenes intercut with other scenes in which the murderers defend their actions. Repeated assertions of Bobo's "defiance" and "taunts" also pepper the screenplay. One imagines United Artists becoming increasingly anxious as to how this film would be received. The first version of Huie's treatment closes with a question: "What should a white man DO when a Negro youth reaches for the hand of a white girl?" The worrying implication is that a racist murderer should be understood, if not condoned. His revised script ends with a somewhat clearer public condemnation of Big Matt: "His neighbors no longer seek his company.... It's not that they wish him ill.... It's just that they feel uncomfortable when he's around. Big Matt can't understand these white folks ... for, as he himself will tell you, he hasn't changed ... not at all."[25] Even if the revised ending nods toward those white southerners extricating themselves from the stranglehold of white supremacist thinking as the result of Till's murder, Huie would admit later that "there seemed no way to make a film about two men who casually murder a boy and then escape punishment with the blessing of their peers."[26]

In 1965 the movie columnist Louella Parsons would report that another of Huie's projects, *Three Lives for Mississippi* (1964), based on the tragic and vicious slaying of activists Michael Schwerner and James Chaney and Mississippi Freedom Summer volunteer Andrew Goodman in 1964, had been bought by an independent, Joseph Besch of Ron Parlo Productions. She posited that Burt Lancaster or Marlon Brando would take the role of the investigative journalist.[27] Unsurprisingly, that film was never made either. Circumspection about how racial terrorism could or should be dramatized was understandable and responsible, but it was also bound up in the image of the South's racial history in the national imaginary that C. Vann Woodward distilled in *The Burden of Southern History* (1955): "The experience of evil and the experience of tragedy are parts of the southern heritage that are as difficult to reconcile with the American legend of innocence and social felicity as the experience of poverty and defeat are to reconcile with the legends of abundance and success."[28] Therefore, some filmmakers would attempt to engage with southern racial change in other ways and outside the region.

One intriguing example is the California-set *Giant* (1956). While the film is remembered mainly for the presence of James Dean in what would be his final role, J. E. Smyth's archival research has found that in the October 1954 version of the script, director George Stevens and the screen writers adapting Edna Ferber's novel "skillfully reinforced some aspects of Jim Crow culture without visualizing the segregation of African Americans in the South." Their attempt to find a way to reflect the *Brown* decision, handed down by the Supreme Court on May 17, 1954, was reworked by April 1955 and would not find its way into the final film.[29] What does remain is an underlying tension between white Texans and Mexican immigrants and thereby an allegorical connection to the situation in the South may be implied – but without the specificity of *Brown*.

In his attempt to reflect the significance of civil rights, Otto Preminger went so far as to add a sequence to *The Cardinal* (1963), the film he based on the picaresque 1950 novel by Henry Morton Robinson. He created a new African American character, Father Gillis (Ossie Davis), who visits the Vatican in 1934 to entreat papal support for desegregating his church in Georgia:

> Quite a few of the folks in my parish, they feel it's time to make some changes. So a bunch of them went and threw a picket line around that white school. Then I got a lot of phone calls and letters with no names signed. And then one night these men with white hoods, they burned my church.

The lone American in the Vatican, the white cardinal of the film's title, supports his plea and follows Gillis back to Georgia where both priests are badly beaten by the Klan for their endeavors. Preminger's insertion of this new storyline,[30] and his cutting directly to the Nazi persecution of Jews and Catholics in Vienna in the next sequence, makes clear his approach to civil rights. That he also imagined a sheriff who supports the priests in bringing the Klan to justice is an acknowledgment that Preminger's understanding of the racial climate was far from simplistic. As an independent and, indeed, a pioneering producer-director, Preminger had more creative control over his material than studio-based directors, but even a B-movie impresario like Roger Corman would come unstuck when he made a film that explored the way in which racist demagogues were stirring up race hatred in white communities.

Independent Projects and Exploitation Movies

The Intruder (1961) was Corman's first serious film. It afforded William Shatner his first starring role as Adam Cramer, based on Charles Beaumont's 1958 novelization of white supremacist John Kasper, a man whom Ralph McGill described as "satanic" and a "Citizens Council Moses,"[31] and who in 1957 spent a week in Clinton, Tennessee, creating trouble for a town that was peacefully desegregating its schools in the wake of the *Brown* decision. Corman was drawn to outsider figures throughout his filmmaking career from "melodramatic madmen" to "objects of ridicule."[32] In Adam Cramer he created a warped psychotic individual who begins as the former and ends as the latter. The shining white suit that Cramer wears in almost every scene was one of the few changes Corman made to Beaumont's source text. The visual effect is of a handsome, shining (if sneering) knight-errant conspiring with a corrupt politician to destroy the town's law-abiding principles and its community leaders. The narrative would slice through that image.

Originally Corman had hoped Cramer would be played by Tony Randall, the laconic film and television actor who had won a Golden Globe for *Pillow Talk* (1959). When financial worries escalated and Edward Small of United Artists decided not to back the film, Shatner's lack of star status became an asset. As an unknown, he does not detract from the uncompromisingly naturalistic feel of the movie, assured by Corman's using only five professional actors with the rest of the cast recruited from townspeople in Charleston, Missouri, over three weeks of filming. The movie was ahead of its time. It was shot as cinéma verité to create a documentary surface, but Corman worried that it would be too obvious a "message picture" and that white audiences would see it as "a slam at us."[33] Certainly, he failed to get commercial backing, and the film failed at the box office too, despite being critically acclaimed at the Venice and Cannes Film Festivals.[34] Corman tried to re-title the film "I Hate Your Guts" in an effort to appeal to the exploitation market, but he lost money and it proved "the greatest disappointment" of his career; an "art film about racial segregation" had, Corman discovered, a limited appeal in the 1960s.[35] *The Intruder* has evolved into a cult success, albeit as the result of Shatner's special place in television history as much as its subject matter, and, like *Nothing But a Man*, on re-release it made the usual comforting civil rights dramas seem all the more whimsical.

The Intruder's key plot device is Cramer's manipulation of the schoolgirl daughter of Tom McDaniel (Frank Maxwell), the editor of the town's newspaper. He seduces her into tricking her new black schoolmate Joe Green (Charles Barnes) into being seen alone with her, and because he trusts her father, a decent man who acts as the town's conscience, Joe is caught in her trap. All the fears of "race mixing" that Cramer has been stirring up are brought to the surface in a vicious confrontation and grotesque preparation to lynch Joe in a children's playground outside the school. Joe is tied to a swing while young white children laugh and he is taunted and punched continually, until traveling salesman Sam Griffin (Leo Gordon) intervenes to save the boy and crush a pathetic and sniveling Cramer. While Joe Green is ultimately the foil in Cramer's scheme, the film is actually structured according to a series of confrontations between white supremacists and white liberal-conformists: Cramer versus McDaniel; Cramer versus Griffin, whose wife he seduces in a disturbing scene of pyscho-sexual manipulation and who reveals Cramer to be a charlatan; and corrupt politician Vern Shipman versus the weak and compromised school headmaster (played by novelist Charles Beaumont). The sheriff, the official face of law and order, is seen only once and is sneeringly ineffectual: "Do you want me to arrest everyone here Tom?" he smiles at the newspaper editor who loses an eye when attacked by a segregationist mob. White men share the frame in antagonism, anger, violence, and, finally, abject humiliation. Diehard segregationists are pitted against racial moderates in a rare depiction of the forces of massive resistance, and the extent to which politicians were powerless to manage the violence they unleashed, and decent white folk suffered in the crossfire.

A byproduct of this approach is that black folk are largely made passive in *The Intruder*, although Corman makes it clear that they are positioned in this way because the threat of racial terrorism is real and pervasive. A cavalcade of cars drives through the black area of the town, replete with Klansmen posing with wooden crosses in the back of pick-up trucks, as if on carnival floats. There can be no resistance to this invasion or reaction to the spectacle. The black citizens watch silently as the symbols of racial terror and paranoia pass through unimpeded. African Americans share symbolic space with Tom McDaniel as the conscience of the film but only Joe Green has a lead role. A black preacher is a solid presence, but only for a few frames when he conducts a short service to support the young people whose task it is to integrate the high school. Later he staggers out of his church when it is bombed to die silently in the arms of Joe Green. Older African Americans are portrayed as fearful of the change that integration portends. Joe's elderly uncle tells him, "Some of you Negroes are going to get some of us niggers killed." A black family drives through downtown and is set upon by another mob fired up by Cramer's speeches. The father gets out of his car and faces them with dignity. As the camera pans around their snarling faces, he quietly asks "Why?" a question a single film could not be expected to answer.

Corman could have exploited his subject matter far more than he did, especially because it took the intervention of the National Guard to settle the crisis that John Kasper had caused in Clinton. But other producers of exploitation movies would press forward with portrayals of murderous mayhem as the drama of civil rights. As I have argued elsewhere, this form of shadow cinema was tasteless and offensive, but it was also the first time that the racial terrorism that black southerners and civil rights workers encountered on a daily basis found cinematic representation.[36] That such films had not been noticed for their depiction of the civil rights movement, sensationalist as it may be, is not surprising. Even though the activism of the Student Nonviolent Committee (SNCC) and the Congress for Racial Equality (CORE) coming together for the Mississippi Project provides the dramatic trigger, that was not evident from a typical exploitation title like *Girl on a Chain Gang* (1964).[37] Huie may have failed to translate his work to the screen but in *Girl on a Chain Gang*, Jerry Gross exploited the circumstances in which Chaney, Schwerner, and Goodman were murdered by Klansmen conspiring with police. The "Freedom Summer Murders," as they came to be known, were just the sort of headline that exploitation films used as material and the tragic murders were dramatized within months of the activists' bodies being discovered on August 4, 1964. *Murder in Mississippi* (1965) would follow the same "plot" as civil rights workers became new exploitation film protagonists. Such films are so thoroughly discomfiting, and so far removed from *The Help* and *The Butler*, that it is difficult to think of them as belonging to the same category of "civil rights fiction films." The "race-sex-hate" dramas that Huie envisaged as possibly moving audiences toward an understanding of the ideology of white supremacy – without the safety of a Brechtian distancing effect – were too raw, too real, and too controversial for Hollywood studios or most independents to take on. Tasteless exploitation movies may seem anomalous in civil rights fiction film history, but they are also very revealing as historical artifacts. With hindsight, civil rights organizers jailed for spurious offenses, tried in kangaroo courts, beaten and assaulted, and even put on chain gangs create sensationalist scenes in such films; but such atrocities actually occurred, as oral testimony and legal affidavits make clear.[38]

Ownership of the Story on Screen

Assessments of the complicated politics of the day like *The Intruder* or *Nothing But a Man*, and exploitation movies, are unusual among films that exploit the drama but pay most attention to ensuring that "mainstream" cinema audiences (tacitly understood to be white) will be moved emotionally by what they see on screen – as long as the mediating character is white.

This has been a delimiting feature and has restricted the scope of most fiction films. When Rob Reiner directed the story of the assassination of Medgar Evers in *Ghosts of Mississippi* (1996), for example, the story he felt qualified to tell was the one with which he could identify personally, thereby making his main protagonist Bobby DeLaughter (Alec Baldwin), the prosecuting attorney in the 1994 retrial of Byron de la Beckwith, rather than Myrlie Evers (Whoopi Goldberg), who had waged a thirty-year campaign to see her husband's killer brought to justice. This was the case despite the fact that Willie Morris, who had pitched the idea for the film, suggested that Goldberg share double-billing with Baldwin.[39] DeLaughter's memoir about the trial would be published on the back of the film as *Never Too Late* in 2001. If it was not too late to tell the story, it was, it seemed, too early for a big budget ($40 million) movie to be made in which Evers's activist-wife could be portrayed as anything other than a grieving widow. The history of the civil rights fiction film is colored by such decisions made by white filmmakers who admit to feeling uncomfortable about taking ownership of the African American freedom struggle on screen. Jonathan Demme, who optioned historian Taylor Branch's book *Parting the Waters: America in the King Years, 1954–1963* (1988) in the 1990s but never made the film, expressed that discomfort when he said, "I questioned more and more my ability to ... stage the kind of brutality that white Americans were visiting on black Americans."[40] Nevertheless, renowned white directors command the biggest budgets with which to tell civil rights stories.

African American producers and directors are forced to contend with the film history I have mapped in this essay. The stories they elect to tell stay closer to history and are often told in documentary forms, as deeply moving history lessons like Spike Lee's *Four Little Girls* (1997) and Charles Burnett's *The Murder of Emmett Till* (2003), or in biopics. Clark Johnson's *Boycott!* (2001) focuses on the Montgomery bus boycott as does Julie Dash's *The Rosa Parks Story* (2002) and both won Emmys and NAACP Image Awards. *Boycott!* has the period feel of a classical Hollywood movie, its cinematography beautifully stylized; but in the film's coda, King (Jeffrey Wright) is imagined into a living trajectory. As Wright walks through the streets of Montgomery in 2001, still performing as King, the credits roll. People on the street are made to experience a shock of recognition and the implication is that "King" could walk again down one of the 500 American streets named in his honor if only his moral presence could be recovered in contemporary society.

Boycott! celebrates the hopeful beginnings of the civil rights movement and is intriguing for what it implies about the intersection of the film text and historical record, and the relationship between film, history, and popular culture. Johnson has commented on the film in a way that explains its visual style and the surprise "ending" when King walks back into the future: "I wanted to approach this in a way that would appeal to [audiences] visually and emotionally rather than just being a history lesson. Every February [during Black History Month], we get to trot out our stories and generally tell them in a politically correct, dry manner that is not, frankly, all that cinematic. I wanted to appeal to my kids and let them understand what went on."[41] *Boycott!* was the first film to foreground Dr. King since Mann's production in 1978. But like Mann's, it was a television movie, an HBO production and a signal of quality but a film with a television budget. It was also a personal project for Johnson, better known as an actor. The role of the actor-director is becoming a significant trope in the evolving history of the African American civil rights fiction film and is reflected in fine movies like Bill Duke's *Deacons for Defense* (2003), another television movie starring Forest Whitaker, and Giancarlo Esposito's *Gospel Hill* (2008) starring Danny Glover and Angela Bassett, with Esposito acting and producing as well as directing. These are important films in civil rights film history, and Duke's story of the Deacons of Bogalusa, Louisiana, in the 1960s complicates the simplistic linear trajectory that Louis's activism is made to follow in *The Butler*. Armed resistance was always necessary in the face of racial terrorism, and in the civil rights era the armed self-reliance of African American communities also protected civil rights workers embedded in rural areas. Such films are too easily overlooked.

Most surprising, perhaps, is that of all the major film production companies, Walt Disney Productions has made a noteworthy intervention into telling civil rights stories. *Song of the South* (1946) elicited a storm of protest from the NAACP for a degrading portrayal of "Uncle Remus," adapted from Joel Chandler Harris's plantation fiction. But on the cusp of the twenty-first century, Disney's source texts would be very different. Its civil rights films stay close to the lives and memoirs of those they portray, from Ernest Green, the first of the "Little Rock Nine" to graduate from Central High, through Ruby Bridges integrating her New Orleans elementary school in 1960, and Sheyann Webb, the youngest of the Selma-to-Montgomery marchers in 1965. In each case, black directors take the helm: African American actor-director Eric Laneuville in *The Ernest Green Story* (1993), Martiniquean Euzhan Palcy for *Ruby Bridges* (1998), and African American independent Charles Burnett for *Selma Lord Selma* (1999). Douglas Brode begins his insightful discussion of how Disney "created" the counterculture with the observation that a recurring image that opens so many Disney films is of "America in transition."[42] Indeed, after a false start with *Perfect Harmony* (1991), Disney celebrates the iconic children on the front lines of a nation in transition at the height of the civil rights movement. Such sure-footed and family-friendly films commemorate rather than comfort, and even succeed in avoiding the "easy-bake" formula.

Civil rights fiction film is contradictory and often frustrating. If one is not to judge it solely by the accuracy of the history that it fictionalizes, it is important to acknowledge, as Brian Ward does, that the civil rights movement has been "pressed into service in film, music, and literature," and that film and television forge "powerful popular notions" of the postwar black freedom struggle for audiences around the world. This "master narrative," and both Ward and I use this gendered term advisedly,[43] is continually being reformulated. It is telling that in *The Butler,* when Louis clashes with his father and is banished from the house, they are arguing about Sidney Poitier's depictions of African Americans on screen, with Louis declaring the actor an "Uncle Tom" and his father admiring him; neither of them recognizes the important role Poitier played by even having the kind of profile that could cause such debate in the 1960s. Civil rights remains a contentious topic especially when filmmakers seek to depict Martin Luther King. Paul Greengrass's script for *Memphis*, a film about the sanitation workers' strike that brought King to Memphis in 1968, was rejected by Universal in 2013. But it may be resurrected. Lee Daniels, director of *The Butler*, is moving ahead to direct *Orders to Kill* based on King's assassination; and while his project *Selma* has stalled, it now has Paramount and Oprah Winfrey on board to produce and David Oyelowo, Louis in *The Butler*, in place to play King. Whether any of these features will be released on the big screen remains to be seen. Steven Spielberg's long-time project to produce a biopic of Dr. King has stalled a number of times since 2009, for example, and Oliver Stone pulled out of directing in January 2014, with tweets about how his script had been rejected by Dreamworks and Warner Bros. and his vision "suffocated" by the King Estate and others who guard King's legacy.[44] Fiftieth anniversaries and national and international commemorations of momentous civil rights events, like the Selma bridge crossing in 2015 and the passing of the Voting Rights Act, and King's death in 2018, will ensure that civil rights fiction films remain in the news.

NOTES

1 Ralph Ellison, *Going to the Territory* (New York: Vintage, 1986), p. 295.
2 Jack Butler, "Still Southern after All These Years," in *The Future of Southern Letters*, ed. Jefferson Humphries and John Lowe (New York: Oxford University Press, 1996), pp. 38, 36.
3 For a different and more detailed reading of the genre, see Sharon Monteith, "Civil Rights Fiction," in *The Cambridge Companion to the Literature of the*

American South (New York: Cambridge University Press, 2013), pp. 159–73; and for a discussion of activist fictions, Sharon Monteith, "SNCC's Stories at the Barricades," in *From Sit-Ins to SNCC: Student Civil Rights Protest in the 1960s*, ed. Philip Davies and Iwan Morgan (Gainesville: University Press of Florida 2012), pp. 97–115.

4   Novels like *The Help* are part of a tradition in contemporary southern women's fiction, as mapped in Sharon Monteith, *Advancing Sisterhood? Interracial Friendship in Contemporary Southern Fiction* (Athens: University of Georgia Press, 2000) and as described in Suzanne Jones, *Race Mixing: Southern Fiction since the Sixties* (Baltimore, MD: Johns Hopkins University Press, 2004).

5   See Allison Graham, "'We Ain't Doin' Civil Rights': The Life and Times of a Genre, as Told in *The Help*," *Southern Cultures*, special issue on *The Help* (Spring 2014): 51–64; and for wider discussion of civil rights cinema, Graham's *Framing the South: Hollywood, Television, and Race during the Civil Rights Struggle* (Baltimore, MD: Johns Hopkins University Press, 2003); and the Introduction and multiple essays on civil rights cinema and individual films in *The New Encyclopedia of Southern Culture: Media*, ed. Allison Graham and Sharon Monteith (Chapel Hill: University of North Carolina Press, 2011).

6   Boxoffice.com's total budget numbers are a combination of production budget figures and estimated domestic P&A costs. http://www.boxoffice.com/statistics/movies/the-butler-2013 (accessed May 25, 2014).

7   David Denby, "Current Cinema: Social History," *New Yorker*, August 26, 2013.

8   Although it should be noted that Winston Groom's novel is more satirical than the 1994 Robert Zemickis film adaptation.

9   Price quoted in Fred Hobson, *But Now I See: The White Southern Racial Conversion Narrative* (Baton Rouge: Louisiana University Press, 1999), p. 129.

10 Elayne Rapping, *The Movie of the Week: Private Stories, Public Events* (Minneapolis: University of Minnesota Press, 1992), p. xii.

11 Coretta Scott King, "Hollywood's Latest Perversion: The Civil-Rights Era as a White Experience," *Los Angeles Times*, December 13, 1988), 7; Reynolds as cited by Scott King.

12 Thomas Cripps, *Making Movies Black: The Hollywood Message Movie from World War II to the Civil Rights Era* (New York: Oxford University Press, 1993), pp. 285–86.

13 Silliphant quoted in Axel Madsen, *William Wyler: The Authorized Biography* (New York: Thomas Y. Crowell, 1973), p. 398.

14 John O. Killens, "Hollywood in Black and White," in *The State of the Nation*, ed. David Boroff (Englewood Cliffs, NJ: Prentice-Hall, 1966), pp. 102–3.

15 Langston Hughes, *I Wonder as I Wander: An Autobiographical Journey* (1956, New York: Hill and Wang, 1993), p. 76.

16 Langston Hughes, "Moscow and Me," *International Literature* 3 (July 1933): 61–66.

17 Information taken from publicity posters for Francia films of Mexico; Anon, "Tenn. State Obscenity Law Upset as Judge Rules for Memphis Exhib," *Motion Pictures Exhibitor*, December 2, 1964. For analysis of French depictions of southern race relations, see Sharon Monteith, "How Bigger Mutated: Richard Wright, Boris Vian and "The Bloody Channels through Which One Pushes Logic to the Breaking Point," in *Transatlantic Exchanges: The South in Europe and Europe*

in the South, ed. Richard Gray and Waldemar Zacharasiewicz (Vienna: Austrian Academy of Arts and Sciences, 2007), pp. 149–66.

18 The American Film Institute Catalog of Motion Pictures Produced in the United States: Feature Films, 1961–1970 (Berkeley: University of California Press/ American Film Institute, 1997), p. 610.

19 Bosley Crowther, New York Times, September 21, 1964; New York Times Film Reviews 1913–1968, Vol. 5 (New York: New York Times/Arno Press, 1970), p. 3491.

20 Roger Ebert, 1997 review in the *Chicago-Sun Times, Roger Ebert's Video Companion* (Kansas City, MO: Andrews McMeel, 1997), p. 889.

21 Langston Hughes, "Is Hollywood Fair to Negroes?" *Negro Digest* 1: 6 (April 1943): 19–21.

22 Harvey G. Cohen, *Duke Ellington's America* (Chicago: University of Chicago Press, 2010), p. 187; Ellington, *Music Is My Mistress* (New York: Da Capo Press, 1973), p. 175.

23 "Writer Discusses 6 Film Properties," New York Times, February 10, 1960: 43. For a critical appraisal of "Wolf Whistle" as pulp fiction and as a screen that seemed to preclude further investigation of Till's murder being necessary, see Sharon Monteith, "Emmett Till's Murder in the Melodramatic Imagination: William Bradford Huie and Vin Packer," in *Emmett Till in Literary Memory and Imagination*, ed. Christopher Metress and Harriet Pollack (Baton Rouge: Louisiana State University Press, 2008), pp. 31–52; and for a reading of Huie's "cycle" of stories, see Christopher Metress, "Truth Be Told: William Bradford Huie's Emmett Till Cycle," *Southern Quarterly* 45.4 (2008): 48–75.

24 The William Bradford Huie Papers, Ohio State University, Box 37, Folder 350, "Wolf Whistle" screenplay dated May 21, 1960, 1. Further references included in the text.

25 The William Bradford Huie Papers, Box 37, Folder 352, "Wolf Whistle" screenplay dated June 29, 1960, 100.

26 Quoted in Howell Raines, *My Soul Is Rested: The Story of the Civil Rights Movement in the Deep South* (New York: Penguin, 1977), pp. 388–89.

27 Louella Parsons, "Film Coming on Martyrs of the Civil Rights Movement," *Washington Post*, April 20, 1965, D6.

28 C. Vann Woodward, *The Burden of Southern History* (Baton Rouge: Louisiana State University Press, 1993, 3rd rev. ed.), p. 21.

29 J. E. Smyth, *Edna Ferber's Hollywood: American Fictions of Gender, Race, and History* (Austin: University of Texas Press, 2009), pp. 204–5.

30 For Preminger's comments, "*The Cardinal*: New Preminger Movie Casts Ossie Davis in Role of Bias-Fighting Dixie Priest," Ebony, December 1963: 125–28, 130.

31 Ralph McGill, The South and the Southerner (Boston: Little, Brown, 1959), p. 271.

32 Mark Jancovich, *Rational Fears: American Horror in the 1950s* (Manchester: Manchester University Press, 1996), pp. 277–79.

33 Roger Corman, *How I Made a Hundred Movies in Hollywood and Never Lost a Dime* (New York: Random House, 1990), 103.

34 Roger Corman, "The Stranger," Sight and Sound, September 1963: 66. The title was ameliorated into *The Stranger* on its U.K. release. Together with producer

brother Gene, Corman financed the film with $80,000. The Motion Picture Association of America (MPAA) refused a Seal of Approval supposedly because of the film's virulent racist language, although the epithet "nigger" had been used in movies that had been awarded the seal.

35 Corman, *How I Made a Hundred Movies*, x.

36 For a more detailed historicized reading of *Free White and 21* (1963), *Girl on a Chain Gang*, and *Murder in Mississippi*, see Sharon Monteith, "Exploitation Movies and the Freedom Struggle of the 1960s," in *American Cinema and the Southern Imaginary*, ed. Deborah E. Clarke and Kathryn McKee (Athens: University of Georgia Press, 2011), pp. 194–218.

37 In *Hollywood's Image of the South: A Century of Southern Films*, compiled by Larry Langman and David Ebner (Westport, CT: Greenwood, 2001), it is passed over as "simply an obscure exploitation drama dealing with civil rights as well as life on a southern chain gang" (173). It can barely be said to deal with the latter but its approach to the former is what makes this movie far more intriguing as a historical artifact than it was as a supposedly "simple" (and, indeed, offensive) drive-in movie.

38 For example, *Mississippi Black Paper* (New York: Random House, 1965) in which fifty-seven black and white citizens provide testimony of police brutality.

39 Willie Morris, *The Ghosts of Medgar Evers: A Tale of Race, Murder, Mississippi, and Hollywood* (New York: Random House, 1998), pp. 86, 108, 112.

40 Quoted in Ann Hornaday, "Waiting for Action," *Washington Post*, 10 July 2007: C01.

41 Quoted in Tom Ticha, "Boycott! History Worth Watching," *Sun Sentinel*, February 24, 2001.

42 Douglas Brode, *From Walt to Woodstock: How Disney Created the Counterculture* (Austin: University of Texas Press, 2004), p. ix.

43 Brian Ward, "Introduction: Forgotten Walls and Master Narratives," *Media Culture, and the Modern African American Freedom Struggle* (Gainesville: University Press of Florida, 2001), p. 8. Ward points to essays in *Gender and the Civil Rights Movement*, ed. Peter Ling and Sharon Monteith (New York: Garland, 1999), which unpack the gendering of the term.

44 A number of Stone's tweets are collected in Dave McNary, "Oliver Stone Falls Out of Martin Luther King Jr. Movie," *Variety*, January 14, 2014, at http://variety.com/2014/film/news/oliver-stone-falls-out-of-martin-luther-king-jr-movie-1201062624/# (accessed May 14, 2014).

8

JEFFREY LAMAR COLEMAN

Civil Rights Movement Poetry

The modern-day civil rights movement of the 1950s, 1960s, and early 1970s has been well documented by way of autobiographies, oral histories, and journalistic and scholarly accounts. While these records are essential to preserving the movement's significance, they in no way come close to exhausting the written and unwritten history of the period. The entire genre of poetry, for example, has not received the attention it deserves. Literally hundreds of poems were written between 1955 and 1975 specifically about the period's social activism and cultural developments. This collection of protest poetry, though often overlooked or neglected, is the most aesthetically exuberant, historically resonant, and poignant of postwar twentieth-century America. The absence of a rigorous, sustained discourse with regard to this poetry is one of the more disturbing facts of contemporary American literary history. This is regretful not only because this particular genre seems to have been abandoned, but also because it is arguably impossible for anyone to fully appreciate or be considered literate about the civil rights movement without at least cursory knowledge of the intersections between cultural politics and cultural productions. Likewise, it is also impossible to have a firm grasp on or be conversant about the continuum of contemporary poetry without familiarity with the rich lines and stanzas that evolved from the most significant social movement of twentieth-century America. With the exception of the omnipresent nature of movement songs such as "We Shall Overcome" or "Keep Your Eyes on the Prize," poetry was the period's most ubiquitous and dominant art form. With respect solely to literary production, poetic compositions stand alone in terms of volume and influence during the civil rights era. While essays, plays, novels, and short stories made substantive and lasting contributions to the fight for equality and justice, poetry was most often the genre that rested on the page once writers retired their pens or typewriters for the day. This poetry clearly warrants increased attention from general readers, students, and scholars. Such attention is indeed required to help establish the poems and the era as formidable sites of literary intellectual inquiry. As is, this bounty of soul-filled and history-rich poetry is a body in search of kindred spirits. Consider this chapter a "state of the field," an acknowledgment of the genre's journey, a celebration of its current status, and a clarion call to action for its critical framing and rightful place in the ever-expanding canon of American letters.

The 2012 publication of *Words of Protest, Words of Freedom: Poetry of the American Civil Rights Movement and Era* from Duke University Press made many of the poems from that period available in a single collection for the first time. While the publication of this anthology is essential to the study of the genre, the volume does not address why the poems went uncollected for approximately seven decades. Although there is more than one explanation for this omission, the primary reason seems to mimic the times themselves. In other words, while Dr. King and other mid-century advocates of democracy were fighting an uphill battle to change policy as well as the hearts and minds of the American people, poets of his generation were engaged in a similar struggle in communities and academia. Indeed, some of the most accomplished poets of the twentieth century captured the indefatigable spirit and political chaos of the 1950s, 1960s, and early 1970s. Amiri Baraka, Gwendolyn Brooks, Lucille Clifton, Lawrence Ferlinghetti, Allen Ginsberg, Nikki Giovanni, Barbara Guest, Robert Hayden, Langston Hughes, Galway Kinnell, Denise Levertov, Philip Levine, Adrienne Rich, Sonia Sanchez, Derek Walcott, Anne Waldman, and Margaret Walker are just a few examples of the American poets who documented the movement in verse. These poets represent different cultural and racial communities, and that was at least a part of the problem. Likewise, the arts often aspire to egalitarian ideals, and that was part of the problem as well. The conflation of these two realities produced fascinating yet troubling accounts of the intersections between race and literature in postwar America – accounts that prove to be highly instructive with respect to the struggle for civil rights, especially for current students and others who have had limited exposure to the history of Jim Crow–era America.

The primary cause of the rupture between the two worlds would appear to be social segregation, which also produced segregation in the arts. The literary world suffered segregation equal to if not greater than society at large during the 1950s, 1960s, and 1970s. Unfortunately for the arts and artists, the reality of segregation and racism often trumped the idealism of freedom and equality. These factors were reflected in the racial discrepancies of the publishing industry. Exclusions of black writers in mainstream anthologies and critical essays during that period have been well documented and do not need to be belabored here more than necessary, but for the sake of those unfamiliar with the type of exclusion or oversight I have in mind, I will offer a few examples.[1] These accounts in no way exhaust or encapsulate the multiple sentiments, criticisms, or politics that were voiced about race and literature. Instead they are noted in order to provide a *sense* of the politics of literary productions and inclusions during the period under discussion.

Robert E. Morsberger's essay "Segregated Surveys: American Literature" reflects the status of the mainstream literary canon during the civil rights era. Published in the March 1970 issue of *Negro American Literature Forum*, "Segregated Surveys" reveals a disturbing trend in American publishing. Morsberger discovered that the 1966 issue of *An Anthology of American Literature*, published by the Bobbs-Merrill Company, contained "no Black selections among its 863 pages" and the Odyssey anthology of American literature published the same year devoted only "thirty-six pages from almost 3000" to African Americans (Phillis Wheatley, Paul Laurence Dunbar, Booker T. Washington, and James Baldwin). Likewise, the four-volume *Viking Portable Library American Literature Survey* included "no Afro-American selections in its 2522 pages." Norton's third edition of *The American Tradition in Literature*, which Morsberger lists as "one of the most distinguished and widely used anthologies," contained 3,834 pages in 1967 but included only two pages of poetry by an African American (LeRoi Jones/Amiri Baraka). "Negro prose and drama are not represented at all. The editors provide no comment even on the existence of Black writers," Morsberger states, "except a half-page introduction to Jones/Baraka. Surely this is disproportionate; 2½ pages by a Black out of 3484 is tokenism with a vengeance."[2] Morsberger offers additional figures, but these few examples alone provide a fair representation of the type of segregation that existed in the mainstream literary community in the late 1960s.

While Morsberger's figures clearly support claims of intentional exclusion of black writers, especially poets, other examples offer more ambiguity. I will briefly detail two additional historically significant occasions concerning the racial politics of literary productions, especially how they relate to the literature produced by African Americans during the civil rights era. The two discussions I have in mind revolve around statements made by Robert Bly in relation to "political" poetry in 1963, and the politics of anthology formation and inclusion, as decided upon by Todd Gitlin, who in 1971 edited an anthology of protest poetry. Taken together, the words of both writers demonstrate how problematic and confusing the subject of race was in the world of poetry, even for whites who appeared to champion progressive ideas, defend protest, and support racial integration in the art form.

An interesting starting point for a discussion of politically charged poetry of the 1950s and 1960s can be found in a 1963 essay by poet and prose writer Robert Bly, whose 1967 collection the *Light Around the Body* won the National Book Award for poetry. While arguing for increased political activism in American verse, Bly asserts: "The poetry we have had in this country is a poetry without even a trace of revolutionary feeling – in either language or politics."[3] Bly claims that "it is startling to realize that in the last twenty years there have been almost no poems touching on political subjects, although such concerns have been present daily."[4] These statements by Bly would come across as extremely curious at any point in American literary history, but given the period, such statements transcend the realm of mere curiosity. Instead, they become highly problematic, bordering on the fine line between ignorance and intentionally elitist proclamations. After all, the "last twenty years" Bly is referring to (1943–1963) include a time when Langston Hughes, Margaret Walker, Gwendolyn Brooks, Robert Hayden, Dudley Randall, Margaret Danner, Naomi Long Madgett, and other African Americans were actively writing and/or publishing poetry that could easily be considered political. The irony of this situation is that Bly and these poets share a great deal in common. For instance, in his only passing reference to race, Bly castigates both the *Kenyon Review* and *Southern Review* for not including political or "revolutionary" poetry. Bly writes, "The guiding impulse in both ... is fear of revolution. As southerners [the editors] act to exaggerate the fear felt by even northerners.... Their holding position in poetry has more resemblance to the attitude of Governor Ross Barnett of Mississippi than most people would be willing to admit."[5]

Bly's allusion to Governor Barnett has direct racial implications, for Barnett opposed integration. Barnett especially opposed James Meredith's attempt to become the first African American student at the University of Mississippi. In fact, on September 13, 1962, three days after the U.S. Supreme Court upheld Meredith's right to be admitted, Barnett declared, "There is no case in history where the Caucasian race has survived social integration.... [Mississippi] will not drink from the cup of genocide."[6] Aside from the brief mention of Governor Barnett, Bly does not discuss the most pertinent political events happening in America, nor does he give any indication of what American writers should write about in order to be considered political or revolutionary. Instead, Bly's focus is on literature and artists abroad. Were the racial, cultural, and social politics of the United States a little too close for comfort for Bly? Perhaps the following comments by Todd Gitlin offer insight into the polemics of crossing or not crossing literary and political boundaries.

Gitlin, author of the influential *The Sixties: Years of Hope, Days of Rage* (1987), and a dozen other works, edited in 1971 *Campfires of the Resistance: Poetry from the Movement*. In the introduction Gitlin writes, "Poetry from the Movement" does not mean simply political poetry, though this anthology includes a lot of poems *about* the political universe – about the war in Vietnam, the American empire, racism, universities, capitalism, the subjugation of women, all forms of American barbarity."[7] Gitlin's sense of politics appears much more explicit than Bly's. However, as Gitlin states, not all of the poems in his collection can be considered political poetry. His qualifier, important in its own right, is soon followed by several others, including this: "One more bias needs explanation. Considering that the black liberation movement has been central to the insurgency of the decade, there are not nearly enough black poets here. The reason is not the usual implicit racism" (xvii).[8] Gitlin does not state how many of the more than fifty poets represented are black, only that his decision not to include many of them was not a racist act. While attempting to explain away the significant absence of African American poets, the editor confesses:

> I had to conclude it would be the height of arrogance for me, white, to exercise my fundamentally white standards to select from other cultures. Arrogance or not, I didn't know how to do it. Maybe I could have been spared this decision if capitalist pricing considerations had not intervened to limit the length of the book. But figuring that the black poetry is beginning to get published where it matters most, I decided to give a fuller representation to the whites, and I sorely hope my motivation will not be misunderstood.[9]

The phrase "where it matters most" is a reference to *two* African American–edited anthologies and a few journals, as if these publications alone represent sufficient publishing forums for African American writers.

The two anthologies Gitlin references are *The New Black Poetry* (1969), edited by Clarence Major and *Black Fire* (1968), edited by Amiri Baraka and Larry Neal. An immediate assumption is that one of these anthologies may contain editorial proclamations or political discourse not necessarily agreeable to Gitlin. This seems to be more than a logical assumption as he specifically points toward these two texts as being indicative of the literary mediums available to African American writers. And in making such a statement, Gitlin seemingly absolves himself of the "responsibility" of providing a fair or equal representation of African American writers, even though his anthology is purportedly a collection of protest poetry that appears to cover many of the areas addressed by civil rights leaders. With these factors in mind, there seems to be much more at play here than liberal feelings of satisfaction that African American poets could be found in two other anthologies. After all, many of the poets selected by Gitlin had also been published elsewhere, a condition that rules out any argument for "new" or "fresh" talent on the editor's behalf. Therefore, the assumption that Gitlin had a problem with the stated politics of Major, Baraka, or Neal is worth pursuing. However, in the ten or so pages of text which serve as Major's introduction to *The New Black Poetry*, there seems to be little or nothing that should cause undue concern for Gitlin or any of his New Left colleagues. That is, unless anyone would be concerned with lines, such as:

> revolutionary black poets feel the urgency of being in a political vanguard. As a matter of fact many of these poets are full-time militant activists. Any droopy concepts of western ideology are already obsolete. Even the best radical white poets today are beginning to question the whole western cultural aesthetic.[10]

Gitlin would not disagree with such sentiments, but there is a chance he would disagree with assertions like, "The new black poetry ... can usually be 'experienced' clearly, anytime by anyone. We do not have to know what the daily life of an ancient Egyptian was like in order to 'feel' the art he produced. Real art, no matter how unique, is never difficult" (Major 12).[11] According to Gitlin, since he is white, he is unable to "experience" or objectively judge literary productions from "other" cultures. Major's introduction does not get much more radical than the lines cited. Was Gitlin practicing racism by excluding some of the leading African American poets of his day, or was he simply being a white liberal sympathetic to the racial and literary politics of both the 1950s and 1960s?

Given the essays by Morsberger and Bly and the introductory comments by Gitlin, it is logical to conclude that the racial climate in America, even in the arts, was not conducive to the publication of an integrated civil rights anthology. Race in America is a volatile minefield we are socialized and conditioned to avoid, as Bly does, or to tread lightly on, as Gitlin does. My point is not to cast aspersions on the two; both have worked to move the art form forward in significant ways. Instead, my goal in highlighting their comments – which were much more left-of-center than those of many of their contemporaries – is to illustrate the tense and often contentious relationship between racial politics and arts during the civil rights era. This tension, which was a byproduct of society's ills, helped to keep poets segregated in many journals and anthologies. The requisite emotional and psychological distancing had to be reached before a sober and integrated account of the period could be relayed in poetry. The argument could be made that the generation that created poetry during the movement years was too affected by the social and racial turbulence of the period to assess and collect the poetry that most accurately represents the era. The impetus for *Words of Protest, Words of Freedom: Poetry of the American Civil Rights Movement and Era* was the desire to bring together as many civil rights–influenced poems and poetry communities as possible, despite the social or racial issues that once segregated them.

Civil rights movement poetry not only represents but also narrates the era. From the 1950s to the 1970s, writers from America and beyond were most active in their attempts to tackle many of the movement's most crucial episodes and turning points. There are poems that address the events, individuals, and social conditions of African Americans from the *Brown* decision through at least the mid-1970s. In fact, the poems from that period could easily lead readers through the tumultuous timeline of the civil rights movement. They allow readers to (re)experience such events as bus boycotts, sit-ins at lunch counters, Freedom Rides, marches, and the evolution of America's racial climate. Overwhelmingly, the poems in *Words of Protest, Words of Freedom* fall into one of two categories: (1) poems that directly focus on crucial movement-related historical moments, and (2) poems that are not necessarily event-specific, but concern themselves with – much like the movement itself – racial oppression and discrimination, or with movement-related social unease of the period as a whole.[12]

For example, poems in the first category chronicle such events as the lynching of Emmett Till in 1955; the Little Rock, Arkansas, school integration crisis of 1957 and 1958; the murder of Mack Charles Parker in 1959; the killing of Medgar Evers in 1963; the Sixteenth Street Baptist Church bombing in 1963; the assassination of John F. Kennedy in 1963; the search for James Chaney, Andrew Goodman, and Michael Schwerner in 1964; uprisings in Harlem (1964), Watts (1965), Newark and Detroit (1967), Orangeburg (1968), and at the Attica Correctional Facility (1971); the assassination of Malcolm X in 1965; the Selma-to-Montgomery voting rights march in 1965; the birth of the Black Panther Party in 1966, and the assassinations of Martin Luther King Jr. and Robert F. Kennedy in 1968.

The poems in the second category, unlike those in the first, are not event-specific but they do offer a broader sense of the social and political climate of the period. The presence of unrelenting violence and death that characterizes the elegiac voice of many poems from the first group is not as evident in this one. Instead, the poems in this grouping, which fall under the subheading of "Struggle, Survival, and Subversion during the Civil Rights Era" in *Words of Protest, Words of Freedom*, speak to a range of issues, including the intracultural debate over the emergence of black nationalism and the continued adherence to traditional civil rights ideology. Additionally, poems in this category chronicle civil rights protests, marches, and demonstrations held in spite of imminent violence, and offer instruction and wisdom to fellow poets and activists. The poems also stress the need for blacks to counteract an array of detrimental issues in the community, especially fiscal inequities. There are also poems that evoke racial conditions and injustices implicitly or metaphorically, often in the process of addressing seemingly unrelated social problems. "For the Union Dead" by Robert Lowell epitomizes this approach by initially addressing the Civil War and later conflating the war and school desegregation. Likewise, Alice Walker's "Be Nobody's Darling" does not directly address the movement but does implore readers to live in the *spirit* of the movement by honoring ancestors and fallen activists.

Taken together, the two categories of poems (event- and non-event-specific) offer an exciting perspective of the United States during its civil rights years, a perspective not previously captured in a single volume of poems, and a perspective that is inherently different and more urgent than those found in other disciplines, such as history and political science. One of the more extraordinary aspects of this particular genre is that it mirrors the movement in terms of its democratic composition of writers. African American poets were not alone in voicing opposition to their status as second-class citizens in America. Writers, regardless of race, and sometimes regardless of nation, contributed to the movement's foundation. The genre was multiracial, multicultural, and multinational long before such nomenclature gained currency in this country. Even more interesting, the writers from this era, as is often the case with artistic periods, were for the most part unaware that they were contributing to a genre. They were not consciously writing verses for the sake of creating civil rights movement poetry. There was no call for submissions of movement-themed poems or poems representative of the period. In fact, most writers were unaware that such a development was taking place, and that a host of other conscientious writers were simultaneously documenting in poetry the most transformative social movement of twentieth-century America. Yet one by one they composed lines and stanzas that complemented each other and formed an ongoing dialogue with each other. This eclectic collection of voices sharing common themes could appear to be an unlikely gathering if one considers that numerous poets hailed from different if not competing schools of poetry, including the Beat, Black Arts, Harlem Renaissance, and Négritude movements, among others. While these movements are quite different in a number of ways, their resistance to the social status quo connects them, and part of that resistance involved the civil rights movement. The Beats, for example, who were mostly white, did not see the need to conform to the overwhelmingly conservative American culture of the 1950s and 1960s, including its sexual and literary practices. As a whole, the Beats did not protest racial conditions in America on a regular basis, but members such as Anne Waldman and Allen Ginsberg broached the subject at times in their writing and during public demonstrations. On the other hand, the Harlem Renaissance and Négritude movements, whose members shared African descent, were primarily concerned with issues of race in America and around the world. The artistic height of the Harlem Renaissance was in the 1920s and 1930s, while the Négritude movement, which was influenced by the energy and philosophy of the Harlem Renaissance and consisted of French-speaking artists and thinkers, was formed in France in the 1930s in opposition to European cultural domination. Négritude members felt that cultural contributions from Africa and her offspring had been too long overshadowed by slavery and colonialism. Simply put, both movements desired to represent the African diaspora, especially in matters relating to race, including issues relevant to civil rights. Langston Hughes is the most prominent member of the Harlem Renaissance in *Words of Protest, Words of Freedom*; Aimé Césaire, Nicolás Guillén, and Léopold Sédar Senghor represent the Négritude movement in the anthology. (These writers and others such as Yevgeny Yevtushenko of Russia attest to the international significance and influence of the civil rights movement.) The Black Arts Movement, formed in the mid-1960s, was the literary representative of the Black Power Movement in America and sought to instill a sense of racial pride in the African American community during the 1960s and 1970s. In poems, novels, plays, and essays, members of the black arts community, including Amiri Baraka and Nikki Giovanni, stressed the significance of black culture and history in a predominantly white society. However, few writers wrote solely in a civil or human rights vein, and some writers were clearly more committed to the movement in verse than others, but when viewed collectively it becomes apparent that a distinctive yet diverse poetic movement was taking shape in the United States and abroad. With the benefit of hindsight and historical perspective we can now view that literary period through the lens of civil rights.[13]

An extraordinary aspect of the civil rights movement is that it inspired ordinary citizens to put down in verse their thoughts and emotions about pivotal historical moments or about the cultural climate of the period as a whole. While many of these poets did not possess the genius of a Langston Hughes or a Gwendolyn Brooks, they did possess an ability to craft meaningful poems. Civil rights movement poets mirror the movement to the extent that well-known and lesser-known (or unknown) individuals worked side by side to sustain a cause. For example, scholars and the general public usually think of King in association with the push for civil rights, but hundreds of unheralded citizens sustained and propelled the movement by participating in sit-ins, marches, and other forms of social protest. These citizens participated because they saw the struggle for equality and democracy as a worthwhile and essential endeavor. The same is true of everyday citizens who decided to pick up a pen or pencil or sit before a typewriter to do *something* to help the cause or to deal with the emotional and psychological impact of the political and social conditions. Although many of the poems collected in *Words of Protest, Words of Freedom* were written by the most influential poets of late twentieth-century America – including writers who would later win prestigious literary prizes, among them the American Book Award, National Book Award, Pulitzer Prize, and Nobel Prize for Literature – this anthology also seeks to honor individuals who never received the same level of recognition.

These writers, the esteemed and the unheralded, believed in the social advancement of African Americans. The civil rights movement's primary objective was to combat racial injustices stemming largely from segregation and to complete the journey toward freedom that began in the Jim Crow era. As previously mentioned, social segregation also produced segregation in the arts. The literary world suffered from this problem in equal if not greater parts than society at large during the 1950s, 1960s, and 1970s. However, numerous poets rejected divisions of this kind, and their attitudes about America were reflected in their art. They rejected the view that blacks deserved to be treated as second-class citizens and that whites, simply by birthright, were entitled to the various riches of American life. The historical period is the dominant rubric that unites the poets, but other aspects of their craft connect them as well. The typical elements of poetry are present, such as hyperbole, satire, irony, personification, and experimentation, but many readers will likely respond to or recall the presence of tragedy in these works. Elegies for those associated with the era are well represented in this genre, starting with Emmett Till in 1955 and ending with Robert F. Kennedy in 1968. Closely tied to the presence of elegies during the period is unpleasant and disturbing imagery. This element appears in many of the elegies but occurs in other poems as well. However, as one becomes more familiar with the poetry written during and about the movement one discovers that in the midst of tragic stanzas there exists the unifying goal, the shared and common hope and dream that America will become America. This dream exists, usually unspoken or unacknowledged on a literal level, as the overriding concern of each poem. The works and their authors do not all agree on how to achieve democracy and equality in America, but the subject is present page after page. In this sense, these poems – poems that recall and record the most life-changing movement of twentieth-century America – are arguably the most *American* poems of the century. They provide a glimpse of Americans at their worst and of Americans at their transcendent best as well.[14]

Likewise, the poets themselves should be remembered and championed for their contributions to the movement and to American poetry. These writers left behind a literary history that directly complements existing accounts in other disciplines, a record of American literature that has for too long been overlooked or not adequately contextualized. In fact these writers left behind poems that in and of themselves could guide readers through many of the defining moments of the civil rights movement. They left behind a collective expression of socially conscious and aesthetically diverse creativity that when viewed as part of the continuum of contemporary American poetry is formidable enough to constitute its own genre. They left behind a twentieth-century legacy of the social and political line and stanza, a legacy that can now be categorized as "Poetry of the American Civil Rights Movement and Era."[15]

The title of King's collection of essays from 1967, *Where Do We Go from Here?*, is quite apropos for this discussion of poetry and the movement. Where, indeed, do we go from here in terms of increased visibility for the literature of the period, carving a niche for it in America's literary history, and ensuring its legacy for the foreseeable future and beyond? Earlier in this chapter the genre of poetry was spoken of as a body in search of kindred souls. Those souls, of course, are readers interested in poetry and/or the civil rights movement. Undoubtedly, some of those readers are scholars and critics who can help initiate and sustain critical discourse about the poetry. Quite frankly, this body provides an exciting, uncommon opportunity for new and established critics. The critical field is a tabula rasa waiting to be inscribed. This statement is not intended to suggest that the poets and poems have not received critical attention from a variety of perspectives (after all, many of the poets are among the most recognized of their generation) or to diminish or negate those contributions, but it is intended to suggest that the poets and poems have not received critical attention as a collective with respect to the civil rights movement. Analyzing and critiquing the poetry from the perspective of the movement is essential to comprehending fully the aesthetic and historical poignancy of the genre. Not often does an already established, internationally recognized area of scholarship like the civil rights movement present new, uncharted avenues of discovery. However, this is exactly the case when it comes to poetry and the movement. Given the worldwide recognition and appeal of the movement, and the international reach of civil rights poetry, coupled with the rich and varied voices of the poems themselves, the possibilities for critical inquiry are virtually limitless. In short, this exciting body of work from an extraordinary historical period offers critics an exceptional opportunity to establish and direct the critical narrative of the field. It is rather unlikely that a similar claim can be made for any other area of twentieth-century American literature. Most, if not all, of the current modes of literary engagement and analyses can be applied to the field of civil rights poetry, especially those involving – broadly speaking – cultural and historical assessments. Furthermore, many of the poems invite interdisciplinary and transgenre critiques. A concern of many poets was to illuminate the interconnectedness of historical and present-day struggles. Such intersections and linkages with regard to the movement and literature are multidimensional and help to situate readers inside or close to the historical sites they discuss. One of the most eloquent examples of a poem that accomplishes this type of polyvocal milieu and audience "relocation" is Michael S. Harper's "Here Where Coltrane Is." A close, succinct examination of the poem can help illustrate the multireferential nature of many civil rights poems and serve as a model – though an admittedly truncated and singular model – of how the era's poetry can be explored.[16]

Harper's extraordinary elegy is a complex interdisciplinary record of how the poet was moved as an artist to create a lyrical response to Coltrane's musical response ("Alabama") to Martin Luther King Jr's oral response (eulogy) to the 1963 bombing of Birmingham's Sixteenth Street Baptist Church. Harper, professor of English at Brown University, the first Poet Laureate of Rhode Island, and twice a nominee for the National Book Award, was drawn to Coltrane's intensity, the struggle for civil and human rights, and a manner in which to unite them artistically. His poem not only weaves together the poet's admiration of Coltrane, jazz, and his interest in social justice, but does so with an exceptionally intriguing and powerful flair. The poem intends to instill in readers memories of all subjects mentioned, from the narrator's early inner discursive conjectures about soul and race to the outer, informing voice of "Alabama" that simultaneously anchors the poem and ushers us to a site of racial hostility and human tragedy. The poem incorporates or alludes to public and artistic responses to the tragedy in Birmingham, and eventually returns to the memory of the violence, and its possible impact on the next generation.

The intricately cohesive nature of the poem, as well as the primary intersections between history, oration, and music are found by way of references to John William Coltrane (1926–1967). The saxophonist, directly and indirectly, is invoked throughout the poem, especially in lines three and four ("memory and modal/songs, a tenor blossoming"), line eleven ("*a love supreme*"), which is the title of one of Coltrane's 1964 albums, and line sixteen ("I play 'Alabama'").[17] The latter utterance is, of course, doubly referential for it not only names Coltrane's tune but also reminds the reader that the song was written in memory of the bombing. Connected to these references, but offstage, as it were, is the fact that music alone was not responsible for Harper's admiration of Coltrane, the kind of admiration that inspired him to write poems in the musician's honor, or call forth the musician or his music as a muse, and title his first collection in 1970 *Dear*

John, Dear Coltrane. Harper's fondness of Coltrane's energy and passion is indeed interesting, for he equates or sees well-defined parallels between the creative musical expression and politicized, societal oppression. This connection explains, at least partially, why Harper was inspired to enter the oral and musical "dialogue" started by King and Coltrane after the Birmingham bombing.

In the poem "Here Where Coltrane Is," the destruction caused by the explosion is inextricably connected to Coltrane's "Alabama," and thus to the events that followed the bombing, namely, the public outcry and Dr. King's eulogy. The narrator's state of contemplation and ongoing struggles to reconcile the historical trauma of the bombing is perhaps most evident in lines eighteen through twenty-one: "skipping the scratches / on your faces over the fibrous / conical hairs of plastic / under the wooden floors." These four lines, economic yet forceful in structure and function, utilize literary devices previously employed by the poet. The first, "skipping the scratches," draws to it the physical, vinyl "record" of "Alabama" from earlier lines ("I play 'Alabama' / on a warped record player"), as well as flows into the following lines of "on your faces over the fibrous / conical hairs of plastic / under the wooden floors." This string of images makes clear that something other than merely listening to Coltrane is happening here. The narrator is now actually "seeing" the four dead girls, and is mentally "skipping the scratches" on their faces, as if attempting to at once remember and forget. But the "memories" do not end here. There is also recollection of the "fibrous / conical hairs of plastic," a phrase that combines, rather cleverly yet gruesomely, the description of human remains ("hairs") entangled with bomb fragments ("fibrous," "conical," "plastic"). All of this is found "under the wooden floors," alluding to the fact that the four bodies were discovered in the basement of the church. While the tone here is decidedly dire, we must remember that the ubiquitous nature of the music is providing a semblance of healing and sustenance for the narrator.

In the midst of memories of destruction, imagination and creativity are being born. "I play Alabama," the narrator says, "on a warped record player." The record player is "warped," metaphorically speaking, because *everything* else also appears out of sync, especially the lack of humanity that occasioned the bombing. This is the primary subject, and pivotal point of the poem, that has been on the narrator's mind since the utterance of "Soul and race / are private dominions" in the opening line. All the while, Coltrane's appropriately melancholic instrumental tune has been playing in the background, guiding and informing the voice and structure of the poem. The interior narrative taking place is shrouded in grief and mourning, caused by the seemingly immediate memory of death, which is also at the heart of

"Alabama." Literary scholar Günter H. Lenz asserts that the poem as a whole is a result of Harper's attempt to transform Coltrane's music into poetry:

> This experiential and aesthetic interaction among the various levels and per-
> spectives of the poem explains why, to Michael Harper, the poet, there is no
> contradiction, no mutual exclusiveness, between the black church, revolution-
> ary politics, and black music. And it confirms to him the continuity of the
> black cultural and communal tradition ... a continuum, however, that by no
> means should be mistaken as simply assuring harmony and happiness but has
> always been characterized, in American history, by suffering, violence, oppres-
> sion, and resistance.[18]

The "suffering, violence, oppression, and resistance," Lenz mentions are the emotions Coltrane and Harper were attempting to translate by way of sax-ophone and stanzas, respectively, for the sake of preserving a collective cul-tural memory.

While "Here Where Coltrane Is" centers on historical references or things past, there is also in the poem a concern for the future that is simultaneously optimistic and foreboding. For example, lines twelve through fifteen, "Oak leaves pile up on walkway / and steps, catholic as apples / in a special mist of clear white / children who love my children," are intended to paint a dream-like picture of racial harmony. What is extremely interesting about this particu-lar section of the poem is the creation of optimism concerning race relations, only to have such optimism immediately obliterated by line sixteen: "I play 'Alabama.'" Alabama then becomes the dominant imagery in the poem (i.e., racial *dis*harmony). Alabama quickly undoes what took so long to build. Like the euphoria after the March on Washington (August 28, 1963), which was undercut by the bomb (September 15, 1963), the dream of interracial solidar-ity too is undercut in Harper's poem by memories of the bombing. The poem deepens its concern for the past, present and future in its closing lines:

> For this reason Martin is dead;
> for this reason Malcolm is dead;
> for this reason Coltrane is dead;
> in the eyes of my first son are the browns
> of these men and their music.

Sascha Feinstein writes that the "ending suggests these men have died because of their race. But it is also a testimony to those who expend themselves for issues broader and more significant than any individual life. For this reason if no other they need to be recognized."[19] While Coltrane definitely suffered due to his race, music, and other factors,[20] he died of liver cancer in 1967, and not as a result of violence as did Martin Luther King Jr. and Malcolm X. However, I feel that Feinstein's assertion concerning individuals who "expend themselves" for "broader and more significant" issues is accurate of all three men. But what about the eyes of the speaker's first son, which carry the "browns / of these men and their music"? Lenz insists that it is this son's responsibility to claim "the black cultural and communal tradition" left by Martin, Malcolm, and Coltrane.[21] Perhaps Lenz's point is valid, but the ambiguous nature of the ending of the poem lends itself to an interpretation that is at once optimistic and despairing. For example, the speaker definitely sees his son as part of a rich cultural history. Nevertheless, this history has resulted in the deaths of this trinity of men. Additionally, as readers we should also consider that the incorporation of Coltrane at this juncture is probably intended to return us to the heart of the poem, which is the deaths of four girls. Taking this into consideration (i.e., references to seven deaths in all), the speaker is most likely placing more emphasis on fear than optimism. As a result, the narrator dreads that the "browns" (race) and correlating blues (experiences) of these men will be handed down to the son (irrespective of the son's talent or achievement) by a traditionally white supremacist culture.

This exploration of Harper's intricate, contemplative poem is obviously not comprehensive but it does provide an example of how the poem, and others, can be explicated and historicized. The intent here is not to exhaust the analytical possibilities of Harper's poem but to present a way of working *toward* in-depth analyses of the cultural productions of the period. Most of the poems, as individual works or as thematic groupings or collectives, are multifaceted and therefore agreeable to a plethora of interpretive models, approaches, and visions, whether established or entrenched or profoundly experimental or emerging. The body of the literature, after several decades of segregation or neglect, has been gathered and is now anxiously awaiting the acknowledgment and attention of kindred souls who appreciate its devotion to and narration of the most transformative social movement of twentieth-century America.

NOTES

1 See Amiri Baraka, "Cultural Revolution and the Literary Canon." *Callaloo* 14.1 (1991): 150–56, and "A Post-Racial Anthology?" *Poetry* 202.2 (2013); Hoyt Fuller, "Racism in Literary Anthologies," *Black Scholar* 18.1 (1987): 35–39; Henry Louis Gates Jr., "The Master's Pieces: On Canon Formation and the African-American Tradition," *South Atlantic Quarterly* 89.1 (1990): 89–111; Linda K. Kerber, "Diversity and the Transformation of American Studies," *American Quarterly* (1989): 415–31; Barbara G. Pace, "The Textbook Canon: Genre, Gender, and Race in US Literature Anthologies," *English Journal* 81.5 (1992): 33–38.

2 Robert E. Morsberger, "Segregated Surveys: American Literature," *Negro American Literature Forum* 4.1 (1970): 4.

3 Robert Bly, "A Wrong Turning in American Poetry," in *Claims for Poetry*, ed. Donald Hall (Ann Arbor: University of Michigan Press, 1986), p. 24.

4 Ibid.

5 Ibid., pp. 24–25.

6 Ross Barnett, "Mississippi Still Says 'Never,'" *The Citizen*, September 1962 (transcript of television and radio address to the people of Mississippi, delivered September 13, 1962).

7 Todd Gitlin, ed., *Campfires of the Resistance: Poetry from the Movement* (Indianapolis: Bobbs-Merrill, 1971), p. xiv.

8 Ibid., p. xvii.

9 Ibid., p. xviii.

10 Clarence Major, ed., *The New Black Poetry* (New York: International Publishing, 1969), p. 15.

11 Ibid., p. 12.

12 Jeffrey Lamar Coleman, ed., *Words of Protest, Words of Freedom: Poetry of the American Civil Rights Movement and Era* (Durham, NC: Duke University Press, 2012), pp. 7–8.

13 Ibid., pp. 9–11.

14 Ibid., pp. 11–13.

15 Ibid., p. 13.

16 A lengthier, more in depth analysis of Harper's poem can be found in Jeffrey Lamar Coleman, "Michael S. Harper's 'Here Where Coltrane Is' and Coltrane's 'Alabama': The Social and Aesthetic Intersections of Civil Rights Movement Poetry," *Journal of Social and Political Thought* 2.1 (2003), http://www.yorku.ca/jspot/ (accessed 23 October 2014).

17 Michael S. Harper, "Here Where Coltrane Is," *Images of Kin: New and Selected Poems* (Urbana: University of Illinois Press, 1977), p. 160.

18 Günter H. Lenz, ed., *History and Tradition in Afro-American Culture* (Frankfurt: Campus Verlag, 1984), p. 29.

19 Sascha Feinstein, *Jazz Poetry: From the 1920s to the Present* (New York: Greenwood Press, 1997), p. 132.

20 See J. C. Thomas, *Chasin' the Trane: The Music and Mystique of John Coltrane* (New York: Doubleday, 1975), p. 82.

21 Lenz, *History and Tradition*, p. 29.

9

ROBERT J. PATTERSON

Gender, Sex, and Civil Rights

On Wednesday, August 29, 2013, the nation commemorated the fiftieth anniversary of the historic March on Washington for Jobs and Freedom in Washington, D.C., with many traveling (and a significant number also returning) to the historic site, where it is estimated that hundreds of thousands of black people congregated to demand full access to America's democratic promises. While several locales throughout the nation remembered this historic moment with festivities and rallies, the nation's official ceremony took place on the same date and in the same location – the steps of the Lincoln Memorial – with President Barack Obama addressing the nation from the same place that Martin Luther King Jr. had done five decades earlier. Those who attended came to reflect on the March's significance; to celebrate the achievements it made possible; and to explore its unfinished business. The main program's featured speakers included media mogul Oprah Winfrey, former president William Jefferson Clinton, civil rights activist John Lewis, and actor-comedian Jamie Foxx. This range of participants was perhaps an acknowledgment that civil rights leadership is not, as historian Belinda Robnett argues, the sole responsibility of one man, who leads the masses to their civil rights by fighting for changes in the nation's laws and public policies.[1] Rather, it confirms, as cultural critic Erica R. Edwards argues in *Charisma and the Fictions of Black Leadership*, that the extraordinary efforts of ordinary men and women animate and sustain movements for civil rights. That is, the inclusion of non-politicians calls attention to the role that each American has in fighting for and ensuring civil rights justice.[2] This chapter examines how the movement still grapples with the need to acknowledge the intersections between race, gender, and sexuality, using first-person writings in particular to reveal how transforming one's way of thinking is intricately linked to political revolution.

The Civil Rights Movement: Phase One and Phase Two

Despite a persistence of racial bias and gender and sexual inequalities today, the diverse speakers at the 2013 March shared a common task: to celebrate the legal, economic, political, and cultural advances that the 1963 March on Washington has made possible. Without a doubt, the energy generated through the 1963 march helped to mobilize demands for civil rights that ultimately led to a more sustained dismantling of the Jim and Jane Crow segregation that *Plessy v. Ferguson* had instantiated in 1896, and that *Brown v. Board of Education of Topeka, Kansas* had begun to undo in 1954. While other significant historical factors contributed to the eventual signing of the Civil Rights Act of 1964, the Voting Rights Act of 1965, and the Civil Rights Act of 1968, the March on Washington catalyzed the nation and local communities to remove legal barriers that were denying African Americans access to the opportunities that might provide them equality. Civil rights historians have acknowledged the removal of Jim and Jane Crow segregation as phase one of the civil rights movement, recognizing that the movement is ongoing and that its goal to achieve equality cannot be met by only eliminating legal obstructions.[3]

Throughout the speeches, however, a narrative of political progress constantly emerged, as speaker after speaker commended America for the progress in race relations it has made, as well as for the material gains that phase one of the civil rights movement afforded. Invoking a central phrase from King's 1963 "I Have a Dream" speech, the "Let Freedom Ring" anniversary celebration likewise challenged American citizens to work collaboratively to achieve the deferred aspects of King's dream. While perhaps underemphasized, this aspect of the speeches deserves examination because it demonstrates that the civil rights movement remains responsible for developing ways to ensure that the equality of access promised by phase one results in an equality of outcome. The movement must also respond to ongoing and newly developing civil rights injustices that infringe on citizens' rights. That is, the program, however unevenly, acknowledged legislative achievements as only part of a larger civil rights agenda, which also includes transforming legal access into material results. Historians have described the transformation of equal access into equal results as one of the main tasks of the civil rights movement's phase two.

While civil rights historians are correct to argue that phase one removed legal obstructions to civil rights justice, contemporary and historical incidents reveal that phase one perhaps has not successfully removed all barriers to legal access to equality; even if laws and policies are not explicitly exclusionary, their application and results certainly are. The discussion seems critical at *this* particular historical moment in which the Supreme Court struck down a significant aspect of the 1965 Voting Acts Right;[4] a Florida jury acquitted George Zimmerman for the murder of Trayvon Martin; black unemployment rates remain disproportionately high; backlash against affirmative action programs has become increasingly more entrenched in public policy; and LGBTQ (Lesbian, Gay, Bisexual, Transgender, and Queer) rights in general, and same-sex marriages in particular, are too-often dissociated from civil rights issues.[5] As is the case in the contemporary moment, historically the legal and political systems have been faced with the question of defining what civil rights are and have contested who and which groups should have access to them. Although civil rights *definitions* are too often cast in terms that are insufficiently complex, and that presuppose that black freedom struggles for civil rights have only been fights for racial rights, phase one and phase two of the movement continue to grapple with the increasingly complicated definitions of civil rights and experiences of civil rights injustices.

Civil Rights Leadership, Intersectionality, and First-Person Writing

Contemporary representations of phase one often identify Martin Luther King Jr. as its sole leader and champion King's desire for integration as the single and most important aspect of his social vision – and of the civil rights movement; however, the King who was "the democratic socialist who advocated unionization, planned the poor people's campaign, and was assassinated in 1968 while supporting a sanitation worker's strike" often gets elided because addressing problems of inequality that subtend American society after phase one challenges the nation and the national conscience.[6] An examination of the anti-capitalist King, for example, demonstrates how King's expansive vision of civil rights not only inextricably tied social class to racial enfranchisement, but also reveals his desire to see the legislative accomplishments of phase one result in the material improvement of black people's living conditions during phase two. Like civil rights activist Bayard Rustin, King, too, desired a package deal, which focused on reducing inequality in housing, employment, and education.[7] By ignoring or otherwise minimizing this aspect of King's vision, several of the day's speakers reconstructed a narrative of political and social progress that not only overestimates the progress America has made regarding civil rights attainment but also fails to recognize the intricate ways that the civil rights movement explicitly and implicitly became simultaneously a fight for class, gender, and sexual rights.

As I argue in *Exodus Politics: Civil Rights and Leadership in African American Literature and Culture*, this framing of civil rights refines the definition of civil rights to focus on what contemporary black feminist thought refers to as an intersectional understanding of identity politics.[8] Take for example the institution of slavery. Without a doubt, American chattel slavery depended on and thrived on the notion that black people's racial identities made them inherently inferior and therefore deserving of subjugation. At the same time, as black queer studies has demonstrated, this inferiority was simultaneously defined by black people's putative inability to conform to gender and sex roles.[9] Discourses of racial inferiority thus have been mutually constituted by gender and sexual ideologies and norms. This point is important because it provides a wide historical context that demonstrates how even the earliest demands for black civil rights – while often articulated in racial (and masculinist) terms – always have been simultaneously articulating and re-articulating, staging and contesting, and pushing forward and moving backward how we understand racial politics and black political concerns, particularly as they converge and diverge along, and in between, the interstices of gender, sexual, and social class locations.

While the 1963 March on Washington for Jobs and Freedom explicitly foregrounded how Jim and Jane Crow (racial) segregation had encroached upon African Americans' political rights, thereby stripping them of educational, housing, and employment opportunities, the movement itself did not explicitly showcase African American women activists, leaders, and organizers who also argued that gender and sexuality were indisputably bound to this civil rights march.[10] Civil rights activist and leader Dorothy Height, for example, who had been a part of President Kennedy's Commission on the Status of Women, and later, thanks to the leadership of Anna Arnold Hedgeman, helped to organize the March on Washington, had "detailed the low wages, poor working conditions, and discrimination that black women faced in the labor market."[11] Although Height, much to the chagrin of her contemporaries, including activist and feminist Pauli Murray, would later propose that this problem could be solved by allowing black men access to the labor market, her participation in the study itself reinforced the notion that race, class, gender, and I would argue sexuality (at least implicitly), were mutually constitutive in producing different material consequences for black women and black men.

Height's work with President Kennedy's Commission not only illuminates one of the many ways that black women had been involved in the civil rights movement's previous and correlative labor movements that fought for black women and men's economic equality; it also provides a historical and political context for understanding the proliferation of first-person narratives that emerge throughout the modern civil rights movement in which black women and men are explicitly staking out their claim for sexual and gender rights, albeit in distinctive, and, at times, adversarial ways. Among these narratives are Malcolm X's *The Autobiography of Malcolm X* (1965), Lorraine Hansberry's *To Be Young Gifted and Black* (1970), Anne Moody's *Coming of Age in Mississippi* (1968), Eldridge Cleaver's *Soul on Ice* (1968), and Angela Davis's *Angela Davis: An Autobiography* (1974).[12]

By drawing attention to how women's *and* men's claims for civil rights were gendered and sexualized, I want to trouble the cultural assumptions that when we speak of gender we speak of women, and when we speak of sexuality we speak of non-heterosexuality. In other words, as black women often fought for rights and had to challenge patriarchal ideas of black heterosexual womanhood that contributed to their disenfranchisement, black men often fought to possess the equivalent of white heterosexual manhood, without necessarily questioning its sexist and heterosexist premises. While acknowledging that this acceptance of patriarchy from black men would engender antagonism between black men and women, this chapter charts the overlap of black men and women whose progressive politics enlarged the scope of civil rights, and ultimately considers how these models might be used to engage twenty-first century civil rights needs that remain unfulfilled during this second phase of the long civil rights movement.[13]

By analyzing Toni Cade Bambara's groundbreaking *The Black Woman: An Anthology* (1970), Kalamu ya Salaam's "Women's Rights Are Human Rights," (1979) and Huey Newton's "A Letter to from Huey to the Revolutionary Brothers and Sisters about the Women's Liberation and Gay Liberation Movements," (1970),[14] all of which were written during the (long) civil rights movement, I demonstrate how such works posited an intersectional definition of civil rights to queer popular understandings that isolated racial rights from sexual and gender rights. That is, these works in particular demonstrated compellingly – in an exemplary way – how notions of civil rights that privileged race over gender and/or sexuality proved inadequate in addressing the complexity of black civil rights disenfranchisement and provided a framework to complicate insufficiently complex ideas about black civil rights. As Kenneth Warren's *What Was African American Literature* evidences, a growing trend in black literary studies in particular (and black studies in general) is calling into question the usefulness of thinking about African American culture and politics through the politics of Jim Crow, as well as defining black cultural production too narrowly as a reaction to white racism and political disenfranchisement. However, the politics of race – that is, how race informs our thoughts, political and personal desires, and public policy – seems central to our understanding of black politics and black identity. While the end of Jim Crow (phase one of the civil rights movement) may have reconstituted the terms under which we understand these relationships, it is politically dangerous and shortsighted to overstate the reach of the end of Jim Crow. These writers position black gendered and sexualized selves in relation to political movements, theoretical paradigms, and personal experiences, and intervene in civil rights and identity politics debates by foregrounding the centrality of cross-cutting political issues to black political debates and black communal transformation. Drawing on earlier formulations of black intersectionality that foregrounded gender and sexual equality as important issues in black political formulations, these activists and writers help engender political solutions that remain attentive to the diversity and complexity of black identities and black political concerns, and their insights might prove useful in addressing the contemporary civil rights problems affecting America.

Race, Gender, and Sexuality in Foundational Texts

Since the mid-1960s, and, as result of the decade's social unrest and political upheaval, the study of black life – vis-à-vis Black Studies, African American Studies, and Ethnic Studies programs and departments – has become increasingly institutionalized within colleges and universities. While these academic units promised to deemphasize the importance of Eurocentric thought, they did not always deemphasize masculinist and/or heteronormative discourses. Without a doubt, the *institutionalization* of black feminism during the 1970s and 1980s, black masculinity studies in the 1990s, and black queer studies during the early 2000s helped correct the tendencies to equate blackness with black heterosexual middle-class manhood. That is, these disciplines advanced academic and popular understandings of black identity as diverse and black identity politics as complicated and sometimes competing. Yet, long before the term "intersectionality" became the analytic rubric for understanding the ways that race, gender, sexuality, and social class overlap in political interests and allegiances, and long before the phrase "non-normative sexualities" was used to demarcate non-heterosexual couplings and to detach sexual performances from sexual identity, black activists, writers, and critics alike were challenging monolithic notions of blackness and black identity politics. Black women in particular have keenly demonstrated how discussions of black civil rights use the language of racial homogeneity to elide the significant ways that gender and sexuality make racial experiences heterogeneous.

A cursory glance at nineteenth-century first-person narratives reveals the long trajectory in which black women writers recognized the commonality of racial suffering and acknowledged how other vectors of identity particularized their social dispossession. For example, Sojourner Truth's famous "Woman's Rights" (1851) and "When Woman Gets Her Rights Man Will Be Right" (1867) highlighted how patriarchy and racism doubly excluded black women from political rights by simultaneously excluding them from the definition of women because of their racial identities and by thinking of women as too incompetent to engage in politics. Harriet Jacobs's *Incidents in the Life of a Slave Girl: Written by Herself* (1861) demonstrates how slavery positions black women in a precarious matrix as the peculiar institution's law does not protect them, thus making rape, poverty, and dependency highly probable. While Anna Julia Cooper's "Womanhood a Vital Element in the Regeneration and Progress of a Race" (1892) foregrounds the need to value black women's roles in shaping the body politic through their roles as mothers, Jarena Lee's *Religious Experience and Journal of Mrs. Jarena Lee, Giving an Account of Her Call to Preach the Gospel* (1842) contests any notion that black women's cultural reach remains consigned to the domestic sphere.[15] In distinct yet mutually constitutive ways, each of these texts functions as a precursor to the different phases of black feminism – double jeopardy (Frances Beale), multiple consciousness (Deborah King), standpoint theory (Patricia Hill Collins), and intersectionality (Kimberlé Crenshaw); each also demonstrates a historical attentiveness to black political cross-cutting issues and argues for an "intersectional" civil rights discourse.[16] While it is important to note that these women were calling for a more expansive notion of civil rights, it is just as imperative to remember that they also were providing models for how society might implement an "intersectional approach" when attempting to redress civil rights grievances.

This chapter began by explicating the significance of the anniversary of the March on Washington to reveal how contemporary civil rights injustices fit within the broader schema of civil rights attainment that black freedom struggles have demanded. Moreover, this long civil rights movement framework contextualizes a historical problem in which black political activity has at best struggled to manage cross-cutting political issues – and, at worst, to ignore them altogether, thus giving rise to black feminist and queer discourses that sought allegiances with black politics. While cross-cutting political issues have always been a central component of black political activity (e.g., Dorothy Height's work), following the 1960s, black political activity became more highly visible in public spheres, and the differing political needs became more forcefully articulated. As political scientist Cathy Cohen explains:

> The public agenda of black communities was once dominated by consensus issues construed as having an equal impact on all those sharing a primary

identity based on race. Now cross-cutting issues structured around and built on the social, political, and economic cleavages that tear at the perceived unity and shared identity of group members are increasingly finding their way into the public spotlight. Cross-cutting issues, while always a part of the historical struggles of marginal groups, are currently generating unprecedented public attention, as African Americans and the multiple issues they confront steadily move into the mainstream of American society.[17]

Cohen's insights are important because they draw attention to three significant points. First, she explains how the myth of scarcity, the notion that America's resources are lacking and/or fleeting, work against formulating political agendas that acknowledge and address cross-cutting issues. Instead, these political, social, and economic cleavages help to form hierarchies of needs (and hierarchies of oppression), which often position middle-class, heterosexual black men's political concerns as the community's most important issues that need to be addressed. Second, she implicitly situates this suppression of cross-cutting issues within black communities' perceptions that conformity to (white) American ideals and norms will result in their empowerment. Third, she suggests that a larger critique of American institutions might prove necessary for black political empowerment across gender, sexual, and class locations to be viable. This point is significant because it helps to explain gender and sexual antagonisms within black communities as not simply black people's unwillingness to address these instances of oppression and discrimination; rather this antagonism is part of a larger cultural phenomenon in which black people have been indoctrinated, even to their own political disempowerment. This issue has been particularly fascinating as it relates to black men, black hetero-patriarchy, and black women's liberations.

While black women undoubtedly played a significant role in foregrounding how gender and sexuality impacted their experiences of racism, black men – in both the nineteeth and twentieth centuries – displayed a range of "progressive gender politics" and argued against black male patriarchal privilege, which further marginalized black women in the public and private spheres. Although debates in black feminist theory have contested what name is most appropriate to describe black men who espouse progressive gender and/or sexual politics – "feminists," "pro-feminists," or "allies to feminism[18] – the emergence of the phrase "black male feminism" into the academic lexicon marks Michael Awkward's courageous theorizing of how a black male feminist analysis might aid the goals of black feminism. "A Black Male Feminist's Place" and Devon Carbado's "Introduction: Where and When Black Men Enter" compellingly demonstrate how black men's intentional engagement and critique of black hetero-patriarchy in order to divest themselves from its alluring pitfalls prove useful in black feminist political goals.[19] Mindful of this context, Frederick Douglass's "I Am a Radical Woman Suffrage Man" (1888), Alexander Crummell's "The Black Woman of the South: Her Neglects and Her Needs" (1883), and W. E. B. Du Bois's "The Damnation of Women" (1920)[20] demonstrate a cultural context in which black men fought for their inclusion in the American body politics, as well as that of black women. As Douglass remarked, "The fundamental proposition of the woman suffrage movement is scarcely less simple than that of the anti-slavery movement. It assumes that woman is herself. That she belongs to herself, just as fully as man belongs to himself – that she is a person and has all the attributes of personality that can be claimed by man, and that her rights of person are equal in all respects to those of man."[21] The suggestion here is not to overstate their disinvestment in patriarchy, nor is it to ahistorically apply Awkward's and Carbado's formulations. Rather, the point is to illuminate the conscious struggle in which black men engaged to insert themselves within a political system that necessarily subjugated women, while using their access within that system to demand more rights for black women.

Race, Gender, and Sexuality in Later Texts

In 1970, author, critic, and political activist Toni Cade (Bambara) published *The Black Woman: An Anthology*, which has become a groundbreaking text in black feminist studies because of its insightful and provocative articulation of the personal, political, economic, spiritual, and social concerns that black women held at the beginning of phase two of the civil rights movement. While this examination of *The Black Woman* pays particular attention to Cade's first-person writings, the volume itself includes a range of genres, including poetry, meeting transcriptions, biographical essays, and social critiques. The contributors, including poet Nikki Giovanni; writers Alice Walker and Shirley Williams; activists Frances Beale, Grace Lee Boggs, and artist Abbey Lincoln, offer provocative responses to address the persisting inequalities that plagued American society. Although many African Americans hoped the 1970s would mark the dawn of a new era in their lives, African American women in particular had experienced firsthand the consequences of sexist and heterosexist logics that circulated in civil rights and Black Power movement discourses, thus hampering the ability for collective black advancement. *The Black Woman* thus offered a doubly significant trenchant critique of American society and black communities. First, it examined the broader institutions of patriarchy and capitalism to demonstrate how both systems threatened the development of thriving black communities, even following the legislative accomplishments that phase one of the civil rights movement made possible. Second, it revealed the pitfalls of black communities' tendencies to privilege black middle-class men's heteronormative ideals as representative of the entire communities' political desires, and rallied against the circumscription and devaluation of black women's roles in empowerment struggles, as well as the tendency to ignore the specific contours of black women's oppression and political concerns.

While Farah Jasmine Griffin rightfully notes, "*The Black Woman* is not a black feminist text as we have come to understand that term," she is equally astute in acknowledging that it "paved the way for an emerging black feminism that came to flower in the late seventies and early eighties."[22] Although Toni Morrison's *The Bluest Eye* (1970) and *Sula* (1973), Alice Walker's *The Third Life of Grange Copeland* (1970), and Gayl Jones's *Corregidora* (1975)[23] became paradigmatic fictive texts in which black women writers demonstrated how sexism and heterosexism undermined the collective empowerment of black women in particular and black people in general, Cade's collection, which included several first-person essays (most of them autobiographical), foreshadowed the concerns the fictive texts engaged by demonstrating how the feminist slogan – the personal is political – functioned in the making of black politics. That is, by demonstrating, for example, how the civil rights movement's desire to help black men "regain their manhood" often meant consigning black women to the private, domestic sphere, *The Black Woman* argued that replicating white American patriarchy was not a radical political act, and this mimicry reinforced the gender antagonisms that were thwarting black people's political progress. Collectively, though, from divergent perspectives and sometimes oppositional points of view, *The Black Woman* calls into question how black liberation movements tend to elevate black men and masculinist concerns, while perpetuating myths about black women's ancillary and subordinate statuses, in order to reimagine a liberation movement and society in which black men and women might work collectively to better the lives of all black people.

In one of the anthology's most thought-provoking essays, "On the Issue of Roles," which Cade herself writes, and which she describes as an autobiographical essay (that may read like a social critique/analysis), she challenges the notion that biology determines social roles by using cross-cultural comparisons of men's and women's roles in African societies to demonstrate that gender roles are socially constructed and not biologically determined. Before demonstrating how gender roles are culturally determined and historically contingent, Cade argues that rigid understandings of gender roles and expectations not only replicate patriarchy's desire to keep women in a subordinate place (and black men, too, for that matter), but also place burdens on men (such as the role of primary breadwinner) that do not acknowledge the specific ways that men and women transgress these binaries in order to thrive. In the opening paragraph, Cade clarifies that the chief problem with relying on "stereotypical" gender roles is that the binary on which those roles are predicated is "antithetical to what [she] was all about – and what revolution for the self is all about – the whole person."[24] For Cade, any form of revolution must begin with the radical ideological reprogramming of the self, and in the case of the black revolution, that reprogramming must eschew the gender politics of that binary which, inflected by capitalism, positions black men and women in antagonistic relationships.

By examining black diasporic attitudes toward women and their roles in society and politics, Cade further bolsters her argument that American gender roles perpetuate racist and capitalist interests; she also provides a blueprint that American black men and women can use to engage in revolutionary, radical political behavior. She illuminates how African tribes honor African women's contribution to politics and African men's contribution to household maintenance to rebuff the American notion that black women's influence should be confined to the domestic sphere while black men remain in the public sphere. Her interrogation of Frantz Fanon's *A Dying Colonialism* adds to this claim by underscoring the necessity for black men and women to move outside of rigid gender roles to truly advance the collective interests of black communities. This example becomes particularly poignant because it shows how the familial unit under discussion has to consciously work against the social norms it has been taught and that it has internalized in order to make genuinely transformative political progress.

Within their newly defined familial roles, where the hierarchies between children and parents, and wife and husband, are disrupted, the family can begin to see itself outside of scripted binaries that inhibit their individual and collective developments. As Cade notes, "The family was no longer a socially ordained nuclear unit to perpetuate the species or legitimize sexuality, but an extended kinship of cellmates and neighbors linked in the business of actualizing a vision of a liberated society. A new person is born when he finds a value to define an actional self and when he can assume autonomy for that self. Such is the task that faces us."[25] Without a self-conscious interrogation of how anti-black, anti-woman, anti-black woman, and capitalistic discourses have corrupted the making of black politics after the civil rights movement's phase one, gender antagonisms will persist and black enfranchisement will remain an underdeveloped possibility.

Cade's analysis thus unhinges several paradigms upon which racist heterosexist patriarchy depends and thrives, and she cautions African Americans, in their rightful request for increased access to citizenship rights and the material benefits that accrue from those rights, to enact a hermeneutics of suspicion toward alluring yet problematic ideologies of capitalism. She, as does Frances Beale in "Double Jeopardy," sees capitalism as a central force in antagonizing black men and black women's relationships by pitting black men and black women against each other in their quest for the scarce resources. She notes, for example, in her discussion of Africa, that "prior to the European obsession of property as a basis for social organization, and prior to the introduction of Christianity, a religion fraught with male anxiety and vilification of women, communities were equalitarian and cooperative."[26] Cade identifies Christianity and capitalism as mutually constitutive in creating hierarchical relationships between men and women in general, and black men and black women in particular, to reinforce how both institutions interlock to produce oppressive conditions.

While Cade is not trying to make claims about the gender relationships throughout the entire continent of Africa, she turns readers' attention to these particular communities to buttress her final admonition against black Americans who want to naturalize sex divisions to think of women as "the helpmate and object because that is the nature of the sexes, because that's the way it's always been, and just because."[27] Cade suggests, "We make many false starts because we have been programmed to depend on white models or white interpretations of non-white models, so we don't even ask the correct questions, much less begin to move in a correct direction." "On the Issue of Roles" demands a more critical analysis of all models that black politics are fashioning themselves upon to ensure black politics do not simply replicate the status quo, albeit in a disguised manner.[28]

While *The Black Woman* first appeared in bookstores and reached audiences within and outside of the academy, Kalamu ya Salaam's "Woman's Rights" first appeared in *The Black Scholar*, an interdisciplinary journal that focused on Black Studies. Its appearance in a Black Studies journal is especially important because, as a field, Black Studies had not been engaged in or receptive to intersectional black feminist analyses, and Salaam's essay offered a refreshing divergence from these trends. Activist, scholar, and cultural critic Salaam argues that (black) women's rights movements are human rights movements to emphasize that both movements demand basic citizenship rights that should be available to everyone regardless of gender. By focusing attention on the category of the human, Salaam instructively challenges the implicit notion that citizenship rights – and civil rights – are privileges and entitlements reserved only for (white) men. On the one hand, Salaam recognizes the ubiquity of this problem, arguing that a global examination of the status of women reveals "the issue of women's rights has and continues to be a central concern of every progressive force in the world, as well as a critical concern of millions of women who daily suffer the degradations and deprivations of sexual chauvinism in its institutional-ized and individual forms."[29] On the other, Salaam's analysis considers how "sexual chauvinism in its institutionalized and individual forms" operates in African American communities, where both the women's liberation and "men against chauvinism" movements are thought to bear little relevance. While the former movement is better known, I use the phrase "men against chauvinism" to describe the task Salaam undertakes in the essay by contex-tualizing it within the broader conversation about black men's relationship to black feminism that animates scholarly debates from the 1990s forward.

Salaam argues that sexism prohibits the development of revolutionary and progressive society because the social stratification on which the system depends denies women the ability to make their own decisions and instead presupposes that women who do are anti-black men as opposed to pro-self. He insists that this limited understanding of women's rights hinges on uncrit-ical investments in capitalism and heterosexual couplings (the nuclear family and/or male-female relationships). As does Bambara, Salaam first argues that in order to achieve an empowered black community in which all of its citi-zens enjoy their privileges, a reordering of the ideological self remains a top priority. Situating his own desire to disrupt a hetero-*patriarchal* system from which he benefits, if only nominally, Salaam notes: "I am concerned about the issue of women's rights because I am striving to be a revolutionary, and without the eradication of sexism there will be no true and thorough going revolution."[30] Two points in the remark deserve further commentary. First, Salaam positions the "revolutionary" and the "sexist" as politically incom-patible positions, disrupting extant civil rights and Black Power discourses that, under the aegis of "revolution," subordinate black women's political needs and aspirations to those of black men. Second, and significantly, Salaam anticipates and responds to questions of why he advocates women's rights.

His response is instructive in that it ultimately reveals not only the entan-glement of sexism, heterosexism, and homophobia, but suggests perhaps that the lack of male allies against chauvinism may in part lie in the fear of having one's sexuality questioned. Citing his historical forefathers as exemplars of men against chauvinism whose allegiances engendered skepti-cism about their sexual desires, Salaam explains, "Douglass was vilified and shunned by former friends who could not understand his concern for the rights of women. I hear Douglass being called a "hermaphrodite" and other terms which questioned his sexuality because of his stand on sexism.... I should rather be called 'hermaphrodite' and other names because of my support than have women continually referred to as 'bitch,' and 'broad' in every day speech."[31] Salaam's point demonstrates how, in his contemporary context, homophobia also functioned with sexism as a means to deter men from promoting anti-patriarchal points of view. At the same time, it highlights the importance of resisting ideologies (sexism and homophobia) that undermine the civil enfranchisement of all people within a community. He must divest himself of patriarchal privilege (the presumption that he is heterosexual and not a "hermaphrodite") in order to empower (black) women.

Although there is an identifiable historical tradition of black men explicitly resisting sexism, it is more difficult to trace a parallel genealogy before the 1970s in which black men resist homophobia. While James Baldwin is one of the most notable exceptions, Huey Newton's short letter, "A Letter from Huey to the Revolutionary Brothers and Sisters," captures an important understanding of how the black liberation, women's liberation, and gay liberation movements share similar goals, which include eradicating oppression and ensuring civil rights. The essay first appeared in *Gay Flames Pamphlet*, which, like many publications emerging in conjunction with gay activist organization such as the Gay Liberation Front (GLF), published first-person writings that articulated gay rights as civil rights. That Newton writes this essay is significant in how it shows the range of thought present in the Black Power Movement and Black Panther Party insofar as Newton eschews homophobia, sexism, patriarchy, and heterosexism, differentiating himself from these problematic ideologies that truncated the political efficacy of the Black Power Movement. Newton thus makes two important interventions, both of which help to conclude this essay and shape the contours of black queer studies. First, by asking the question, "What made them homosexuals?" Newton draws attention to the nature versus nurture debate in sexuality, where arguments that framed sexuality as biologically determined undermined the notion that gay and lesbians chose their sexuality and therefore could become heterosexuals and obtain the rights denied them. After clarifying his non-investment in either argument, Newton elaborates, "whatever the case is, we know that homosexuality is a fact that exists and we must understand it in its purest form; that is, a person should have the freedom to use his body whatever way he wants to."[32] For Newton, the debate between biology and choice obfuscates the point that everyone – heterosexual and non-heterosexual – makes choices about how he or she exercises his or her sexuality, and that both sets of choices deserve equal social and political privileges.

Second, as does Bambara, Newton redefines our understanding of what it means to be revolutionary by focusing on constructing new models and frameworks for organizing society. Like Bambara, Newton's discussion of sexuality reminds that "we haven't established a revolutionary value system; we're only in the process of establishing it. I don't remember us ever constituting any value system that said that a revolutionary must say offensive things toward homosexuals or that a revolutionary must make sure that women not speak out about their own particular kind of oppression."[33] By connecting homophobia and sexism, Newton suggests that a revolutionary system, one that radically differs from the system it is trying to subvert, must not replicate those pathological ideologies. Equally important, he also explicates the intricate relationship that sexism and homophobia have, as they operate through each other.

The modern civil rights movement catalyzed other social movements, including the (white) second wave feminist movement and the (white) gay and lesbian movement, while also turning attention to how intra-racial relations grappled with the politics of gender and sexuality as they intersected with those of race. And while black feminism and black queer studies, as academic disciplines, gave rise to more formalized discussions of these relationships, antagonisms, and possibilities, the first-person writings of civil rights activists – throughout history – reveal a long-term, sustained engagement with cross-cutting political issues. As phase two of the civil rights movement continues in the twenty-first century, it will progress only by rethinking what "revolutionary" politics really are, and how enacting a revolutionary politics foregrounds models of civil rights that keep a keen eye on cross-cutting issues and developing policies and practices that do not reinstitute any form of oppression. We should not, like early conversations that phrased feminism and gay rights as a "white" issue, presume that black civil rights are heteronormative or masculinist; such a move would undo the important work scholarship and activism has done to underscore cross-cutting issues' importance.

NOTES

1 See Belinda Robnett, *How Long? How Long? African-American Women in the Struggle for Civil Rights* (New York: Oxford University Press, 1997). Robnett points out that to understand the complexity of men's and women's civil rights leadership, it is important to understand formal leadership versus bridge leaderships. Whereas the former refers to the activities in which men typically engaged, which includes holding titled positions and making media appearances, the latter includes the everyday organizational and mobilizing tactics that women engaged in to raise consciousness and promote activism within local communities.

2 See Erica Edwards, *Charisma and the Fiction of Black Leadership* (Minneapolis: University of Minnesota Press, 2012). Edwards argues against the notion that leadership is a supernatural gift (charisma) available only to black men, demonstrating how this very notion defies the democratic claims that black political movements seek by creating a gender hierarchy that privileges black men and their political concerns – both in black freedom struggles and society.

3 The concept of phasing draws attention to civil rights historians' desire to understand the legal aspect of the civil rights movement (the classical phase or phase one), which deemed it necessary to remove Jim and Jane Crow segregation, as connected to the implementation aspect (phase two), which desired to achieve equal results and outcomes. See Charles Hamilton, "Federal Law and the Courts in the Civil Rights Movement," in *The Civil Rights Movement in America*, ed. Charles Eagles (Jackson: University Press of Mississippi, 1986), pp. 97–117.

4 While the striking of any aspect of this act seems like a setback to civil rights, the court specifically noted that the federal government no longer has to monitor locales that historically have been known for voter obstruction. Immediately following this ruling, several states, including North Carolina, moved to amend their voting laws to make it more difficult for black people to participate in the electoral process.

5 The backlash against affirmative action programs demonstrates the resistance the broader society has toward implementing the goals of phase one of the civil rights movement, particularly if affirmative action is thought of as "instrumental to rethinking and retooling American democracy and economic equality" and "designed to monitor inequality, reduce poverty, and to redress the centuries-long exploitation and social degradation of African Americans." Aliyyah Abdur-Rahman, *Against the Closet: Black Political Longing and the Erotics of Race* (Durham, NC: Duke University Press, 2012), p. 134.

6 Jacquelyn Dowd Hall, "The Long Civil Rights Movement and the Political Uses of the Past," *Journal of American History* 91 (2005): p. 1234.

7 In "From Protest to Politics," Bayard Rustin charts the movement from integration during the classical phase to implementation during phase two as central to the movement's continued progress. Bayard Rustin, "From Protest to Politics," in *Time on Two Crosses: The Collected Writing of Bayard Rustin*, ed. Devon Carbado and Donald Weise (San Francisco: Cleis Press, 2003), pp. 116–29.

8 Robert J. Patterson, *Exodus Politics: Civil Rights and Leadership in African American Literature and Culture* (Charlottesville: University of Virginia Press, 2013).

9 For further exploration of black queer studies' engagement with the interrelation between civil rights, gender rights, and sexual rights, see Darieck Scott, *Extravagant Abjection: Blackness, Power, and Sexuality in the African American Literary Imagination* (New York: New York University Press, 2010); E. Patrick Johnson and Mae Henderson Johnson, eds., *Black Queer Studies: A Critical Anthology* (Durham, NC: Duke University Press, 2007), and Abdur-Rahaman, *Against the Closet*.

10 For more in-depth investigations of black women's leadership and participation in the civil rights movement, see Vicki L. Crawford, Jacqueline Rowe, and Barbara Woods, eds., *Women in the Civil Rights Movement: Trailblazers and Torchbearers, 1941–1965* (Bloomington: Indiana University Press, 1993); Barbara Ransby, *Ella Baker and the Black Freedom Movement: A Radical Democratic Vision* (Chapel Hill: University of North Carolina Press, 2003); and Paula Giddings, *When and Where I Enter* (New York: Perennial, 2001).

11 William Jones, *The March on Washington: Jobs, Freedom, and the Forgotten History of Civil Rights* (New York: W.W. Norton, 2013), p. 166.

12 Malcolm X, *The Autobiography of Malcolm X* (New York: Ballantine, 1987); Lorraine Hansberry, *To Be Young Gifted and Black* (New York: Vintage, 1996); Anne Moody, *Coming of Age in Mississippi: Anne Moody's Classic Autobiography of Growing Up Poor and Black in the Rural South* (New York: Bantam Dell, 1992); Eldridge Cleaver, *Soul on Ice* (New York: Dell, 1999); and Angela Davis, *Angela Davis: An Autobiography* (New York: International Publishers, 2013).

13 The phrase "long civil rights movement" is used to argue that the civil rights movement did not simply develop during the mid-twentieth century, but rather had been occurring since dispossessed Africans first began fighting to reclaim their freedom. See Hall, "The Long Civil Rights Movement," 1233–63; also see Leon Litwack, "Fight the Power! The Legacy of the Civil Rights Movement," 75.1 *Journal of Southern History* (2009): 3–28.

14 Toni Cade (Bambara), ed., *Black Woman: An Anthology* (New York: Washington Square Press, 2005); Kalamu ya Salaam, "Women's Rights Are Human Rights," in *Traps: African American Men on Gender and Sexuality*, ed. Rudolph Byrd (Bloomington: Indiana University Press, 2001), pp. 113–18; Huey Newton, "A Letter from Huey Newton to the Revolutionary Brothers and Sisters about the Women's Liberation and Gay Liberation Movements," in *Traps*, ed. Byrd, pp. 37–45.

15 Sojourner Truth, "When Woman Gets Her Rights Man Will Be Right," in *Words of Fire: An Anthology of African-American Feminist Thought*, ed. Beverly Guy-Sheftall (New York: New Press, 1995), pp. 37–38; Truth, "Woman's Rights," p. 36. Harriet Jacobs, *Incidents in the Life of a Slave Girl, Written by Herself*, ed. Kwame Appiah (New York: Modern Library, 2000); Jarena Lee, *Religious Experience and Journal of Mrs. Jarena Lee, Giving an Account of Her Call to Preach the Gospel* (Philadelphia: P. S. Duval, 1849); Anna Julia Cooper, "Womanhood a Vital Element in the Regeneration and Progress of a Race," in *A Voice from the South* (New York: Oxford University Press, 1988), pp. 9–47.

16 Kimberlé Crenshaw, "Mapping the Margins: Intersectionality, Identity Politics, and Violence against Women of Color," *Stanford Law Review* 43 (1991): 1241–99; Patricia Hill Collins, *Black Sexual Politics: African Americans, Gender, and the New Racism* (New York: Routledge, 2004); Deborah King, "Multiple Jeopardy, Multiple Consciousness: The Context of Black Feminist Ideology," in *Words of Fire*, ed. Beverly Guy-Sheftall, pp. 294–318; Frances Beale, "Double Jeopardy: To Be Black and Female," in Words of Fire, ed. Beverly Guy-Sheftall, pp. 146–56.

17 Cathy Cohen, *The Boundaries of Blackness: AIDS and the Breakdown of Black Politics* (Chicago: University of Chicago Press, 1999), p. 8.

18 Farah Jasmine Griffin, "Conflict and Chorus: Reconsidering Toni Cade's *The Black Woman: An Anthology*," in *Is It Nation Time? Contemporary Essays on Black Power and Black Nationalism*, ed. Eddie S. Glaude Jr. (Chicago: University of Chicago Press, 2002), pp. 113–29.

19 Michael Awkward, *Negotiating Difference: Race, Gender, and the Politics of Positionality* (Chicago: University of Chicago Press, 1995); Devon Carbado, "Introduction: Where and When Black Men Enter," in *Black Men on Race, Gender, and Sexuality: A Critical Reader*, ed. Devon Carbado (New York: New York University Press, 1999), pp. 1–13.

20 Frederick Douglass, "I Am a Radical Woman Suffrage Man," in *Traps*, ed. Byrd, pp. 37–45; Alexander Crummell, "The Black Woman of the South: Her Neglects and Her Needs," in *Traps*, ed. Byrd, pp. 46–57; W. E. B. Du Bois, "The Damnation of Women," in *Traps*, ed. Byrd, pp. 58–70.

21 Douglass, "I Am a Radical Woman Suffrage Man," p. 43.

22 Griffin, "Conflict and Chorus," p. 118.

23 Toni Morrison, *The Bluest Eye* (New York: Knopf, 1970); Toni Morrison, *Sula* (New York: Knopf, 1973); Alice Walker, *The Third Life of Grange Copeland* (New York: Harcourt Brace Jovanavich, 1970); and Gayl Jones, *Corregidora* (Boston: Beacon Press, 1986).

24 Toni Cade (Bambara), "On the Issue of Roles," in *The Black Woman: An Anthology*, ed. Bambara, pp. 123–25.

25 Ibid., p. 133.

26 Cade (Bambara), "On the Issue of Roles," p. 126.

27 Ibid.

28 Ibid., p. 133.

29 Salaam, "Women's Rights," p. 111.

30 Ibid., p. 114.

31 Ibid.

32 Huey Newton, "A Letter from Huey Newton," p. 282.

33 Ibid.

IO

BARBARA MCCASKILL

Twenty-First-Century Literature: Post-Black? Post–Civil Rights?

Patriotic hymns and anthems can be meaningful barometers of Americans' shifting connections with particular national identities, however far removed from actuality they may be. In order to celebrate the country as a symbol of freedom from tyranny, for example, Samuel Francis Smith's "America" (1832) invokes the peacefulness and protectiveness of nature and of natural elements – mountains, woods, trees, breezes. From the mountains to the prairies to the "oceans, white with foam" that buttress against enemies in Irving Berlin's "God Bless America" (1918), the landscape appears as an expansive, verdant green that is at once orderly, harmonious, and reassuring. In these lyrics, the beauty of America rests in its implied generosity, in its eagerness to extend an overabundance of foods, mineral resources, and open spaces to the outstretched and open arms of humanity.

By contrast, an anthem to the landscapes of the civil rights movement would track a different cast of images. Its scenery would gesture to a centuries-long, compassion-short, American story that instead has been disorderly, messy, and disquieting. A river meandering through rural Mississippi, the downtown public park shading the "Magic City," a bridge spanning sultry Selma, and even the iconic arches guarding the school in the southern college town where I teach and write – all these would pay tribute to a divided America loathe to let love heal the hate of racism, or to shine a little light of hope and freedom through the barricading storm clouds of despair. They would inscribe an America traumatized by such events as the 1955 lynching of Emmett Till, the 1963 "D Day" youth protests against segregation in downtown Birmingham, 1965's "Bloody Sunday" when Alabama police and state troopers attacked activists marching for voting rights, and the 1961 desegregation of the University of Georgia by two young academic standouts from Atlanta's all-black high schools, Charlayne Hunter and Hamilton Holmes.

From commemorating the birthday of Martin Luther King Jr. as a national holiday and erecting a statue of him on the National Mall, to staffing civil rights movement museums and leading educational tours throughout the

Deep South, Americans have acknowledged the legacy of such places as battlegrounds and turning points in the long African American freedom struggle. Even as we lay claim to dreams of an inclusive, tolerant, multiracial, multicultural society, we reflect upon how such sites remind us of the ugly, unfinished histories of exploitation and abuse in the name of race and of racial, sexual, and cultural markers of difference. Over one-half century has passed since the milestone legislations of the movement, and concurrent with discussions of the gains and losses represented by a post–civil rights, post-racial society, a conversation about the strengths and disadvantages of post-blackness has emerged.

As Michael Eric Dyson writes, "post-black" is a term that resists any definition of African American identity and culture that begins with an inflexible or essential idea of authentic blackness. It "points, instead, to the end of the reign of a narrow, single notion of blackness." Paul C. Taylor traces the term, what many critics refer to as "post-soul," to the curator Thelma Golden, who implied that for post–civil rights black artists "the traditional meanings of blackness ... are too confining. New meanings have emerged, new forms of black identity that are multiple, fluid, and profoundly contingent, along with newly sophisticated understandings of race and identity." By associating the term with black identity formation "outside of a U.S. context," L. H. Stallings also includes Diasporic Africans, as well as African Americans, within its frame of reference. A "post-black" point of view in either case means to follow the premise that there is no single, fixed, legitimate way of being, thinking, acting, or reacting like a black person. The collateral legacy of the African American freedom struggle has been to challenge "myths of unity," as Dyson calls them, that historically have mobilized African Americans around the central good work of defeating slavery and Jim Crow – as well as the stereotypes that both institutions have imposed upon generations of black people. An ongoing goal has been to materialize a nation where all Americans, including African Americans, stand free and able to choose or change allegiances based on affiliations that embrace class, religion, sexual orientation, education, and politics. One of the struggle's logical outcomes, then, has been to question prescriptions from within the black community and outside of it that require all group members to adopt, unilaterally and uncritically, the same tastes, interests, and priorities for themselves and their posterity, especially when such uniformity never has been the case.[1]

In a move toward understanding the racial and social politics of this post-black era, Lila Quintero Weaver's graphic novel *Darkroom: A Memoir in Black and White* (2012), Natasha Trethewey's memoir *Beyond Katrina: A Meditation on the Mississippi Gulf Coast* (2010), and Tayari

Jones's novel *Silver Sparrow* (2011) raise the ghosts of Jim Crow and segregation that haunt America. Adhering to Brian Norman's definition of post–civil rights narratives, they "return to the nation's Jim Crow past in order to disrupt easy proclamations of a coherent and binding multiethnic culture where competing ideas of civic and pluralistic citizenship are no longer at war."[2] Weaver, Trethewey, and Jones remember Jim Crow days when African Americans found common ground and a shared identity in protesting against oppression and racial stereotyping. Rather than remaining in this moment, however, they explore the possibilities of the post-black experience, of "learning to ignore the white gaze, along with the added burden of disregarding the censoring black one."[3] *Darkroom,* for example, critiques and rejects the southern white gaze by recollecting how a grammar school history textbook titled *Know Alabama* (1961) masqueraded for an informed history of the state.[4] It told a wild fiction that painted plantation slavery as a rosy antebellum world of kind masters and happy slaves, only to be dragged under by Reconstruction's terrible tide of predatory northern carpetbaggers, traitorous southern scalawags, and "uppity" African American candidates running for and winning political offices. "This is often the way collective, cultural memory works," Natasha Trethewey reflects in her memoir, "full of omissions, partial remembering, and purposeful forgetting. People on both sides of a story look better in a version that leaves out certain things."[5]

To varying degrees, African Americans responded to such omissions and erasures by shaping collective identities that engendered power, pride, and self-esteem. Where the twenty-first-century literary productions of Weaver, Trethewey, and Jones take these civil rights movement histories is to ramp up more capacious and variant meanings of blackness, during what Roopali Mukherjee calls this current "historical moment in which neither cultural practices nor political solidarities cohere predictably along racial lines."[6] Rooted in local places in Alabama, Mississippi, and Georgia, *Darkroom, Beyond Katrina,* and *Silver Sparrow* do not directly advocate either for or against post-blackness. Nonetheless, even as they acknowledge the incompleteness of the freedom struggle, they illuminate conversations about the fluidity and firmness of African American identity that the civil rights movement set in motion.

Weaver's *Darkroom* conjures the zeitgeist of a childhood spent "deep in the heart of Dixie" from first grade through high school, when "Jim Crow hadn't yet surrendered to the inevitable, but his days were numbered."[7] Most of the narrative's action is set from 1961 to 1965 in Marion, a "charming" central Alabama college "town of 3,200" that Weaver remembers as "neatly divided between black and white" (19). According to the Perry County census figures of 1960, 65.8 percent of residents are African American, and

34.2 percent of residents are white: that is, until the Quinteros arrive from Buenos Aires, Argentina. The darkroom of the title is the segregated South of the 1950s and 1960s. A provincial place "simmering with racial strife" (62), it is also a metaphor for segregation as an existential idea, a "'way of life'" (63). From cradle to grave based on two – and only two – races, everything is bifurcated into black and white: theaters, buses, restaurants, schools, amusement parks, hospitals, restrooms, even churches and the cemeteries that shoulder them. "Dividing lines between one race and the next" govern who does or does not attain social, economic, and educational mobility (88).

Midway through her memoir, the author explores these meanings by literally plunging readers into a dark room. Fourteen thickly blackened or black-bordered pages follow "Marion's darkest hour" (27) – a night-time voter registration march in 1965 that ends with murder and that inspires the celebrated walk from Selma to Montgomery. At one of the town's African American churches, activists gather to hold a mass meeting featuring songs and prayers, to prepare their bodies, minds, and spirits for facing violence and even death at the hands of segregationists. The pastor shares an implied comparison between the town outside the church doors and the darkroom of racial apartheid. "Remember what the prophet Isaiah said," he warns them. "'The people that walked in darkness have seen a great light.'[8] One day, by God's grace, the white man will see the light and emerge from his dark cell" (154). The marchers then spill out onto a pitch black emptiness filled quickly by sounds of clubs cracking bones, as white "policemen, sheriff's deputies, and state troopers brutalize" them (161). A sickening "shot in the dark" rings out (169). A twenty-seven-year-old black man named Jimmie Lee Jackson has been mortally wounded as he seeks shelter for his mother and grandmother away from the mob.

The darkroom of Jim Crow also includes violence that is both misogynistic and emasculating. Black women of Marion are objectified around town as the targets of unsolicited and lascivious catcalls. In her study *At the Dark End of the Street*, Danielle L. McGuire explains that these rituals of shaming, hatred, and subjugation belonged to a spectrum of racist crimes ranging from ogling and fondling to sexualized assaults and interracial rape. They gained traction from "white stereotypes of black women's uninhibited sexuality" and from whites' perceptions that African American women "lure men into raping them."[9] Likewise, to punctuate a litany of stories about Ku Klux Klan violence and other vigilantism, Weaver draws the image of a black man dangling at the end of a lynch rope – somebody's husband, son, uncle, nephew, father (195).

In addition to symbolizing such terror, the darkroom is the literal space in the Quintero household where Nestor, a college teacher, preacher, and photographer, makes art from empty pages. As with the Mexican painter Frida Kahlo's father Guillermo, Nestor's brush is his camera. This place, the South, is his canvas. "Every house we ever lived in had a makeshift dark-room," the author recalls (22). As a space where blank sheets of photo-graphic paper, dipped in chemical baths, miraculously seem to flower into snapshots documenting family and community members, her father's dark-room encompasses a process of incubation, composition, and growth as well as a final, often unanticipated, outcome. It signals the transformative power of anti-racist movements, or how such mobilizations catalyze people to gather momentum behind the project of eliminating prejudice and stereotyp-ing, abandoning the constrictiveness of such moral menaces in order to open themselves to "the full tonal range" of humanity and human nature (17).

The heterogeneous Quinteros are the antitheses of narrow attitudes that traffic in disunity and dim the darkroom of segregation. Among the mother, father, two sisters, and one son, differences abound. Weaver's mother Nelly comes from "pure" and privileged "European stock" (83), while her father Nestor is a *trigueño* or mixed-race person, from the Spanish word *trigo* for "wheat" (83), who descends from impoverished, indigenous peoples. Defiantly, Nelly and Nestor have married, even though social conventions mandate their apartness. Yet they remain "tether[ed] to the old country" through poetic letters and photographs "that took on the feel of fairy tales" (110, 111), through home-cooked meals featuring *empanadas, paella, pan dulce, dulce de leche*, and other Latin American savories, and through their insistence on speaking their native Spanish not only at home but also (to the great irritation of their children) in public places like the supermarket for all the town to hear. Ginny, the Quinteros' popular older daughter, who "gave brains glamour," introduces her siblings to an America "brimmed over with the stuff of dreams," from leggy Barbie dolls and the rocking LPs of Chubby Checker to bouffant hairdos and the protest anthems of Harry Belafonte and Joan Baez (64, 39). By contrast, their youngest daughter, Lissy, endures notoriety and swallows embarrassment at her all-white school after being branded "the girl with nigger lips" (79).

These distinctions among the Quintero family members expose the illogic of segregation. Its mainstay is a false perception that confirms the existence of clearly defined, visibly delineated borders between and within racial and ethnic groups. Such nonsense falls apart "when reality fails to accommodate those neat categories" (88). The memoirist Weaver anticipates this more complex understanding of identity by defining herself as neither American nor Argentine, since "most southerners had no idea how to label us" (86). Instead, she centers her selfhood on a global scale, as a cosmopolitan "shut-tling back and forth between my two worlds" while bearing witness to sweeping social and cultural changes (122). Reinforcing this notion of world citizenship, *Darkroom* appropriates an image reminiscent of the old RKO Radio Pictures' opening logo of a radio tower transmitting Morse code signals atop a rotating globe. In the place of a radio tower, however, Weaver substitutes a heavy-winged jet plane: trawling between northern and southern hemispheres, suspended above clouds and mountains, puttering around the planet. The planes and planets visually intertwine the Quinteros' memories of physical migrations between the hemispheres. Yet they also function as shorthand for the family's iconoclastic, fluid self-definitions that such migrations both disclose and obscure.

"The rules that governed race relations were written down nowhere," Weaver writes, "but you were supposed to know them anyway. You had to get educated. For one thing, violations could be very costly" (76). She pays this cost during the period of school integration, when she enrolls in summer classes at the Marion Military Institute and begins to befriend and date its first African American cadet. As their relationship becomes public, disapproving chatter in both the white and black communities reaches her father, who teaches at the Institute, and the school's commandant, and the men succeed in breaking up the couple. Weaver's exposure to the "raised eyebrows" and "sidelong glances" of black and white southerners who have been slow to shake off the burden of Jim Crow (220) suggests a version of the "racial fidelity," as Dyson writes, that historically has pressured African Americans to prioritize group solidarity over personal preferences and self-interest.[10] The town's destructive reaction to Weaver's relationship points to the sources of such pressures in fears of change, suspicions of difference, and desires to preserve power. It also points to the debate over whether or not a post-black, diverse idea of African American community and culture has been gained at the cost of a shared rhetoric of racial identity that focuses group energies and frames a unified, if illusory, vision for advancement.

In August 1969, just before Weaver began negotiating the racial polarities of a desegregated high school, "just a year after the beaches [of Mississippi's coast] were fully integrated" (45), and thirty-six years before Hurricane Katrina, the storm named Hurricane Camille rumbled through Natasha Trethewey's childhood home of North Gulfport, Mississippi. As she writes in her memoir *Beyond Katrina*, North Gulfport is "one of two historically African American communities that sprang up along the Mississippi Gulf Coast after emancipation" (85). It is where Trethewey, who became a U.S. poet laureate, once lived with her mother and grandmother, Gwendolyn Turnbough Trethewey and Leretta Dixon Turnbough. With "its liquor stores and car washes, / trailers and shotgun shacks / propped at the road's edge; /

its brick houses hunkered / against the weather" (73), modest, working-class North Gulfport identified African Americans collectively as a persistent and unified people – laboring hard, moving along the margins of prosperity to make a way out of no way, proving a united front against poverty and crime and other odds stacked against them. After Camille swept through the city, "more than six thousand residential and commercial buildings were destroyed and many more damaged. The local death count was 132" (44). Yet, many North Gulfport residents had remained throughout the storm, to ride it out, unscathed, in their homes, and the resilient neighborhood recovered and rebuilt itself.

"The past can only be understood in the context of the present," writes Trethewey, "overlapped as they are, one informing the other" (51). While Weaver demonstrates how we have arrived at discussions of post-blackness out of the black and white tensions of segregation, Trethewey suggests an origin story that is grounded not so much within this binary as in a hybrid, multicultural definition of America and the American dream that politics, money, and environmental pollution now conspire to erase. "The idea of America is inscribed on the landscape of North Gulfport," she writes, "streets called Jefferson, Madison, Monroe, Florida, Arkansas, Alabama, the names of presidents and states" (21). Other "names of towns, shopping malls, and subdivisions bear witness to vanished Native American tribes, communities of former slaves, long-ago industrial districts and transit routes" (33). Who remembers, she muses, that African Americans were barred from the Gulf's seafood industry as it took off in the 1890s, with those positions going to "Yugoslavs and Slovenians … as well as other men, women, and children of European descent, many of whom were Polish immigrants brought in from Baltimore and Acadians transported from Louisiana?" (35).

For twenty-first-century residents of the city and of the Mississippi Gulf Coast, the promise of "new jobs" and "new revenues" from the dockside gaming industry has arrived. However, due to the impact of residential and commercial development on the natural wetlands, along with such opportunities has come the threat of "the erosion" of both coastal culture and the coast itself (13). To reboot the economic mechanisms of seaside cities such as Gulfport and Biloxi in the wake of Katrina, many commercial and political interests have concentrated their investment capital and labor on shore-side casinos and other tourist attractions and corporate enterprises. They have priced out former residents of historic black communities who cannot afford to meet new construction standards for rebuilding their homes and businesses, they have redistricted neighborhoods so that property taxes have soared to unaffordable rates "even as property values have declined" (86), and they have paved the way for the environmental demise of these places. As a symbol of such cascading erasures in the devastating aftermath of Katrina's 2005 landfall, Trethewey's brother Joe stands in the middle of Jefferson Street in North Gulfport, "wildly" trying "to flag down an emergency vehicle zooming right by." Oblivious to him, it is destined for less "isolated" areas (21). Throughout *Beyond Katrina,* Joe's rising and falling fortunes parallel the "competing narratives" of remembering and forgetting that characterize the "sleepy little towns" along Mississippi's Gulf Coast (11, 45).

By presenting Joe as a symbol of the tension between the cultural memory and cultural erasure that both predates and follows Katrina, Trethewey also invites readers to consider the multiple, at times conflicting, identities that are evoked by the term "post-black." Seizing opportunities provided by the booming dockside gaming industry, by "renovating existing hotels and ... constructing new ones" (46), Joe made mad money before Katrina struck. As markers of prosperity finally rose in chronically under-resourced North Gulfport – "street lights" and "the Walmart, fast-food restaurants, motels, gas stations, and convenience stores, up to the new outlet mall" (48) – Joe entrepreneurially restored family properties and rented the shotgun houses to a steady stream of tenants. "A hard worker – efficient and likeable" (43), he had honed his skills for years as a young man hustling construction jobs in hotels and casinos along the coast. A striver's litany inserts Joe into the classic narrative of American identity where hard work, creativity, and initiative shape character; all three are rewarded; and an individual is limited only by the extent and originality of his or her dreams. Immediately after Katrina, Joe was also the epitome of industry:

> In the weeks following the storm, Joe busied himself, like a lot of coast residents, aiding the efforts to get food and water to victims. He unloaded trucks, stacked boxes of supplies, handed out diapers and water bottles, clothing and canned goods, to people lined up in the heat. He patched what he could of Miss Mary's roof.... He got a job directing traffic, standing on the highway waving a flag. He got a job removing debris, clearing the roadways, sorting through the remnants of life before Katrina. He stood in line for a check. He got a job cleaning the beach. (50)

Joe's whirlwind of activity after Katrina associates him with qualities of post-black masculinity, where simplistic stereotypes of African American men as either victims or criminals have yielded to possibilities limited only by their imagination and predilections. Evenly offering help to both anonymous "coast residents" as well as a longtime neighbor, he circulates boundlessly and porously among roadways and neighborhoods and beaches. Even though he does not neglect to claim "a check," he does not wait for the government to swoop down and rescue him with a Federal Emergency Management Agency (FEMA) trailer and public assistance. Instead, he lifts himself out of the storm's ruins by dialing up his energy and staying alert for opportunities. He is a post-black man who loves the members of his African American community, but whose stake in his own survival is not derived or expressed exclusively from in-group allegiances to them.

Because he loses all of his rentals as a result of Katrina's destruction, Joe's life takes a turn for the worse. Unmoored from his old social networks, ineligible "for the kinds of programs that had helped businesses and wealthier citizens get back on their feet," he traffics cocaine and is picked up by the police (91). On July 14, 2008, he begins an imprisonment that will last at least three years before he can apply for parole. He enters a carceral environment that drives home the fact that African American men too frequently have found themselves on the losing side of the criminal justice system, a history rooted in the bigotry of slavery and Jim Crow. Since desegregation, African American men continue to be disproportionately represented among this country's inmate populations, in part because of mandatory minimum and habitual offender policies that mete out harsh sentences. As of 2001, according to the NAACP, one in six African American men had served prison or jail time.[11] In addition, retrogressive definitions of African American masculinity, internalized by the inmates themselves, seem to have reversed the hands of time. Gang affiliations and repeat visits to the pen are markers of respect and belonging to many inmates, and a bewildered Joe wonders why they do not "aim at other accomplishments to be proud of," like getting released and never, ever returning to these cell blocks again (106).

In letters to his sister, Joe's incarceration aligns eerily with Jim Crow's darkroom. "Inside these walls there's a different world entirely," he discloses, "a world that consists of its own unwritten laws and rules" (112). He complicates this perception by not being helpless or passive and by attempting to gain some autonomy and control even within the prison's regulated and surveilled regimes. In the days of segregation, to retain a modicum of dignity and power, African Americans often made sacrifices like walking to work or school, instead of sitting or standing in the colored section at the back of the bus, or going thirsty to avoid using a segregated water fountain. Similarly, Joe reinvents a numbing inmate work detail – "eight miles a day doing roadwork – free labor for the state of Mississippi" (113) – into his own personal exercise program. Within the confining prison routines, he also maintains a sense of assertion and freedom by referring to "convicting" activities, as the inmates call them, like "hand washing my clothes in the sink and boiling my bottled water to make coffee," as actions of "creativity or ingenuity" (106).

He cannot literally change the terms and conditions of his sentence, but he does find meaning through this daily slog by approaching it as an opportunity for exercise rather than as wasted time and unrequited labor. He thus exemplifies the "liberating pursuit of individuality" that the sociologist Orlando Patterson has described as inherent in the idea of post-blackness.[12]

In his correspondence, Joe's nostalgic memories of an idyllic African American childhood run counter to perceptions of African Americans as pawns at the mercy of systemic degradations and as failed men and women. Instead, he has experienced a happy, picture postcard, all-American childhood. He had two parents, a "wonderful and supportive family," and an abundance of friends; and he lived in "a big house in a nice neighborhood" (107). His reminiscences follow what David Lee Ikard and Martell Lee Teasley describe as the post-black project of placing "a high premium on community and moral values."[13] His fondly remembered images shift criminality from its associations with blackness and black male identity to their sources in other social problems. The swagger that he encounters among his fellow prisoners, as Joe understands it, is a response to poverty and exclusion, not a demonstration of what all black men must be and become.

Because of its recognition of America's histories of erasure and silencing, *Beyond Katrina*'s venture into post-blackness does not fall into the trap that Ikard and Martell accuse a post-*racial* society of creating: of blaming social ills on those Americans who have been most disempowered by them and absolving the privileged of any and all accountability for such inequities. Joe acknowledges his responsibility for his incarceration and his complicity in his own undoing. At the same time, demonstrating that post-blackness exists in tandem with a world where racism "happens in places where we don't expect it to happen," he is skeptical of the conclusion that African Americans' expansive choices for self-definition mean that America is now colorblind.[14]

America, in other words, still remains race-based. What *Beyond Katrina* proposes as a necessary next step is a membership in a new community rooted in social action. Rather than what people have anointed as legitimate tastes and behaviors that define a racial group, Trethewey calls for a heightened involvement among everyone in "public discourse of difficult events" (102). Conversations about such national debacles as the botched emergency response to Hurricane Katrina can lead to solutions that directly confront the stark challenges of poverty, unemployment, hunger, environmental collapse, cultural erasure, and race and class stratification – all of which hobble America's ability to deliver on its promises.

Joe was "born and raised half his life in Atlanta" (45), and it is this city that inspires meanings of post-blackness in Tayari Jones's *Silver Sparrow*.

Like Harlem and Washington, D.C., Atlanta historically has been associated with examples of African American educational aspiration, class mobility, and financial success. Spelman College (founded 1881) and Morehouse College (founded 1867) are two storied and prestigious institutions that anchor a consortium of world-renowned schools of higher education established originally by and for black people. Also, during the 1930s and 1940s, the African American neighborhood of Sweet Auburn in downtown Atlanta became nationally known for its prosperous businesses and lively entertainment attractions. The offices of one of the wealthiest African American corporations, the Atlanta Life Insurance Company (founded 1905), and the pressroom of the *Atlanta Daily World* (founded 1928), the largest circulating black-owned newspaper in the South, were located in this community. Dr. Martin Luther King Jr., a Morehouse College graduate, was born and raised here, and here he founded the Southern Christian Leadership Conference that spearheaded desegregation actions and helped vault him to an international stage. A white mayor, William B. Hartsfield (1890–1971), once boasted that Atlanta was "the city too busy to hate," its residents so absorbed by the mutual project of economic and cultural growth that they allegedly had no time to distract themselves with the pettiness of racial tensions. In the 1980s, two African American mayors worked hard to make this claim a reality: Andrew Young (b. 1932), who once marched alongside King in boycotts and protests, and Maynard Jackson (1938–2003), an architect of what has become one of the world's major transportation hubs, Hartsfield-Jackson International Airport. They elevated Atlanta to an international stage as a symbol of the inclusive, sophisticated, and capital-infused New South.[15]

In the Atlanta of *Silver Sparrow*, subtler vestiges of racial intolerance also remain, such as store managers who eye African American shoppers suspiciously and assume that they plan to boost merchandise.[16] Yet the city's frame of reference is the affluence and assertion of *The Cosby Show,* not the shuffling stereotypes of *Amos 'n' Andy.*[17] Much has changed since the restrictive social policies of the first half of the twentieth century, and black Atlantans can select from an expanded range of services, neighborhoods, schools, and personal and professional roles. In the novel, African Americans drive "gangsta lean"[18] in sleek and speedy European imports like Jettas as well as old school Lincolns, Cadillacs, Coupe de Villes, and Buicks, their radios tuned to classical music or the R&B falsetto sounds of Smokey Robinson and Al Green. They can pilot their vehicle of choice to Paschal's, the historic black-owned restaurant where activists like King and Young once met to strategize over plates of southern fried soul food (49), or they can book a special occasion meal at the posh, white-owned

Mansion. They can enroll their college-bound children in prep schools like Woodward Academy, or they can encourage them to attend public-funded magnets such as Benjamin Mays High, named after a Morehouse College president and mentor to Dr. King.[19] In the Atlanta of *Silver Sparrow,* the racially bifurcating Jim Crow labels have disappeared, and colorblind NO SMOKING signs that apply uniformly to everyone have replaced them. The city is thus an appropriate setting for the novel's evocation of post-blackness and post-black identities.

Silver Sparrow's two adolescent protagonists and narrators, Dana Lynn Yarboro and Bunny Chaurisse Witherspoon, along with their mothers, Gwendolyn Beatrice Yarboro and Laverne Witherspoon, present a range of African American female identities that together compose a palette of post-blackness. The outgoing, pretty Dana is a gifted high school science and honors student with "waterfall hair" who has placed an Ivy League college degree in her sights (210). Yet she also rebels against her role as an obedient daughter and high-achieving student. She sneaks out to indulge in marijuana joints, strawberry wine coolers, peppermint schnapps, and monthly "pee-in-a-cup pregnancy tests" with her best friend Ronalda Harris; to shoplift cosmetics and condoms; and to love and risk "a reputation" with her older, arrogant boyfriend, Marcus McCready III (113, 105). Dignified, lovely, and proper, like "a strand of pearls" or "a dark-skinned Lena Horne" (19, 313), Dana's mother Gwendolyn Yarboro is a hard-working licensed practical nurse who wonders aloud why she once permitted the task of "learning to be a wife" to keep her on the periphery of movement activity, even though she benefited from it (24). She was the "very first colored" woman to work the gift-wrap counter in Atlanta's downtown Davison's department store (18).

Dana's doppelganger, the introverted, "stay-at-home" Chaurisse Witherspoon, is similarly squeaky clean on the surface (146). An "entertaining, and adoring" daddy's girl (he has nicknamed her Buttercup), she attends a performing arts high school and helps out afternoons and weekends in her mother's beauty salon (192). Where Dana is a "silver" beauty who augments her natural attractiveness and sparkling personality with "a smoothed on layer of pretty from a jar," Chaurisse describes herself as an ordinary girl who really does need that "Pretty in a Jar," and she sports a synthetic hair weave to prove it (197, 196). Yet, like Dana, Chaurisse has flirted with "a reputation for being a fast-tailed girl," having lost her virginity at age fourteen to a minister's son (188). Desperate "to shine" like the "natural beauties" she calls "silver girls," she describes herself as "not much to look at," and she agonizes constantly about her chubbiness, plain appearance, loneliness, and lackluster hair (197, 295).

Chaurisse's casual, maternal, hard-working mother Laverne is a licensed cosmetologist who proudly owns her business. At the Pink Fox, she crisply presses, perms, straightens, and Jheri curls other black women's hair and listens long days to her clients' confessions. At the end of the novel, however, Laverne's spirit has been "shattered" by a revelation that leaves her no "stronger than a cracked plate,"[20] even as her daughter Chaurisse urges her to be more *black* by resolving "to fight back" instead of whining and crying and indulging in "hard mourning" (315, 314, 311). What has left Laverne "heavy as a sandbag" is the unraveling of a secret that has knotted together all four of the mothers and daughters since the girls were infants (313). Her husband, James Alexander Witherspoon Jr., is a bigamist. He has been a "double duty daddy" with two marriage licenses, two wives, and two daughters (4).

James married Laverne first in front of a Marietta, Georgia, judge. When their daughter Chaurisse was three days old, to give his "outside child" (75) Dana a connection to her real father, he married Gwendolyn in front of a Birmingham, Alabama, judge (Gwendolyn retained her surname Yarboro from a previous marriage). James hid his infidelity from Chaurisse and Laverne, but Dana and Gwendolyn knew all along about the Witherspoon women and made a tacit agreement with James to steer clear of them. Yet they quickly broke this pact, shadowing and spying on James's first family, "nervous and excited, like rookie cops," and keeping tabs on the time and money James spent on them (108).

Silver Sparrow raises themes of legitimacy and authenticity and realness that ripple through conversations about post-blackness. Throughout the novel, Jones uses imagery to reference the secrets that people conceal from each other in the name of keeping up appearances of prosperity and perfection, of blending in with the crowd, and of hiding ugly or unsightly realities. For example, like the wigs and weaves of Laverne and Chaurisse, Gwendolyn and Dana tote Louis Vuitton designer knock-offs, or "LV" bags as they call them. Because the English letters can be taken for Roman numerals, they create a faux continental glamour (199). Similarly, when Dana is five years old she tries to camouflage her missing top teeth by "a plan to slide a folded piece of paper" in the gap (10). When Dana is older, on a visit to her grandmother's rural Alabama home, she observes "still and impassive" sheets hanging on the clothesline in order to cover the lingerie, underwear, and other "secret things" that "you didn't want visible from the street" (143, 144). Such camouflage and fakery is what the idea of post-blackness works against. It proposes that a monolithic notion of African American identity hides a more dynamic range of black subjectivities that are equally authentic, even though everyone may not be comfortable with them.

In all three of these novels, the sense of collective identity that post-blackness challenges is critiqued but never dismissed. In the freedom songs of *Darkroom*'s marchers, in the love-thick families and neighborhoods of *Beyond Katrina*, in the ethnic malls and debutante balls of *Silver Sparrow,* there are effable cultures that black southerners have created and sustained, even if a sense of connectivity or group consciousness may be elusive. As cultural theorists such as Nelson George, Tricia Rose, and Mark Anthony Neal have ventured in their discussions of post-modern African American artists and aesthetics, the new standpoints of "post-black" and "post-soul" have returned us to the movement's old idea of growth through dialogue.[21] This ongoing conversation about blackness is rooted in received identities, even while they are called into question, redefined, and even rejected.

NOTES

1 Michael Eric Dyson, "Tour(é)ing Blackness," Foreword to Touré, *Who's Afraid of Post-Blackness? What It Means to Be Black Now* (New York: Free Press, 2011), pp. xvii, xvi; Paul C. Taylor, "Post-Black, Old-Black," *African American Review* 41.4 (Winter 2007): 626; L. H. Stallings, "Sonics of Sex (Funk) in Paul Beatty's *Slumberland*," in *Contemporary African American Literature: The Living Canon*, ed. Lovalerie King and Shirley Moody-Turner (Bloomington: Indiana University Press, 2013), p. 191.

2 Brian Norman, *Neo-Segregation Narratives: Jim Crow in Post–Civil Rights American Literature* (Athens: University of Georgia Press, 2010), p. 15.

3 Orlando Patterson, "Race Unbound" (reprinted as "The Post-Black Condition"), Review of Touré, *Who's Afraid of Post-Blackness? What It Means to Be Black Now,* New York Times, September 25, 2011: BR1.

4 Frank L. Owsley, John Craig Stewart, and Gordon T. Chappell, *Know Alabama: An Elementary History* (Northport, AL: Colonial Press, 1965).

5 Natasha Trethewey, *Beyond Mississippi: A Meditation on the Mississippi Gulf Coast* (Athens: University of Georgia Press, 2010), p. 20. Subsequent page references given in the text.

6 Roopali Mukherjee, "Bling Fling: Commodity Consumption and the Politics of the 'Post-Racial,'" in *Critical Rhetorics of Race*, ed. Michael G. Lacy and Kent A. Ono (New York: New York University Press, 2011), p. 178.

7 Lila Quintero Weaver, *Darkroom: A Memoir in Black and White* (Tuscaloosa: University of Alabama Press, 2012), p. 63. Subsequent page references given in the text.

8 "The people walking in darkness have seen a great light; a light has dawned on those living in the land of darkness" (Isaiah 9:2), *The Holy Bible*, King James Version (Nashville, TN: Holman Bible Publishers, 2009).

9 Danielle L. McGuire, *At the Dark End of the Street: Black Women, Rape, and Resistance – A New History of the Civil Rights Movement from Rosa Parks to the Rise of Black Power* (New York: Knopf, 2010), pp. 93, 274.

10 Dyson, "Tour(é)ing Blackness," p. xvii.

11 National Association for the Advancement of Colored People, Criminal Justice Fact Sheet, http://www.naacp.org/pages/criminal-justice-fact-sheet (accessed May 13, 2014).

12 Patterson, "Race Unbound," BR1.

13 David H. Ikard and Martell Lee Teasley, *Nation of Cowards: Black Optimism in Barack Obama's Post-Racial America* (Bloomington: Indiana University Press, 2012), p. 28.

14 Henry Louis Gates Jr., quoted in Touré, *Who's Afraid of Post-Blackness?*, p. 259.

15 For historical studies of Atlanta's black communities during the twentieth century, see Frederick Allen, *Atlanta Rising: The Invention of an International City, 1946–1996* (Marietta, GA: Longstreet Press, 1996); Ronald H. Bayor, *Race and the Shaping of Twentieth-Century Atlanta* (Chapel Hill: University of North Carolina Press, 2000); Tomiko Brown-Nagin, *Courage to Dissent: Atlanta and the Long History of the Civil Rights Movement* (New York: Oxford University Press, 2012); Winston A. Grady-Willis, *Challenging U.S. Apartheid: Atlanta and Black Struggle for Human Rights, 1960–1997* (Durham, NC: Duke University Press, 2006); Alexa B. Henderson, *Atlanta Life Insurance Company: Guardian of Black Economic Dignity* (Tuscaloosa: University of Alabama Press, 2003); and Gary M. Pomerantz, *Where Peachtree Meets Sweet Auburn: A Saga of Race and Family* (New York: Penguin Books, 1997).

16 Tayari Jones, *Silver Sparrow: A Novel* (Chapel Hill: Algonquin Books of North Carolina, 2011). Page number references given in the text.

17 *The Cosby Show* (1984–1992) was a popular sitcom that starred comedian Bill Cosby (b. 1937) and Phylicia Rashad (b. 1948) as an affluent, stylish African American couple. He played a doctor; she played a lawyer; together they performed as the loving parents of five beautiful children. This groundbreaking series disrupted conventional depictions in television and film of black American households as underprivileged, dysfunctional, single-parent headed, and poor. On the other hand, for its perpetuation of racial stereotypes, the *Amos 'n' Andy* television show (1951–1953), starring Alvin Childress (1907–1986) and Tim Moore (1887–1958), sparked a protest led by the NAACP. For an analysis of prime time television programs featuring African Americans from *Amos 'n' Andy* to *The Cosby Show*, see Marlon Riggs, *Color Adjustment* (San Francisco: California Newsreel, 1992).

18 "Gangsta lean" describes a driving style that was popularized among hip, urban African American men beginning in the 1970s and 1980s. The driver steers the wheel with one hand, usually the left, and leans the body in the opposite direction.

19 Benjamin Elijah Mays (1894–1964) served as a beloved president of Morehouse College from 1940 to 1967. His body is buried on the campus grounds. See Benjamin E. Mays, *Born to Rebel: An Autobiography* (Athens: University of Georgia Press, 2003).

20 This metaphor alludes to the 1937 novel *Their Eyes Were Watching God* by Zora Neale Hurston (1891–1960). In order to protect her from the racism and sexism of the Jim Crow South, the character Nanny encourages her orphaned granddaughter Janie to seek security in a loveless marriage. Broken and sorrowful, she begs the resistant teen to "Have some sympathy fuh me. Put me down easy, Janie, Ah'm a cracked plate." *Their Eyes Were Watching God*, in Zora

Neale Hurston: Novels and Stories, ed. Cheryl A. Wall (New York: Library of America, 1995), p. 190.

21 See Nelson George, *Buppies, B-Boys, Baps, and Bohos: Notes on Post-Soul Black Culture* (Cambridge, MA: Da Capo Press, 2001); Tricia Rose, *Black Noise: Rap Music and Black Culture in Contemporary America* (Middleton, CT: Wesleyan University Press, 1994); and Mark Anthony Neal, *Soul Babies: Black Popular Culture and the Post-Soul Aesthetic* (New York: Routledge, 2001).

GUIDE TO FURTHER READING

This list is intended as a starting point for research on civil rights movement literature. It includes works cited by contributors and selected supplemental resources in civil rights movement literature and history.

Primary Resources

Armstrong, Julie Buckner, and Amy Schmidt, eds. *The Civil Rights Reader: American Literature from Jim Crow to Reconciliation.* Athens: University of Georgia Press, 2009.

Baldwin, James. *Blues for Mister Charlie: A Play.* 1964. Reprint, New York: Vintage, 2013.

   The Fire Next Time. 1963. Reprint, New York: Vintage, 1993.

   Going to Meet the Man: Stories. 1965. Reprint, New York: Vintage, 2013.

   Notes of a Native Son. 1955. Reprint, Boston: Beacon Press, 2012.

Bambara, Toni Cade. *These Bones Are Not My Child.* 1999. Reprint, New York: Vintage, 2009.

Bambara, Toni Cade, ed. *Black Woman: An Anthology.* 1970. Reprint, New York: Washington Square Press, 2010.

Baraka, Amiri/LeRoi Jones. *The Autobiography of LeRoi Jones.* New York: Freundlich, 1984.

   Dutchman and the Slave: Two Plays. New York: Harper Perennial, 1971.

   Transbluesency: The Selected Poetry of LeRoi Jones/Amiri Baraka, 1961–1995. New York: Marsilio Publishing, 1995.

Baraka, Amiri, and Larry Neal. *Black Fire: An Anthology of Afro-American Writing.* 1968. Reprint, Baltimore: Black Classic Press, 2007.

Beckham, Barry. *Runner Mack.* New York: Morrow, 1972.

Bell, Madison Smartt. *Soldier's Joy.* New York: Penguin, 1990.

Bradley, David. *The Chaneysville Incident.* New York: Harper Perennial, 1990.

Brooks, Gwendolyn. *The Essential Gwendolyn Brooks.* Ed. Elizabeth Alexander. New York: Library of America, 2005.

Brown, Rosellen. *Civil Wars.* New York: Knopf, 1984.

   Half a Heart. New York: Picador, 2001.

Brown, Wesley. *Darktown Strutters*. 1994. Reprint, Amherst: University of Massachusetts Press, 2000.

Butler, Jack. *Jujitsu for Christ*. 1986. Reprint, Jackson: University Press of Mississippi, 2013.

Butler, Octavia. *Kindred*. 1979. Reprint, Boston: Beacon Press, 2004.

Campbell, Bebe Moore. *Your Blues Ain't like Mine*. New York: Putnam, 1992.

Chaze, Elliot. *Tiger in the Honeysuckle*. New York: Scribner's, 1965.

Chesnutt, Charles. *The Marrow of Tradition*. 1901. Reprint, New York: Penguin, 1993.

Cleaver, Eldridge. *Soul on Ice*. 1968. Reprint, New York: Delta, 1999.

Clifton, Lucille. *The Collected Poems of Lucille Clifton, 1965–2010*. Rochester, NY: BOA Editions, 2012.

Coleman, Jeffrey L., ed. *Words of Protest, Words of Freedom: Poetry of the American Civil Rights Movement and Era*. Durham, NC: Duke University Press, 2012.

Cruse, Howard. *Stuck Rubber Baby*. 1995. Reprint, New York: Vertigo, 2010.

Davis, Angela. *Angela Davis: An Autobiography*. 1974. Reprint, New York: International Publishers, 2013.

Demby, William. *Beetlecreek*. 1950. Reprint, Jackson: University of Mississippi Press, 1998.

Douglas, Ellen. *Can't Quit You, Baby*. New York: Penguin, 1989.

Dove, Rita. *On the Bus with Rosa Parks: Poems*. New York: W.W Norton, 1999.

Du Bois, W. E. B. *The Souls of Black Folk*. 1903. Reprint, New York: Penguin, 1996.

Edwards, Junius. *If We Must Die*. 1961, Reprint, Washington, DC: Howard University Press, 1984.

Ellison, Ralph. *Invisible Man*. 1952. Reprint, New York: Vintage, 1995.

Faulkner, William. *Intruder in the Dust*. 1948. Reprint, New York: Vintage, 1991.

Ford, Jesse Hill. *Liberation of Lord Byron Jones*. 1965. Reprint, New York: Little, Brown, 1965.

Forman, James D. *Freedom's Blood*. London: Franklin Watts, 1979.

Fowler, Connie May. *Sugar Cage*. New York: Washington Square Press, 1993.

Fuller, Charles. *A Soldier's Play*. New York: Hill and Wang, 1982.
      Zooman and the Sign. New York: Doubleday, 1982.

Gaines, Ernest J. *A Gathering of Old Men*. New York: Vintage, 1992.
      A Lesson before Dying. New York: Vintage, 1997.

Griffin, John Howard. *Black like Me*. 1962. Reprint, New York: Signet, 2010.

Grooms, Anthony. *Bombingham: A Novel*. New York: Free Press, 2001.

Haas, Ben. *Look Away, Look Away*. New York: Simon and Schuster, 1964.

Hansberry, Lorraine. *A Raisin in the Sun*. 1960. Reprint, New York: Vintage, 2004.
      To Be Young Gifted and Black. 1969. Reprint, New York: Vintage, 1996.

Harper, Frances E. W. *Iola Leroy, or, Shadows Uplifted*. 1892. Reprint, New York: Penguin, 2010.

Harper, Michael S. *Images of Kin: New and Selected Poems*. Champaign-Urbana: University of Illinois Press, 1977.

Hayden, Robert. *Collected Poems: Robert Hayden*. New York: Liveright, 1985.

Hopkins, Pauline. *Of One Blood, or the Hidden Self*. 1902. Reprint, New York: Washington Square Press, 2004.
      Contending Forces, or a Romance Illustrative of Negro Life North and South. 1900. Reprint, New York: Oxford University Press, 1991.

Hughes, Langston. *The Collected Poems of Langston Hughes*, ed. Arnold Rampersad and David Roessel. New York: Vintage, 1995.

Huie, William Bradford. *The Klansman*. New York: Delacourte Press, 1967.

Johnson, Charles. *Dreamer*. New York: Scribner's, 1999.

Johnson, James Weldon. *The Autobiography an Ex-Colored Man*. 1912. Reprint, New York: Penguin, 2010.

Johnson, Mat, and Warren Pleece. *Incognegro: A Graphic Mystery*. New York: Vertigo, 2009.

Jones, Madison. *A Cry of Absence*. Baton Rouge: Louisiana State University Press, 1989.

Jones, Tayari. *Silver Sparrow: A Novel*. Chapel Hill: Algonquin Books of North Carolina, 2011.

Jordan, June. *Directed by Desire: The Collected Poems of June Jordan*. Port Townsend, WA: Copper Canyon Press, 2007.

Kiker, Douglas. *The Southerner*. New York: Rinehart Press, 1957.

Killens, John O. *'Sippi*. New York: Thunder's Mouth Press, 1988.

Kincaid, Nanci. *Crossing Blood*. Tuscaloosa: University of Alabama Press, 1999.

King, Woodie, and Ron Milner, eds. *Black Drama Anthology*. New York: New American Library, 1972.

Larsen, Nella. *Passing*. 1929. Reprint, New York: Penguin, 2003.

Lee, Harper. *To Kill a Mockingbird*. 1960. Reprint, New York: Harper Perennial, 1993.

Lester, Julius. *All Our Wounds Forgiven*. 1994, Reprint, New York: Arcade Books, 2002.

Lorde, Audre. *Collected Poems of Audre Lorde*. New York: W.W. Norton, 2000.

Sister Outsider: Essays and Speeches. New York: Crossing Press, 2007.

Zami: A New Spelling of My Name – A Biomythography. New York: Crossing Press, 1987.

Malcolm X, with Alex Haley. *The Autobiography of Malcolm X: As Told to Alex Haley*. 1965. Reprint, New York: Ballentine Books, 1987.

McCullers, Carson. *Clock without Hands*. New York: Houghton Mifflin, 1961.

McGruder, Aaron, Reginald Hudlin, and Kyle Baker. *Birth of a Nation: A Comic Novel*. New York: Crown, 2004.

Moody, Anne. *Coming of Age in Mississippi*. New York: Laurel Books, 1968.

Morrison, Toni. *The Bluest Eye*. 1970. Reprint, New York, Vintage, 2007.

Beloved. 1987. Reprint, New York: Vintage, 2004.

Song of Solomon. 1977. Reprint, New York: Vintage, 2004.

Nelson, Marilyn. *Faster Than Light: New and Selected Poems, 1996–2011*. Baton Rouge: Louisiana State University Press, 2013.

Newton, Huey. "A Letter from Huey Newton to the Revolutionary Brothers and Sisters about the Women's Liberation and Gay Liberation Movements." In *Traps: African American Men on Gender and Sexuality*, ed. Rudolph Byrd. Bloomington: Indiana University Press, 2001, 37–45.

Nordan, Lewis. *Wolf Whistle*. 1993. Reprint, New York: Algonquin Books, 2003.

Nunez, Elizabeth. *Beyond the Limbo Silence*. New York: Ballentine, 2003.

Parks, Suzan-Lori. *Getting Mother's Body*. New York: Random House, 2004.

Perkins, Kathy, and Judith Stephens, eds. *Strange Fruit: Plays on Lynching by American Women*. Bloomington: Indiana University Press, 1998.

Petry, Ann. *The Street*. 1946. Reprint, New York: Houghton Mifflin, 1946.

Randall, Dudley. *Roses and Revolutions: The Selected Writings of Dudley Randall*, ed. Melba Joyce Boyd. Detroit: Wayne State University Press, 2009.

Rice, Anne, ed. *Witnessing Lynching: American Writers Respond*. New Brunswick, NJ: Rutgers University Press, 2003.

Rogers, Lettie Hamlett. *Birthright*. New York: Simon and Schuster, 1957.

Salaam, Kalamu ya. "Women's Rights Are Human Rights." In *Traps: African American Men on Gender and Sexuality*, ed. Rudolph Byrd. Bloomington: Indiana University Press, 2001, 113–18.

Sanchez, Sonia. *Shake Loose My Skin: New and Selected Poems*. Boston: Beacon Press, 2000.

Sanders, Dori. *Clover*. New York: Ballentine, 1991.

Schuyler, George. *Black No More*. 1931. Reprint, New York: Dover, 2011.

Senna, Danzy. *Caucasia*. New York: Riverhead, 1998.

Shange, Ntozake. *For Colored Girls Who Have Considered Suicide/When the Rainbow Is Enuf*. 1980. Reprint, New York: Scribner's, 1997.

Siddons, Anne River. *Heartbreak Hotel*. New York: Harpertorch, 1976.

Smith, Anna Deavere. *Twilight: Los Angeles, 1992*. New York: Anchor Books, 1994.

Smith, Lillian. *Killers of the Dream*. 1949. Reprint, New York: Norton, 1994.

Strange Fruit. 1944. Reprint, New York: Harvest Books, 1992.

Spencer, Elizabeth. *The Voice at the Back Door*. 1956. Reprint, Baton Rouge: Louisiana State University Press, 1994.

Stockett, Katherine. *The Help*. New York: Einhorn Books, 2009.

Styron, William. *The Confessions of Nat Turner*. 1967. Reprint, New York: Vintage, 1992.

Trethewey, Natasha. *Beyond Mississippi: A Meditation on the Mississippi Gulf Coast*. Athens: University of Georgia Press, 2010.

Walker, Alice. *The Color Purple*. 1982. Reprint, New York: Mariner Books, 2006.

Meridian. 1976. Reprint, New York: Harcourt, 2003.

Walker, Frank X. *Turn Me Loose: The Unghosting of Medgar Evers*. Athens: University of Georgia Press, 2013.

Walker, Margaret. *This Is My Century: New and Collected Poems*. Athens: University of Georgia Press, 1989.

Weaver, Lila. *Darkroom: A Memoir in Black and White*. Tuscaloosa: University of Alabama Press, 2012.

Whitehead, Colson. *The Intuitionist*. New York: Anchor Books, 2000.

Whitt, Margaret E., ed. *Short Stories of the Civil Rights Movement: An Anthology*. Athens: University of Georgia Press, 2006.

Williams, John A. *The Man Who Cried I Am: A Novel*. Boston: Little, Brown, 1967.

Wilson, August. *Fences*. New York: Plume, 1986.

Two Trains Running. New York: Plume, 1993.

Wright, Richard. *Black Boy: A Record of Childhood and Youth*. 1945. Reprint, New York: Harper Perennial, 2007.

Native Son. 1940. Reprint, New York: Harper Perennial, 2005.

Uncle Tom's Children. 1938. Reprint, New York: Harper Perennial, 2008.

York, Jake Adam. *A Murmuration of Starlings*. Carbondale: Southern Illinois University Press, 2008.

Persons Unknown. Carbondale: Southern Illinois University Press, 2010.

Secondary Resources

Abel, Elizabeth. *Signs of the Times: The Visual Politics of Jim Crow*. Berkeley: University of California Press, 2010.

Alexander, Michelle. *The New Jim Crow: Mass Incarceration in the Age of Colorblindness*. New York: New Press, 2012.

Anadolu-Okur, Nilgün. *Contemporary African American Theater: Afrocentricity in the Works of Larry Neal, Amiri Baraka, and Charles Fuller*. New York: Routledge, 2011.

Armstrong, Julie Buckner, Susan Hult Edwards, Houston Bryan Roberson, and Rhonda Y. Williams, eds. *Teaching the Civil Rights Movement: Freedom's Bittersweet Song*. New York: Routledge, 2002.

Cha-Jua, Sundiata, and Clarence Lang. "The 'Long Movement' as Vampire: Temporal and Spatial Fallacies in Recent Black Freedom Studies." *Journal of African American History* 92.2 (Spring 2007): 265–88.

Colbert, Soyica Diggs. *The African American Theatrical Body: Reception, Performance, and the Stage*. New York: Cambridge University Press, 2011.

Collier-Thomas, Bettye, and V. P. Franklin, eds. *Sisters in the Struggle*. New York: New York University Press, 2001.

Crawford, Vicki L., Jacqueline Rowe, and Barbara Woods, eds. *Women in the Civil Rights Movement: Trailblazers and Torchbearers, 1941–1965*. Bloomington: Indiana University Press, 1993.

Cripps, Thomas. *Making Movies Black: The Hollywood Message Movie from World War II to the Civil Rights Era*. New York: Oxford University Press, 1993.

Crosby, Emilye, ed. *Civil Rights History from the Ground Up: Local Struggles, a National Movement*. Athens: University of Georgia Press, 2011.

Dabbs, James McBride. *Civil Rights in Recent Southern Fiction*. Atlanta: Southern Regional Council, 1969.

Dittmer, John. "The Civil Rights Movement." In *The African American Experience: An Historical and Bibliographical Guide*, ed. Arvarh E. Strickland and Robert E. Weems. Westport, CT: Greenwood Press, 2001, 352–67.

Local People: The Struggle for Civil Rights in Mississippi. Champaign-Urbana: University of Illinois Press, 1995.

Dray, Philip. *At the Hands of Persons Unknown: The Lynching of Black America*. New York: Random House, 2002.

Duck, Leigh Anne. *The Nation's Region: Southern Modernism, Segregation, and U.S. Nationalism*. Athens: University of Georgia Press, 2006.

Edwards, Erica. *Charisma and the Fiction of Black Leadership*. Minneapolis: University of Minnesota Press, 2012.

Eagles, Charles. "Toward New Histories of the Civil Rights Era." *Journal of Southern History* 66 (2000): 815–48.

Eagles, Charles, ed. *The Civil Rights Movement in America*. Jackson: University Press of Mississippi, 1986.

Fabre, Geneviève, and Robert O'Meally, eds. *History and Memory in African-American Culture*. Oxford: Oxford University Press, 1994.

Gayle, Addison Jr., ed. *The Black Aesthetic*. Garden City, NJ: Anchor Books, 1971.

Glaude, Eddie Jr. *Is It Nation Time? Contemporary Essays on Black Power and Black Nationalism*. Chicago: University of Chicago Press, 2002.

Goldsby, Jacqueline. *Spectacular Secret: Lynching in American Life and Literature*. Chicago: University of Chicago Press, 2006.

Graham, Allison. *Framing the South: Hollywood, Television, and Race during the Civil Rights Struggle*. Baltimore, MD: Johns Hopkins University Press, 2003.

Gray, Jonathan W. *Civil Rights in the White Literary Imagination: Innocence by Association*. Jackson: University Press of Mississippi, 2013.

Gwin, Minrose. *Remembering Medgar Evers: Writing the Long Civil Rights Movement*. Athens: University of Georgia Press, 2013.

Haddox, Thomas F. "Elizabeth Spencer, the White Civil Rights Novel, and the Postsouthern." *MLQ: Modern Language Quarterly* 65.4 (December 2004): 561–81.

Hale, Grace Elizabeth. *Making Whiteness: The Culture of Segregation in the South, 1880–1940*. New York: Pantheon, 1998.

Hall, Jacquelyn Dowd. "The Long Civil Rights Movement and the Political Uses of the Past." *Journal of American History* 91 (2005): 1233–63.

Hobson, Fred. *But Now I See: The White Southern Racial Conversion Narrative*. Baton Rouge: Louisiana State University Press, 1999.

Johnson, Charles. "The End of the Black American Narrative." *American Scholar* 77.3 (Summer 2008): 32–42.

Jones, Suzanne. *Race Mixing: Southern Fiction since the 1960s*. Baltimore, MD: Johns Hopkins University Press, 2006.

Joseph, Peniel E. *The Black Power Movement: Rethinking the Civil Rights-Black Power Era*. New York: Routledge, 2006.

——— *Waiting 'Til the Midnight Hour: A Narrative History of Black Power in America*. New York: Henry Holt, 2007.

——— "Waiting till the Midnight Hour: Reconceptualizing the Heroic Period of the Civil Rights Movement, 1954–1965." *Souls: A Critical Journal of Black Politics, Culture, and Society* 2.2 (Spring 2000): 6–17.

King, Martin Luther Jr. *Where Do We Go from Here: Chaos or Community?* New York: Beacon Press, 2010.

——— *Why We Can't Wait*. Boston: Beacon Press, 2011.

King, Richard H. "The Civil Rights Debate." In *A Companion to the Literature and Culture of the American South*, ed. Richard Gray and Owen Robinson. Malden, MA: Blackwell, 2004, 221–37.

——— *Civil Rights and the Idea of Freedom*. New York: Oxford University Press, 1992.

——— "Politics and Fictional Representation: The Case of the Civil Rights Movement." In *The Making of Martin Luther King and the Civil Rights Movement*, ed. Brian Ward and Tony Badger. New York: Washington Square Press, 1996, 162–78.

Lawson, Steven F. "The Long Origins of the Short Civil Rights Movement." In *Freedom Rights: New Perspectives on the Civil Rights Movement*, ed. John Dittmer and Danielle McGuire. Lexington: University of Kentucky Press, 2011, 9–37.

Litwack, Leon F. "'Fight the Power': The Legacy of the Civil Rights Movement." *Journal of Southern History* 75.1 (February 2009): 3–28.

Malcolm X. *Malcolm X Speaks: Selected Speeches and Statements*, ed. George Breitman. New York: Grove Press, 1994.

McGuire, Danielle L. *At the Dark End of the Street: Black Women, Rape, and Resistance – A New History of the Civil Rights Movement from Rosa Parks to the Rise of Black Power*. New York: Knopf, 2010.

Melosh, Barbara. "Historical Memory in Fiction: The Civil Rights Movement in Three Novels." *Radical History Review* 40 (Winter 1988): 64–76.

Metress, Christopher. *The Lynching of Emmett Till: A Documentary Narrative*. Charlottesville: University of Virginia Press, 2002.

"Making Civil Rights Harder: Literature, Memory, and the Black Freedom Struggle." *Southern Literary Journal* 40.2 (Spring 2008): 138–50.

Miller, Keith D. "On Martin Luther King Jr. and the Landscape of Civil Rights Rhetoric." *Rhetoric and Public Affairs* 16.1 (Spring 2013): 167–83.

Mitchell, Koritha. *Living with Lynching: African American Lynching Plays, Performance, and Citizenship, 1890–1930*. Champaign-Urbana: University of Illinois Press, 2011.

Monteith, Sharon. *Advancing Sisterhood? Interracial Friendship in Contemporary Southern Fiction*. Athens: University of Georgia Press, 2000.

"Exploitation Movies and the Freedom Struggle of the 1960s." In *American Cinema and the Southern Imaginary*, ed. Deborah E. Clarke and Kathryn McKee. Athens: University of Georgia Press, 2011, 194–218.

"Civil Rights Fiction." *The Cambridge Companion to the Literature of the American South*, ed. Sharon Monteith. New York: Cambridge University Press, 2013, 159–73.

"The 1960s Echo On: Images of Martin Luther King Jr. as Deployed by White Writers of Contemporary Fiction." In *Media, Culture, and the Modern African American Freedom Struggle*, ed. Brian Ward. Gainesville: University Press of Florida, 2001, 255–72.

"Revisiting the 1960s in Contemporary Fiction: "Where Do We Go from Here?" *Gender and the Civil Rights Movement*, ed. Peter Ling and Sharon Montieth. New Brunswick: Rutgers University Press, 2004, 215–38.

"SNCC's Stories at the Barricades." In *From Sit-Ins to SNCC: Student Civil Rights Protest in the 1960s*, ed. Philip Davies and Iwan Morgan. Gainesville: University Press of Florida, 2012, 97–115.

Norman, Brian. *The American Protest Essay and National Belonging: Addressing Division*. Albany: State University of New York Press, 2007.

Neo-Segregation Narratives: Jim Crow in Post–Civil Rights American Literature. Athens: University of Georgia Press, 2010.

Norman, Brian, and Piper Kendrix Williams, eds. *Representing Segregation: Toward an Aesthetics of Living Jim Crow, and Other Forms of Racial Division*. Albany: State University of New York Press, 2010.

Patterson, Robert J. *Exodus Politics: Civil Rights and Leadership in African American Literature and Culture*. Charlottesville: University of Virginia Press, 2013.

Patterson, Robert J., and Erica R. Edwards. "Black Literature, Black Leadership: New Boundaries, New Borders." *South Atlantic Quarterly* 112 (2013): 217–19.

Payne, Charles M. *I've Got the Light of Freedom: The Organizing Tradition and the Mississippi Freedom Struggle*. Berkeley: University of California Press, 2007.

Pollack, Harriet, and Christopher Metress. *Emmett Till in Literary Memory and Imagination*. Baton Rouge: Louisiana State University Press, 2008.

Reid, Margaret Ann. *Black Protest Poetry: Polemics from the Harlem Renaissance and the Sixties*. New York: Peter Lang, 2001.

Richardson, Riché. *Black Masculinity and the U.S. South: From Uncle Tom to Gangsta*. Athens: University of Georgia Press, 2007.

Robnett, Belinda. *How Long? How Long? African-American Women in the Struggle for Civil Rights*. New York: Oxford University Press, 1997.

Rojas, Fabio. *From Black Power to Black Studies*. Baltimore, MD: Johns Hopkins University Press, 2007.

Romano, Renee C., and Leigh Raiford. *The Civil Rights Movement in American Memory*. Athens: University of Georgia Press, 2006.

Rushdy, Ashraf H. A. *The End of American Lynching*. New Brunswick, NJ: Rutgers University Press, 2012.

Smethurst, James. *The Black Arts Movement: Literary Nationalism in the 1960s and 1970s*. Chapel Hill: University of North Carolina Press, 2005.

Sundquist, Eric. *To Wake the Nation: Race in the Making of American Literature*. Cambridge, MA: Harvard University Press, 1993.

Thomas, Brook. *Civic Myths: A Law-and-Literature Approach to Citizenship*. Chapel Hill: University of North Carolina, 2007.

Touré. *Who's Afraid of Post-Blackness? What it Means to Be Black Now*. New York: Free Press, 2011.

Trodd, Zoe, ed. *American Protest Literature*. Cambridge, MA: Harvard University Press, 2006.

Ture, Kwame/Stokely Carmichael, and Charles Johnson. *Black Power: The Politics of Liberation*. New York: Vintage, 1992.

Van Deburg, William L. *New Day in Babylon*. Chicago: University of Chicago Press, 1992.

Walker, Melissa. *Down from the Mountaintop: Black Women's Novels in the Wake of the Civil Rights Movement, 1966–1989*. New Haven, CT: Yale University Press, 1991.

Ward, Brian. *Media, Culture, and the Modern African American Freedom Struggle*. Gainesville: University Press of Florida, 2001.

Warren, Kenneth. *What Was African American Literature?* Cambridge, MA: Harvard University Press, 2011.

Whitt, Margaret Earley. "Using the Civil Rights Movement to Practice Activism in the Classroom." *PMLA* 124 (2009): 856–63.

Woolfork, Lisa. *Embodying Slavery in Contemporary Culture*. Champaign-Urbana: University of Illinois Press, 2008.

INDEX

Cambridge Companions to...

AUTHORS

Edward Albee edited by Stephen J. Bottoms

Margaret Atwood edited by Coral Ann Howells

W. H. Auden edited by Stan Smith

Jane Austen edited by Edward Copeland and Juliet McMaster (second edition)

Beckett edited by John Pilling

Bede edited by Scott DeGregorio

Aphra Behn edited by Derek Hughes and Janet Todd

Walter Benjamin edited by David S. Ferris

William Blake edited by Morris Eaves

Jorge Luis Borges edited by Edwin Williamson

Brecht edited by Peter Thomson and Glendyr Sacks (second edition)

The Brontës edited by Heather Glen

Bunyan edited by Anne Dunan-Page

Frances Burney edited by Peter Sabor

Byron edited by Drummond Bone

Albert Camus edited by Edward J. Hughes

Willa Cather edited by Marilee Lindemann

Cervantes edited by Anthony J. Cascardi

Chaucer edited by Piero Boitani and Jill Mann (second edition)

Chekhov edited by Vera Gottlieb and Paul Allain

Kate Chopin edited by Janet Beer

Caryl Churchill edited by Elaine Aston and Elin Diamond

Cicero edited by Catherine Steel

Coleridge edited by Lucy Newlyn

Wilkie Collins edited by Jenny Bourne Taylor

Joseph Conrad edited by J. H. Stape

H. D. edited by Nephie J. Christodoulides and Polina Mackay

Dante edited by Rachel Jacoff (second edition)

Daniel Defoe edited by John Richetti

Don DeLillo edited by John N. Duvall

Charles Dickens edited by John O. Jordan

Emily Dickinson edited by Wendy Martin

John Donne edited by Achsah Guibbory

Dostoevskii edited by W. J. Leatherbarrow

Theodore Dreiser edited by Leonard Cassuto and Claire Virginia Eby

John Dryden edited by Steven N. Zwicker

W. E. B. Du Bois edited by Shamoon Zamir

George Eliot edited by George Levine

T. S. Eliot edited by A. David Moody

Ralph Ellison edited by Ross Posnock

Ralph Waldo Emerson edited by Joel Porte and Saundra Morris

William Faulkner edited by Philip M. Weinstein

Henry Fielding edited by Claude Rawson

F. Scott Fitzgerald edited by Ruth Prigozy

Flaubert edited by Timothy Unwin

E. M. Forster edited by David Bradshaw

Benjamin Franklin edited by Carla Mulford

Brian Friel edited by Anthony Roche

Robert Frost edited by Robert Faggen

Gabriel García Márquez edited by Philip Swanson

Elizabeth Gaskell edited by Jill L. Matus

Goethe edited by Lesley Sharpe

Günter Grass edited by Stuart Taberner

Thomas Hardy edited by Dale Kramer

David Hare edited by Richard Boon

Nathaniel Hawthorne edited by Richard Millington

Seamus Heaney edited by Bernard O'Donoghue

Ernest Hemingway edited by Scott Donaldson

Homer edited by Robert Fowler

Horace edited by Stephen Harrison

Ted Hughes edited by Terry Gifford

Ibsen edited by James McFarlane

Henry James edited by Jonathan Freedman

Samuel Johnson edited by Greg Clingham

Ben Jonson edited by Richard Harp and Stanley Stewart

James Joyce edited by Derek Attridge (second edition)

Kafka edited by Julian Preece

Keats edited by Susan J. Wolfson

Rudyard Kipling edited by Howard J. Booth

Lacan edited by Jean-Michel Rabaté

D. H. Lawrence edited by Anne Fernihough

Primo Levi edited by Robert Gordon